Winning Moves
Cases in Strategic Management

Alfred A. Marcus, Ph.D.

Carlson School of Management
University of Minnesota

Marsh Publications
Lombard, Illinois

Library of Congress Cataloging-in-Publication Data

Marcus, Alfred Allen, 1950-
  Winning moves: cases in strategic management / Alfred A. Marcus-1st ed.
    p. cm.
  Includes bibliographical references and index.
  ISBN 0-9713130-2-4 (alk. paper)
  1. Strategic planning-Case studies. 2. Management-Case studies. 3. Competition-Case
  studies. I. Title.
  HD30.28.M35275 2005
  658.4'012-dc22
                                    2004030529

Manufactured in the United States of America

10   9   8   7   6   5   4   3   2

∞ PRINTED ON ACID-FREE PAPER

CONTENTS

PREFACE

The premise of the text is that most companies have at least one main competitor, what Intel co-founder Andy Grove refers to as the entity about which they worry constantly; this entity may shift over time, but generally these rivalries are fairly enduring and they help define companies. The classic example would be Coke and Pepsi (Case 7), but there are many other good examples as well. Of course, most companies have more than a single competitor, but a company's future is often molded out of the play back and forth with a key contender that resembles the company in some significant respects. Winning the war with this company is critically important. If winning can be achieved for long periods of time, the company has come close to an important goal, that of attaining sustained competitive advantage.

But how many companies are really able to sustain long-term competitive advantage? Typically, the two firms in question make alternating moves back and forth. One company gains temporary advantage only to be followed by the other company advancing. This casebook focuses on these back and forth moves between companies, which are central to strategy. The cases will allow you and your students to learn from the contrasting approaches each pair of firms has taken and might take to this battle. Your students will be able to analyze and criticize past moves and strategize future moves.

Winning Moves will enable you to structure your classroom case exercises in the form of a contest between firms. Of course, this contest is played out against a broader context. Each case provides relevant information about this broader context. It offers pertinent facts about each firm's macroenvironment, industry structure, resources and capabilities, and company positioning. After considering all of these factors, your students can then decide what they would do next. Consider organizing your case exercises in the form of one group of students taking the side of one company and another group taking the side of the other company. You can ask the two groups of students what they would do. Then, you and the class can speculate about how the competitive interaction between these firms will turn out.   In the process, your students will gain a hands-on grasp of many important strategy issues.

I have written this volume because too many strategy casebooks focus on only a single company rather than examining the ongoing interaction between pairs of competitors, thereby failing to enable students to see "strategy in action." My approach is to follow the interaction between competitive companies over a period of time with respect to classic competitive battles, applying a framework that is common to the way strategy is taught and practiced. The challenge for students of strategy is to put themselves in the position of the top-management team of these ongoing contending parties and develop a series of competitive actions that the top-management team should make next in the belief that these moves are likely to lead to sustained competitive advantage. A critical dilemma that runs through all the cases is the extent to which a company should exploit its existing businesses or explore for new opportunities. To better deal with a dilemma such as this, I suggest that your students take the following steps. They should:

1. Examine the *external environment* for evidence of opportunities and threats.
2. Assess their companies' *internal strengths and weaknesses* to gauge the extent to which the companies are capable of competing in this environment.
3. Consider how to better *position and reposition* their companies.
4. Contemplate the *advantages and disadvantages* of mergers and acquisitions for acquiring new and/or additional resources and capabilities and/or entering new businesses.
5. Assess *globalization's* impacts on their companies' ongoing operations and determine whether "going global" will offer new opportunities.
6. Look at entirely *new products and markets* and better business models, determine how difficult it would be to transition to these products, markets and/or models, and decide to what extent and how they might do so.
7. Consider how to *consolidate gains* their companies have achieved or how to avoid losses their companies might sustain, then move on to the next opportunity.

With this framework in mind, your students should be able to make better moves. They should have a clearer understanding of what moves to take in response to the actions of key competitors. The book is organized around the premise that some cases better illustrate critical strategy than others. Hence, there are cases dealing with such diverse topics as industry analysis, resources, capabilities, and competencies, positioning, globalization, corporate leadership, innovation, and the judo metaphor that has been used to describe strategic interaction. The cases in the book are organized systematically so that students will understand these topics as they are played out in some of the most interesting recent rivalries in corporate history.

Many of the cases in this volume raise the issue of the importance of online retailing and the Internet as a source for consumer information. I have provided an addendum that can be used in cases such as Barnes & Noble vs. Amazon.com, Dell vs. Gateway, Best Buy vs. Circuit City, and Wal-Mart vs. Spartan. Your students can examine the Internet landscape and analyze key trends in online retailing that might result in competitive advantage for those who possess the resources and knowledge to operate effectively in this space.

Acknowledgments

I want to acknowledge the many students I have had in the strategic management courses at the Carlson School of Management and the Master of Technology Management program at the University of Minnesota. These students have been instrumental in testing these cases for use in the classroom and for sharpening my sense of what should be included in them. I also want to thank Christopher Morgan and Bryan Maser, who were the main authors of the Ecolab vs. JohnsonDiversey case.

I also want to thank the INCAE Business School in Costa Rica for their encouragement and hospitality while I worked on *Winning Moves* during my tenure there in the winter of 2004.

My sincere appreciation goes to the following reviewers, who offered valuable suggestions and feedback as I developed the cases: Ilan Alon, Rollins College; Peng Chan, California State University, Fullerton; Dante Di Gregorio, University of New Mexico; and Sarah J. Marsh, Northern Illinois University.

Alfred A. Marcus

CASE 1

Exploring and Exploiting
Intel versus AMD[1]

If stock market performance is used as a guide, as of July 17, 2003, AMD had fought Intel to a near draw for five years. From 2000-2002, AMD actually did much better than its large and accomplished competitor, Intel. While Intel had been moving from exploiting its existing strengths to exploring for new business opportunities to fuel its growth, AMD had set its sights on Intel's existing businesses, especially its highly profitable microprocessor business. Being small—a tenth the size of Intel—gave AMD flexibility and focus.

To make up for Intel's heft, AMD had alliance partners, most notably the Taiwanese company Via, which made chipsets (see the "Glossary of Computer Terminology" below), and UMC, with whom AMD had formed a manufacturing partnership in Texas. Jerry Sanders, AMD's flamboyant, controversial, and combative founder and chair, had said that while Intel was a "gorilla," AMD was a "virtual gorilla."

In its ongoing battles with Intel, AMD was counting on the alliances it had formed with other companies and the fact that it was an underdog and had the support of some customers, who did not want Intel to be too strong. The company was also pinning its hopes on a new technology, called "Hammer," which it had introduced. AMD touted "Hammer" as the only chip able to *flawlessly* run 32-bit *and* 64-bit software (see the glossary below), unlike Intel's competing product, the Itanium, which efficiently ran *just* 64-bit software.

---

1. This case was written by Alfred Marcus, University of Minnesota, Carlson School of Management. Copyright © 2005 by Marsh Publications LLC. All rights reserved.

A glossary of computer terminology

Bus. This component is the set of conductors that connect to the functional units in the computer such as external memory, peripherals, and networks. Higher bus speeds mean higher computer speed.

Chipset. All components communicate with the CPU through the chipset; it is the hub of data transfer. The chipset is usually second in size to the CPU.

Direct random access memory (DRAM). This component temporarily stores information from the system, applications, and data that are currently in use. It determines how many programs can be run simultaneously and how quickly they perform.

Eight through 64-bit architectures. This is the number of binary digits or information bits a microprocessor can retrieve from memory at one time.

Flash memory. This is a small memory device that holds a lot of data and is mainly found in personal desk assistants (PDAs), wireless phones, and laptops.

Hard drive. This is where the operating system, applications, files, and data are kept when they are not in use. Capacity is measured in gigabytes (GBs), with 1 GB = approximately 1000 megabytes (MBs). It is where the computer's permanent memory is stored.

Microprocessor or central processing unit (CPU). This component interprets information from various devices and executes commands, such as telling a printer to print. The faster the processor is, the faster the computer works.

As with AMD, Intel had serious issues to deal with. Intel could go only so far in pushing back AMD with price wars (discounts of >40 percent on the Pentium4), sending lawyers after AMD's partner, Via, and offering advertising subsidies for exclusive deals with original equipment manufacturers (OEMs') such as Dell and Hewlett Packard (HP). It could not concentrate only on protecting its core microprocessor business from AMD's attacks, and by "throwing spaghetti against the wall to see what sticks." Intel had to find the right balance between exploiting its existing strengths and exploring for new opportunities in a business climate that was less promising than that of the late 1990s.

For Intel it may have made sense to concentrate on exploring for new business opportunities when the market was flush and the Internet economy looked as though it had no limits, but the tech economy had been in an extremely serious slide and Intel had to now decide what to do about its core business. There were signs that Intel's execution had been poor and that the company had been thinly stretched. Did Intel have to regain its focus before AMD made too large an inroad on its core market?

The question was not just what Intel or AMD would do, but what they *both* would do and how their actions would affect each other. Where was the competition between these two companies heading?

The Recent Performance of Intel and AMD

In 2001, in the semiconductor industry total growth plummeted by 32 percent. Intel reported that its sales declined 21 percent, while AMD's decline was 16 percent (see Appendix A: Exhibits 1-3).

Between 2000–2002, AMD had outperformed Intel in stock market return, stacking up gains of 14.8 percent compared to Intel's returns of 4.9 percent. But for the 10 years from 1992–2002, Intel's share prices increased by 35.6 percent per year, while AMD's grew by just 6.1 percent per year.

The period 1998–2001 had been a very good one for Intel, but starting in 2001, the company had experienced a reversal in fortune. The 1998–2001 period was a continuation of more than 12 years in which Intel posted average revenue growth in excess of 20 percent per year. The year 2000 was the best in the company's history, with sales of $33.7 billion and net income that grew by 44 percent. But the following year was a tough one for the technology industry as a whole, and especially for Intel, because its 2001 revenues, $26.5 billion, were down 21 percent from 2000, and net income, at $1.3 billion that year, was 88 percent less than the $10.5 billion it earned in 2000.

AMD was far smaller than Intel: In 2002 it had $2.7 billion in revenues to Intel's $26.8 billion. Also, unlike Intel, it was not profitable in 2002 when the company lost $1.3 billion while Intel earned $3.1 billion. In fact, AMD had not been profitable during most of the 1990s. In other ways, however, AMD was the mirror image of Intel. AMD kept up with its larger competitor in microprocessors (Intel's architecture division), flash memory, and networking (Intel's wireless communications group). A high percentage of both companies' sales came from overseas, especially the Asia–Pacific region. AMD had been chipping away at Intel's dominance in this region for some time. Overall, its unit market share in microprocessors jumped from under 6 percent in 1996 to over 20 percent in 2001 (see Table 1.1).

TABLE 1.1   Unit market share in microprocessors

Worldwide PC shipments		
Year	Intel	AMD
1998	86.7%	6.6%
1999	80.9	14.1
2000	83.1	16.7
2001	77.6	22.1

Source: Brent Schlender, "Intel Unleashes Its Inner Attila," Fortune, October 15, 2001.

AMD's revenue market share soared from 2 percent in 1996 to nearly 10 percent in 2001, meaning that it was gaining not just at the lower end of the market, what Intel's Chairman of the Board Andy Grove called "segment zero," but also at the higher end. In 2000, Intel climbed back from 30 percent of the market in the lower-end sub-$1,000 computer microprocessor market in 1999 to over 62 percent, but the company was having difficulty moving forward in the upper end of the market.

The Evolution of Intel's Strategy

Intel's strategy had evolved through three stages: (1) computer memory, (2) microprocessors, and (3) its attempt to branch out into other products. During this evolution, the company also experienced numerous moments of great change when it had to overturn assumptions and make rapid adjustments. Andy Grove referred to these as "inflection points." The first of those adjustments was computer memory, which is discussed below.

The first stage: computer memory

Dynamic random access memory (DRAM) is the most common kind of computer memory. It controls short-term computer operations including the software applications, the number of these applications open at the same time, and the processing speed.[2] Intel invented DRAMs in 1971. Initially, a technically sophisticated product, DRAMs quickly became a commodity that required little specialized marketing and distribution. DRAMs acquired the nickname "jelly-beans," and the primary consideration in their purchase was price. In 1985, Intel—facing its first inflection point—decided to abandon DRAMs, the main source of its profits and revenues at the time.

2. DRAMs are comparable to short-term memory, while memory in the hard drive is comparable to long-term memory.

Japanese manufacturers—NEC, Mitsubishi, Fujitsu, Hitachi, and Oki—had captured 80 percent of the world DRAM market, and firms from Korea—Samsung and Hyundai—were not far behind. Intel's executives reasoned that U.S. companies could not compete with large, vertically integrated Japanese and Korean firms that were the beneficiaries of substantial government subsidies.

U.S. firms bonded together temporarily in 1987 in a government-sponsored consortium called Sematech to fight the foreign firms. Intel was a member, as was IBM, AT&T, and Motorola. However, just one U.S.company survived in this business—Micron Technology. Increasingly, the world's DRAM production belonged to the Japanese and Koreans. Andy Grove wrote that getting through inflection points involves fear, grieving, chaos, denial, and acceptance. "You have to do away with established practice and established people. You have to tear things apart."[3] The next stage was microprocessors.

The second stage: microprocessors

During the 1990s, Intel obtained more than 80 percent of its revenue and nearly all of its profits from microprocessors. A microprocessor is a complex electronic circuit in a computer that moves instructions from such devices as hard disks, floppy disks, CD-ROMs, remote Internet servers, and plug-in cartridges to the point at which they are carried out. The first microprocessors had thousands of transistors. The most recent have millions residing on a tiny chip of silicon no bigger than the size of a fingernail.

Along with Robert Noyce, coinventor of the microprocessor, and Andy Grove, Gordon Moore was another Intel founder. In 1972, four years after the company began, he made the prediction that there would be exponential growth in the number of transistors per integrated circuit and therefore a doubling in microprocessor speed every 18 months. Intel helped make this prediction, known as "Moore's Law," a reality (see Figure 1.1 and Table 1.2).

Intel started to work on microprocessors when Busicom, a Japanese calculator maker, asked it for an integrated circuit. Intel suggested a general-purpose, programmable circuit that would function like a central processing unit (CPU). The device it developed was powerful and sophisticated. The project to develop this device, which started in 1969, took longer than expected. Meanwhile, lower prices in the cal-

---

3. "Global Executive: Intel's Andy Grove on Competitiveness," *Academy of Management Executive* 13, no. 1, 1999, p. 18.

FIGURE 1.1   Moore's Law and Intel's microprocessors

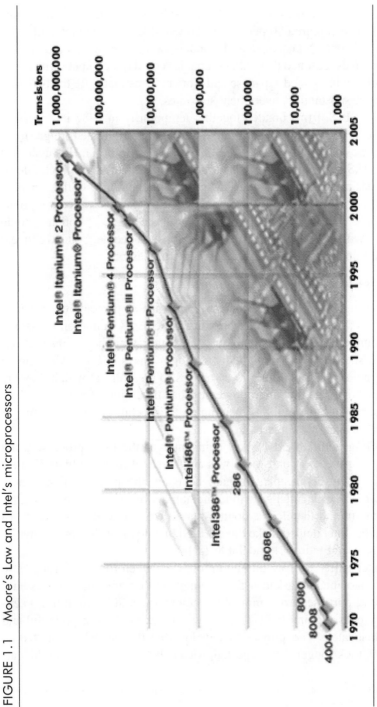

Source: Intel Website (http://www.intel.com/research/silicon/mooreslaw.htm).

TABLE 1.2   Microprocessors' growth in speed

Intel's microprocessor models	Year of introduction	Number of transistors in microprocessor
4004	1971	2,250
8008	1972	2,500
8080	1974	5,000
8086	1978	29,000
286	1982	120,000
386	1985	275,000
486	1989	1,180,000
Pentium	1993	3,100,000
Pentium II	1997	7,500,000
Pentium III	1999	24,000,000
Pentium 4	2000	42,000,000

Source: Adapted from Ramon Casadus-Masnnel and Michael Rukstad, "Intel Corporation: 1997–2000," Harvard Business School Case 9-702-420, p. 8.

culator market made the idea of putting a microprocessor into a calculator obsolete, but Intel realized that what it had created had more uses. The company returned development costs less to Busicom in exchange for commercialization rights, and went on to develop a series of microprocessors, worth billions of dollars, based on its early design.

IBM played a key role in commercializing Intel's microprocessor. In 1981, it selected the 8086 (see Table 1.2 above) for its personal computer (PC). Together with Microsoft's operating system, this microprocessor became the backbone of the PC. IBM, however, did not want Intel to be the sole supplier. Therefore, it required the company to license its design to other chipmakers. The first companies to receive a license from Intel were National Semiconductor, Zilog, NEC, Fujitsu, and AMD. All of them dropped out of the business except AMD. Cyrix and NexGen bought the licenses of the other companies when they expired or were amended.

As the central processing unit (CPU) of the PC, the microprocessor was the most critical factor in a PC's performance. From the beginning, the manufacturers' main goal was to enhance performance. Each model they brought out had more transistors and ran faster than previous ones.

In 1993, Intel introduced the first Pentium processor. Early models ran at speeds of 60 MHz and 66 MHz. Ultimately, new versions of the Pentium would run at speeds in excess of 3 GBs. The Pentium's initial launch was shaky, however, and Andy Grove describes it as another inflection point. The problem was that some of the chips contained a flaw. Over many calculations the chips made mistakes. The computer approximated an answer rather than giving the precise one. Intel had to fix this problem by recalling affected systems. Later versions did not have the flaw, but the incident left its mark on the company.

Nonetheless, the Pentium quickly became the processor of choice for most users. Intel reclaimed the speed crown from competitors like IBM and Motorola and established its strong brand identity of Intel Inside. Within a matter of years, the power of PC processors rose dramatically. The relentless rise in speed provided users with sufficient power to cope with Windows' hungry systems. Intel's dominance reached its zenith in August 1996 with the release of a 200 MHz variant of the Pentium.[4]

Battles with AMD. In 1997, it seemed as if Intel had virtually no competition, the main exception being AMD, a company that had a long and tortured relationship with Intel. Like Intel's leaders, Jerry Sanders, founder of AMD, was an alumnus of Fairchild Semiconductor. From 1987 to 1995, while Intel grew from $1.9 billion to $16.2 billion in revenues, AMD's sales went from just $1 billion to $2.5 billion.

In 1987, Sanders sued Intel for monopolistic practices, claiming that Intel had kept critical technology out of AMD's reach and stifled competition by offering customers advertising subsidies they could not refuse in exchange for exclusive supply deals. In 1995, the suit ended in arbitration. The arbitration ended with Intel agreeing not to try to take away AMD's license to make microprocessors as long as AMD did not make microprocessors that simply plugged into the socket on a PC motherboard designed for Intel's chips.

Intel now counted on its architecture, which had become a de facto standard, to maintain its dominance. The agreement meant that AMD could not design microprocessors to fit this architecture. Thus, the only way AMD could compete was by creating its own chipset (see "The Glossary of Computer Terminology" above) and having its own design for a motherboard.

Intel had always produced chipsets of its own. It sold them along with its microprocessors. AMD, which had to start from scratch and did not have the capability to make chipsets and lacked its own architecture, had substantial barriers to overcome. AMD therefore was severely handicapped when it tried to build a Pentium clone from

4. The Pentium Pro had a multiprocessor system that could accommodate up to four processors, which made it suitable for NT servers. In January 1997, Intel introduced the Pentium MMX. It was marketed as a revolutionary processor with refinements that made it better for multimedia applications, graphics, and sound.

scratch, which would mimic all, or nearly all, of the Pentium's functions. Called the K5, AMD was five months late in delivering this product to the customer, Compaq, which had ordered most of them. Compaq was not at all happy with this result as in doing business with AMD, it had alienated Intel from whom it also bought CPUs.

AMD's executives quickly recognized that they could not compete with Intel by themselves. Therefore, in early 1996, AMD bought another chipmaker, NexGen, which had a license to make microprocessors, and it combined what it considered NexGen's superior intellectual property with its own superior production expertise. To compete with Intel, AMD also had to work very closely with the Taiwanese microprocessor and chipset maker, Via. Jerry Sanders reasoned that if his company could not be a real gorilla like Intel, it could be a virtual gorilla. Using its new capabilities, AMD created a second Pentium clone, the K6, in 1997. The K6 in most respects was equivalent to Intel's Pentium Pro, but sold at a much lower price.

At the same time that AMD came out with the K6, Cyrix, an even smaller company than AMD (it had revenues under $0.5 million), brought out the MediaGX. The MediaGX did not have the bells and whistles of the PII, but it was a workable, inexpensive microprocessor.[5] Intel lost ground to both AMD and Cyrix because their cheap microprocessors created the phenomenon of the sub-$1,000 PC. Andy Grove referred to this development as another inflection point. The sub-$1,000 market showed PC owners that they did not have to spend over $1,000 to get a reasonable machine—one that offered a fast processor and full features such as a sound card and a decent monitor. For Intel, the threat was to the high margins it had sustained when it was the sole or nearly sole microprocessor provider (see Table 1.3).

Lower processor prices meant less profits for producers and lower-end product prices for customers. AMD was challenging the entire business model on which Intel depended (see Table 1.4).

Though this threat was real, Intel did not react immediately. Intel's executives thought they could win back customers with speed. Neither AMD nor Cyrix was in a position at that time to match what Intel was doing.[6] But Intel's executives soon real-

5. Via later bought the rights to Cyrix technologies and marketed them under the Via Cyrix label.

6. Intel had been developing an improved version of the Pentium Pro, which ultimately became the Pentium II (PII), but it did not deliver the PII until after AMD had launched the K6. It continued to work on the PII. Early versions were available at speeds of 233 MHz and 266 MHz. In autumn 1997, Intel put enhancements in the PII that allowed for speeds in excess of 266 MHz. Soon new versions moved the speed of PIIs up to 450 MHz.

TABLE 1.3   Gross margins earned by Intel and its rivals

Product	When introduced (Dec. 1997)	Published Price	Est. mfg. cost	Est. gross margin
PENTIUM PRO, 200-MHz	Nov. 1, 1995	$487	$144	70%
PENTIUM, 200-MHz	June 10, 1996	106	40	62
CYRIX MEDIAGX, 180-MHz	Feb. 20, 1997	81	45	44
AMD K6, 166-MHz	Apr. 2, 1997	84	70	17
PENTIUM II, 266-MHz	May 7, 1997	530	103	81
PENTIUM MMX, 233-MHz	June 2, 1997	300	50	83

Source: Andy Reinhardt and Ira Sager, "Intel," *Business Week,* December 12, 1997, p. 70.

TABLE 1.4   Typical system price with the processors of Intel and its rivals

Product	When introduced	Typical system price	Processor cost (percent)
PENTIUM PRO, 200-MHz	Nov. 1, 1995	$3,190	15.3%
PENTIUM, 200-MHz	June 10, 1996	1,252	8.5
CYRIX MEDIAGX, 180-MHz	Feb. 20, 1997	799	10.1
AMD K6, 166-MHz	Apr. 2, 1997	1,040	8.1
PENTIUM II, 266-MHz	May 7, 1997	2,363	22.4
PENTIUM MMX, 233-MHz	June 2, 1997	1,655	18.1

Source: Andy Reinhardt and Ira Sager, "Intel," *Business Week,* December 12, 1997, p. 70.

ized that processing power was not the only thing that consumers wanted. With new PC buyers, especially, price was a very important concern.

Thus, the scene was set for Intel's most dramatic change in direction since its 1985 exit from DRAMs. Intel could not let Cyrix and AMD dominate what Andy Grove called "segment zero" or the sub-$1,000 PC market. The company decided that it had to have its own low-budget processor. In April 1998, it launched the Celeron as its reply to growth in this sector. The Celeron built on the advances Intel had made with the Pentium. The new microprocessor was essentially a Pentium II with the plastic casing removed, which lowered the costs (see Figure 1.2).

The first Celerons were slow and clunky and Intel won just 30 percent of the market, but the company quickly increased their speed with a second version (code-named Mendocino) with which it won more than 60 percent of the market. Intel beat back the segment-zero threat AMD had posed by turning the Celeron into a credible alternative to the K6.

FIGURE 1.2   The Celeron microprocessor: Pentium II with plastic casing
removed

Source: pc.watch.impress.cu.jp. . . /98069/celeron.jpg.

In the summer of 1998, Intel also introduced the Xeon. It was meant solely for the high-end server/workstation market and was not intended for use by the home consumer. The price tag for the Xeon started at $700 for a 400 MHz model and rose to $3,000 for a 450-MHz model. The Pentium III (PIII), introduced shortly thereafter, offered the ultimate in processing power—clock speeds of up to 550 MHz. With the launch of the Xeon and the PIII, Intel had a full-fledged segmentation strategy. For the low end of the market, it offered the Celeron; for the high end, it offered the Xeon; and for the middle it had the PIII (see Appendix C, Exhibit 5).

The Athlon. Intel's battles with AMD, however, were not over. Having failed to dislodge Intel from the low end of the market, AMD now took aim at the middle portion. If the game Intel was playing was speed, AMD could play it too. The virtual gorilla now felt that it had accumulated enough experience and capabilities to go after Intel.

Both AMD and Intel were pushing hard for a doubling of clock speed. According to Moore's Law, one of them would be able to soon reach the 1-GHz level. The prize would go to the company that would clear this hurdle first. That company would be recognized as the most technically able. For AMD, always operating in Intel's shadow, it was a prize certainly worth striving for: It would give AMD the legitimacy of not being only a low-cost producer.

Indeed, AMD arrived at the speed of 1 GHz in March of 2000, a short period of time before Intel. For the first time in 19 years, someone other than Intel had the world's fastest processor. This event was another inflection point in Intel's history. Since the launch of the K6 around the same time as the Pentium II in 1997, AMD had tried to match Intel step for step. Intel—which previously operated as if it had no competition—now had to take AMD seriously. The Athlon was AMD's strongest offering to date; it had speed, power, and low cost.

Just as the Celeron had sealed off the K6, Intel's aim was to seal off the Athlon. It pushed forward, still hoping to get the better of AMD in the speed battle, despite a recall of the Pentium III that showed that this processor had reached its design limits. Intel was determined not to be bested by AMD. It moved to the next generation of processors, the Pentium 4 (P4). The P4 was based on a new design, which Intel branded "NetBurst." Ultimately, this design enabled the P4 to run at speeds of 1.5 GHz to 3 GHz and better.

With the P4, it appeared that Intel at last had a processor that could rival the Athlon. But the P4's first year in production was not a resounding success. Early P4s received lukewarm receptions from PC enthusiasts. The first version was not a huge hit in the retail market, though it did do well in the corporate PC and workstation market. The next year Intel doubled the P4's clock speed to 2.0 GHz. This jump from 1 GHz to 2 GHz in about 18 months continued to show the relevance of Moore's Law.

Intel's hope was that this advance would bring consumers back to the company. However, many consumers were now more interested in the speed of their Internet connections than in the speed of their processor. Industry experts found it hard to say whether the 2.0 GHz P4 was any better than a 1.4 GHz Athlon. AMD started to question how Intel was measuring speed. From the user's perspective, was there any real advantage to the 2.0 GHz P4? To keep its market share, AMD lowered Athlon's price by up to 50 percent.

In response, Intel discounted the P4 by 40 percent to 85 percent. It granted special advertising subsidies, and gave volume discounts to customers who signed up for exclusive deals. Intel also went after AMD's partner, Via, suing it in an effort to prevent Via from making chipsets for the P4 as long as it was working with AMD. At the same time, Intel continued to improve the P4. The company increased the speed of the processor to up to 3.06 GHz, as promised, and it lowered production costs.

The fact that the P4 was faster than Athlon was hard to contest.[7]

---

7. In gaming and professional uses, it had closed whatever performance gaps existed. In multitasking applications, the P4 generally had better results. In any test that used Adobe Photoshop, the P4 won, but games like POV-RAY and Unreal Tournament still ran better on Athlon.

Even more impressive was the fact that it also was inexpensive enough that it could be offered in sub-$1,000 PCs. Clearly, Intel had retaken the performance and price lead from AMD, but it had been a brutal struggle in which Intel had squeezed its competitor so that its profit margins on the Pentium 4 were relatively modest. Moreover, most customers still believed that the Athlon XP, which ran at 1.8 GHz and sold at a discount, was nearly as good as the P4.

The third stage: branching out

Had Intel reached the end of the line in the microprocessing business? While engaged in this epic struggle with AMD for domination of the microprocessor market, Intel did not remain still. It was busy in other areas. Was this preoccupation with so many different areas the reason that Intel had been almost overtaken by AMD? Microprocessors provided Intel with 80 percent of its revenues and almost all of its profits. The other areas made modest contributions to the bottom line. But Intel hoped that they could be important contributors in the future.

During the time when the battle with AMD over processors was raging, Intel was paying increasing attention to other ventures. The company was exploring for new business opportunities precisely at the moment when its core business was under vigorous attack. With the benefit of hindsight can we say that Intel should have *either* dedicated itself to defending its existing turf *or* fully reached out to find new opportunities. Trying to do both simultaneously was a hard balancing act.

Craig R. Barrett became chief executive officer (CEO) of Intel in 1997. He had been chief operating officer (COO) under Andy Grove. A former professor of engineering at Stanford, he was credited with creating Intel's excellence in manufacturing. Barrett was largely responsible for Intel's ultraefficient fabrication plants (fabs). However, in 1997, when he became Intel's new chief executive, he launched a strategy to move Intel beyond PCs and into such markets as communications, information appliances, and Internet services. But by 2001, about 40 percent of Intel's more than $10 billion in new investments had yielded nothing (see Table 1.5). Intel had to cut back. Not only were the investments not paying off, but Intel was alienating some of its most important customers, whose territory it had entered. In networks, its competitors included IBM, Lucent, Motorola, Texas Instruments, and Broadcom. In wireless, they were Ericsson, Lucent,

TABLE 1.5   The failure of Intel's investments to yield a profit (in millions)

	2001	2000	1999
Intel architecture business (including microprocessors and chipsets)			
Revenues	$21,446	$27,301	$25,459
Operating profit (loss)	6,252	12,511	11,131
Intel communications group			
Revenues	2,580	3,483	2,380
Operating profit (loss)	(735)	319	437
Wireless communications and computing group			
Revenues	2,232	2,669	1,264
Operating profit (loss)	(256)	608	(96)
All other			
Revenues	281	273	286
Operating profit (loss)	(3,005)	(3,043)	(1,705)
Total			
Revenues	26,539	33,726	29,389
Operating profit	$ 2,256	$10,395	$ 9,767

Source: Intel company reports.

Motorola, and Nokia. In communications, they were 3Com, Nortel, and Cisco.

Intel stopped making network servers and routers after some of its biggest chip customers, including Dell and Cisco, started to complain that it was competing against them. In 2001, Intel also exited from other businesses. The company shut down a service for broadcasting shareholder meetings and training sessions over the Web, an e-commerce and hosting service for small and midsize businesses, and an information-appliance business. It also had to cut 5,000 jobs, mainly through attrition, because of the bad economy. Critics—of whom there were many—maintained that Intel had moved into too many new markets, losing its focus.

Barrett admitted that Intel had stumbled and taken its eye off the ball, but he maintained that Intel's distractions were behind it and that the company had gained a new focus. He defended himself, claiming that there were indeed "side effects" of pushing forward at a breakneck pace. Intel had to retreat from many ventures, but a number of them, although not profitable in 2001, continued to show promise. Intel had to sow the seeds for its future.

Barrett pointed to new ventures that were bearing fruit. Intel was still committed to powerful, high-margin chips that sold for up to 40 times the price of a PC microprocessor. These were the new Itanium

FIGURE 1.3   The Centrino brand

Source: article.pchome.net/2003/06/16/centrino.jpg.

processors for servers. Acceptance might be slow, because of the need to rewrite software to take advantage of 64-bit processing instead of the more common 32-bit processing, but Barrett was convinced that ultimately the Itanium would succeed. The Itanium was a joint project with HP that had taken longer to come to market than anticipated. The development costs had far exceeded what Intel had expected.

Outside of servers, the best growth prospect was in the wireless group, where Intel had made inroads with a "wireless Internet on a chip," which it called Centrino. In 2003, wireless was starting to take off and the Centrino was being sold for use in laptop computers. Intel planned to spend more than $300 million to build the Centrino brand around the theme of becoming "unwired." Intel was working with McDonald's, Borders, Hilton hotels, and other stores, airports, and hotels to become wireless "hot spots" and to display Centrino logos and other signage so that consumers would know about wireless access.

Intel's President and COO, Paul Otellini, maintained that the company had learned important lessons from its failures. He pointed to the Centrino as being critical to Intel's future (see Figure 1.3). Here was an initiative that AMD could not match.

In 2000, Andy Grove, who remained the chair of Intel's board, said that "capacity is strategy." He pointed out that the company was committed to spending $10 billion on its fabs, and pushing the state-of-the art in manufacturing technology. Grove considered Intel's excellence in manufacturing to be a major strength. As an expert in manufacturing, Barrett was remodeling Intel's plants, introducing the latest production technologies to help cut costs. Grove believed that AMD would not be able to match this effort. Increasingly, it would have to rely on partners such as UMC, which would require AMD to outsource its manufacturing. As the only fully integrated chipmaker, Intel would have a substantial advantage over its competitors. AMD would have a hollow core, which Intel could exploit.

Intel also was spending heavily on R&D. It hoped to make the technical differences in its products more pronounced so that it could raise its prices. As part of the technical excellence strategy, the Intel Capital division would continue to invest in leading edge smaller companies, whose success was closely tied to that of Intel.

With respect to all these initiatives, Intel remained self-questioning and critical. It held onto its culture of tough, rigorous debate and disagreement. Nothing had been resolved with finality, and given the uncertainties in the tech economy, the company was keeping its options open.

AMD's Responses

Meanwhile, AMD also was not sitting still. It was focused on one goal, betting that its Hammer technology could outdo the Itanium.

AMD, the world's leading supplier of flash memory for cell phones, decided in 2003 to fold that business into Fujitsu's flash memory operations. With the telecom market sliding, AMD did not consider flash memory a promising business. The memorandum of understanding with Fujitsu consolidated the two companies' operations into a single entity.

With flash memory off the plate, no products existed to divert AMD from being single-minded and devoted to but one goal—to commercialize the Hammer. This 64-bit processor was fully compatible with, and increased the performance of, existing 32-bit software, as opposed to Intel's Itanium, which was not fully compatible with 32-bit software and did not efficiently run this software. There were two commercial versions of the technology: Opteron processors for the server and workstation markets, and Athlon 64 processors for the desktop and mobile markets.

Intel had started developing the Itanium in 1994. Its aim was to get into the lucrative market for servers that powered corporate networks and the Internet. It dubbed its processor a "Sun-killer," because the Itanium would compete with Sun's 64-bit chip. A 64-bit chip can process data in twice the chunks as ordinary processors. The idea was great, but the Itanium did not live up to expectations. When launched two years late in 2001, it had to run software then in existence, most of it written for 32-bit processors, at a speed one-fifth as fast as a Pentium 4.

In 1999, AMD made the decision to develop its own 64-bit chip, the "Hammer," but with one critical difference: It would be fully compatible with old 32-bit software. Thus, AMD believed that the Hammer was the ideal chip for the transition from a 32-bit to a 64-bit world. It was convinced that the Hammer-based Opterons and Athlon 64s would do very well. Indeed, it was betting the company on this likelihood. As one analyst wrote:

> For AMD, it's the bottom of the 9th inning (end of the game of baseball for non-Yanks), the bases are loaded, and there's a batter going up to the plate. His name is Opteron (or Athlon 64 in the PC version), and he needs to score. He's got a lot of people cheering for him in the press and a select group of elite fans that need his 64-bit power. Will he have the power to score big? Not just a couple of runs, but hitting a home run and bringing everyone in. He'd better, because if AMD doesn't win this particular inning, it's going to end up in the minors or just plain out of the league (CBS Marketwatch, April 23, 2003).

AMD was operating on the edge. The Hammer had to succeed. To be able to compete with Intel in the microprocessor market, AMD had to continue to form close relationships with designers and manufacturers of chipsets, motherboards, and other components. It had to have these alliances because its agreement with Intel did not allow it to have features compatible with Intel's microprocessors. It had to be a virtual gorilla to take on Intel, which it considered the real gorilla.

AMD's new CEO was Hector de Jesus Ruiz, a native of Mexico and former Motorola employee. His plans were not to tear up the company or make dramatic shifts in strategy, but to execute flawlessly the strategy of bringing Hammer to market. His goal was to keep making chips like Hammer that were more functional than Intel's.

The ultimate aim was for AMD to boost its share of the PC processor business from 20 percent to 30 percent. AMD could crack the more lucrative server and high-end commercial desktop with Hammer technology because of Intel's Itanium faux pas. AMD could then gradually leave the lower-margin consumer segment, which it had pioneered, but where the margins were too low for it to prosper.

Ruiz had said that AMD was "going to win through innovation and better technology." He was "shocked" by Intel's hardball tactics, and was appreciative that the federal government was closely monitoring Intel.[8]

---

8. Paul Keegan, "Man with a Hammer," *Business 2.0*, November 2002.

What to Do Next?

Analysts commented that AMD had put all of its eggs in one basket, while Intel was still looking for greener pastures. In their view, Intel's strategy might be flawed, and looking for greener pastures might be Intel's ultimate undoing. But was AMD's strategy with its singular focus any more likely to be successful? While AMD was concentrating exclusively on Intel, Intel had a host of companies with which it was competing and with which it had to contend.

AMD had to figure out how it could make this situation work to its advantage. What options did it have open to it? How would Intel respond? Could AMD stay the course and prevail against an opponent that had beat back every advance it had made to this point? Could it think three or four moves ahead of Intel? Intel too had decisions to make. It had to decide how to thwart the threat that AMD posed to its dominance.

Intel was making some important decisions. In 2004, it was backing away from the development of chips for big screen, high definition, rear-projection television using a novel technology called liquid crystal on silicon (LCOS). The company's executives did not think that the returns available justified this investment. Intel would not be competing with Texas Instruments (TI) in this lucrative part of the consumer electronics market. TI's digital light-processing technology had been the first mover. Since 1996, TI had captured the business of more than 50 TV manufacturers. Intel's top executives concluded that the resources dedicated to LCOS would be better shifted to extending its core computer chip business into other consumer products. Instead of LCOS, Intel decided to put more emphasis on Centrino, boosting the speed of its laptop package with a new and faster Pentium M processor. The new processor ran at a clock speed of 2.1 GHz and was priced at $637 for 1,000 unit quantities. The introduction of the new and faster processor followed price cuts on its older and somewhat slower Pentium processors that now sold at $423 for 1,000 unit quantities. The prices of other Pentium models were lowered from 13 percent to 30.5 percent.

Intel's repricing of its processors was coming at the same time that AMD's Athlon 64 was getting rave reviews in PC technical magazines. *PC Advisor,* for instance, wrote on Oct. 22, 2004 (PC Advisor Internet site) that the Athlon 64 was "the fastest desktop processor ever." Though its core clockspeed was 1 GHz slower than the Pentium 4, it offered "powerful performance beyond the reach of its rival . . ." Both companies would have to meet the next technological leap forward—dual core products that put the circuitry of two microprocessors on a single piece of silicon. Any other way of moving ahead with Moore's Law seemed out of the question, as power leakage and other problems were making it harder to achieve high clock speeds using conventional methods. Dual core chips offered the advantage of running two sets of software at once. For example, one could use Microsoft's word processor at the same time that an antivirus software was running in the background. Microsoft and other software producers such as Linux suppliers Novell and Red Hat had promised to charge a single price for the software that ran dual core technology, while Oracle and IBM were charging for dual core products as if they were two chips. For dual core technology to be successful, Intel and AMD would have to work very closely with the software developers. The future of their dual core technology depended on the type of alliances they could forge with these companies.

Questions for Discussion

1. For a company like Intel, what does it mean to find the right balance between exploration and exploitation?
2. What does it mean to be a "virtual gorilla"? Why was being a virtual gorilla critical to AMD's success?
3. What role do price wars play in this industry?
4. What role do the courts play in this industry?
5. What is "segment zero"? How did Intel beat back AMD's challenge in segment zero?
6. How long can a company like Intel "throw spaghetti against the wall to see what sticks"?
7. What does "inflection point" mean? How many inflection points has Intel faced? How effective was it in dealing with these inflection points? Why was it effective?
8. When and why did it become counterproductive for Intel and AMD to keep chasing after microprocessing speed?
9. How important were chipsets and motherboard architecture to Intel's dominance? How did AMD overcome these factors?
10. What was Moore's Law? How did it motivate and provide Intel with a vision?

11. What does Andy Grove means when he says "only the paranoid survive?"

12. Why was the Hammer so important to AMD? What would it mean to AMD if the Hammer failed? Why did AMD have to ensure that it would succeed? How could Intel counter the Hammer? What should it do in response to this initiative by AMD?

Exercises

1. What is the competitive challenge AMD faces from Intel? How should AMD fend off this challenge? Analyze the situation and give advice to management.

2. What is the competitive challenge Intel faces from AMD? How should Intel fend off this challenge? Analyze the situation and give advice to management.

Video

"The View from the Top: Taking Risks at Intel." Films for the Humanities and Social Sciences, FFH 4560, 1994.

Bibliography

Alsop, Stewart. "Can AMD Avoid the Intel Graveyard?" *Fortune*. April 14, 1997:169.

Casadesus-Masnaell, Farmon, and Michael Rukstad. "Intel Corporation. 1997–2000." Harvard Business School Case 9-702-420, November 2001, p. 8.

Clark, Don. "Microsoft Sets Pricing Policy on Next Generation of Chips." *The Wall Street Journal*. October 19, 2004:B3.

Edwards, Cliff, and Ira Sager. "Can CEO Craig Barrett Reverse the Slide?" *Business Week*. October 15, 2001:80.

Einhorn, Bruce, Adam Aston, and Cliff Edwards. "Getting in Intel's Face." *Business Week*. November 5, 2001:96B.

Grove, Andy. "Intel's Andrew Grove on Competitiveness." *Academy of Management Executive* 13, no.1 (1999):15.

_____. *Only the Paranoid Survive*. NY: Doubleday: 1999.

Kirkpatrick, David, and Christopher Tkaczyk. "See This Chip?" *Fortune*. February 17, 2003:52.

Reinhardt, Andy. "Meet AMD's Rags-to-Riches Heir Apparent." *Business Week*. October 2, 2000:112.

_____. "Intel Inside Out," *Business Week*. December 4, 2000:116.

Schlender, Brent. "Intel Unleashes Its Inner Attila." *Fortune*. October 15, 2001:168.

Appendix A

EXHIBIT 1   Ten years of Intel's annual performance (in millions)

Year	Net revenue	Gross margin	Research & development	Operating income
2002	$ 26,764	$ 13,318	$ 4,034	$ 4,382
2001	26,539	13,052	3,796	2,256
2000	33,726	21,076	3,897	10,395
1999	29,389	17,553	3,111	9,767
1998	26,273	14,185	2,509	8,379
1997	25,070	15,125	2,347	9,887
1996	20,847	11,683	1,808	7,553
1995	16,202	8,391	1,296	5,252
1994	11,521	5,945	1,111	3,387
1993	8,782	5,530	970	3,392

Source: Intel company reports.

EXHIBIT 2   Intel's annual income statement 1998–2002 (in millions of U.S. dollars except for per-share items)

	2002	2001	2000	1999	1998
Total revenue	26,764	26,539	33,726	29,389	26,273
Cost of revenue	13,446	13,487	12,650	11,836	12,088
Gross profit	13,318	13,052	21,076	17,553	14,185
Selling/general/ admin. expenses, total	4,334	4,464	5,089	3,872	3,076
Research & development	4,034	3,796	3,897	3,111	2,509
Unusual expense (income)	20	198	109	392	165
Total operating expense	22,382	24,283	23,331	19,622	17,894
Operating income	4,382	2,256	10,395	9,767	8,379
Net income	3,117	1,291	10,535	7,314	6,068

Source: Yahoo! Finance (http://finance.yahoo.com).

EXHIBIT 3   AMD's annual income statement 1998–2002
(in millions of U.S. dollars except for per-share items)

	2002	2001	2000	1999	1998
Total revenue	2,697.0	3,891.8	4,644.2	2,857.6	2,542.1
Cost of revenue	2,105.7	2,589.7	2,514.6	1,964.4	1,718.7
Gross profit	591.4	1,302.0	2,129.6	893.2	823.4
Selling/general/ admin. expenses, total	670.1	620.0	599.0	540.1	419.7
Research & development	816.1	650.9	641.8	635.8	567.4
Unusual expense (income)	330.6	89.3	0.0	38.2	0.0
Total operating expense	3,922.4	3,950.0	3,755.5	3,178.5	2,705.8
Operating income	(1,225.4)	(58.3)	888.7	(320.9)	(163.6)
Net income	(1,303.0)	(60.6)	983.0	(88.9)	(104.0)

Source: Yahoo! Finance (http://finance.yahoo.com).

Appendix B

EXHIBIT 4   Pentium processors*

Processor	Clock speed	Bus speed	Clock multiplier
P 60	60 MHz	60 MHz	1x
P 66	66	66	1
P 75	75	50	1.5
P 90	90	60	1.5
P 100	100	66	1.5
P 120	120	60	2
P 133	133	66	2
P 150	150	60	2.5
P 166	166	66	2.5
P 200	200	66	3
P Pro 166	166	66	2.5
P Pro 180	180	60	3
P Pro 200	200	66	3
P 200 MMX	200	66	3
P 233 MMX	233	66	3.5
PII 233	233	66	3.5
PII 266	266	66	4
PII 300	300	66	4.5
PII 333	333	66	5
PII 350	350	100	3.5
PII 400	400	100	4
PII 450	450	100	4.5

Source: Intel Website (http://www.intel.com).

*Clock speed is the rate at which the internal logic operates. It is measured in units of hertz, or cycles processed per second. Bus speed is speed of access. The clock multiplier is the number of instructions executed per cycle.

Appendix C

EXHIBIT 5   The Celeron and its successors.

Processor	Clock speed	Bus speed	Clock multiplier
Celeron 266	266 MHz	66 MHz	4.0
Celeron 300	300	66	4.5
Celeron 300 A	300	66	4.5
Celeron 333 A	333	66	5.0
Celeron 366 A*	366	66	5.5
Celeron 400 A*	400	66	6.0
Celeron 433 A*	433	66	6.5
Celeron 466	466	66	7.0
Celeron 500	500	66	7.5
PII Xeon 400	400	100	4.0
PII Xeon 450	450	100	4.5
PIII Xeon 500	500	100	5.0
PIII Xeon 550	550	100	5.5
PIII 450	450	100	4.5
PIII 500	500	100	5.0
PIII 550	550	100	5.5

Source: Intel Website (http://www.intel.com).

CASE 2

Industry Analysis
Barnes & Noble versus Amazon.com[1]

Leonard Riggio, founder, chair, and CEO of Barnes & Noble, transformed bookselling into a giant industry, relying on the philosophy that people bought books based on emotion. Shopping, Riggio believed, was a recreational activity. In 1999, he concluded that the Internet would account for 20 percent of all sales and that his company had to plunge in and compete vigorously in this market.

Fortune's May 2003 cover story featured Riggio's arch-rival Jeff Bezos, founder, chair, and CEO of Amazon.com, jumping on a trampoline. The story remarked that during the Internet bubble, Bezos' "oversized personality made him seem fun and inspiring," but "when Amazon.com's stock price fell and its losses continued to mount, . . . his behavior made him look clueless."[2]

The industry in which Barnes & Noble and Amazon.com competed was changing rapidly. How attractive was this industry? What position should these companies occupy? This case provides an analysis of the bookselling industry and the positions Amazon.com and Barnes & Noble held within it (see Table 2.1).

The Performance of Amazon.com, Barnes & Noble, and Barnes & Noble.com

In September 2003, Amazon.com had greater market capitalization than Barnes & Noble and Barnes & Noble.com, an Internet company

1. This case was written by Alfred Marcus, University of Minnesota, Carlson School of Management. Copyright © 2005 by Marsh Publications LLC. All rights reserved.
2. Fred Vogelstein, "Mighty Amazon," *Fortune*, May 26, 2003, p. 20.

TABLE 2.1   A comparison of major booksellers with regard to a number of key indicators (September 2003)

	Amazon.com	Barnes & Noble	Barnes & Noble.com	Borders
Market cap($)	17.8B**	1.7B	384.3M*	1.54B
Employees	7,500	39,000	990	15,500
Revenue growth	26.0%	8.2%	4.5%	3.7%
Revenue ($)	3.9B	5.3B	422.8M	3.5B
Gross margin	24.6%	26.9%	23.5%	26.1%
Operating margins	3.2%	5.3%	-14.3%	5.08%
Net income ($)	-85.9M	127.0M	-15.7M	104.1M

Source: Yahoo! Finance (http://finance.yahoo.com).
*M=million
**B=billion

that Barnes & Noble started in 1999.[3] Amazon.com.had faster revenue growth than Barnes & Noble.com, but its gross margins and operating margins were not as good as those of Barnes & Noble and it lost money ($85.9 million), while Barnes & Noble made money ($127 million). (See the appendix for further performance analysis of these companies and of Borders, another bookseller with whom they competed.)

From 1998–2003, Amazon.com's stock outperformed Barnes & Noble, though it had a rougher ride. Barnes & Noble.com's stock performance bounced back and forth like that of Amazon.com.

The business press had a hard time understanding these companies. Initially, it believed Barnes & Noble would "crush" Amazon.com, but by the middle of 2003, it was doling out effusive praise for Amazon.com and calling Bezos a genius.

The bookselling industry

In the bookselling industry, competition was intense, growth was sluggish, profit margins were slim, and the product was a commodity. Like any industry, this one can be understood in terms of customers, substitute products, competitors, suppliers, and new entrants.

Customers

More than 2.5 million books were sold each year beginning in the late 1990s, but many were bought on impulse and barely read. Most books were sold in the Christmas season and on weekends. The biggest

---

3. In 1998, Barnes & Noble sold 18 percent of Barnes & Noble.com in an initial public offering (IPO). It jointly owned the remaining 64 percent with the German media conglomerate Bertelsmann (owner of Random House). In 2003, it bought out the portion Bertelsmann owned.

buyers were between the ages of 35 and 75; their average annual house-hold income exceeded $75,000. Consumers spent $19.5 billion on books in 2003, an increase from $18.8 billion in 2002. New York investment bank Veronis Suhler Stevenson predicted annual growth of 1.9 percent through 2008, compared to a 2.9 percent rate during the previous five years. The market was divided as follows:

Tradebooks: about 37 percent
College and K-12 textbooks: about 21 percent
Professional books: about 16 percent
Mass-market paperbacks: about 9 percent
Religious books: about 7 percent

The rest of the market consisted of book clubs and mail order catalogs (Barnes & Noble had both), subscription reference books such as ency-clopedias, and university press books.

Slow growth. Bookstores coped with their situation in a variety of ways. They relied on bestsellers like *Harry Potter* to generate traffic, but bestsellers were only 3 percent of their sales and consumers were increasingly buying them from mass-merchandise retailers such as Wal-Mart and Costco. To combat this threat, bookstores tried to create a special feel in their stores. Some stores decked themselves out like small- or full-scale libraries. In most stores, it was common to have places to sit—comfortable chairs and/or writing tables. The stores tried to create a "literary climate"; they had readings by famous authors, and other events. They usually had pleasant music—jazz or classical—in the background. As well as book selection, retailers paid a great deal of attention to décor, layout, furniture, display, and signage.

Customers cared about selection, service, and location, but the amenities listed above were among the most important reasons they kept coming back. Without an enjoyable and pleasant climate for browsing, bookstore executives and owners believed that they would lose out to mass-merchandise retailers.

Substitutes

There were numerous alternatives to spending time in a bookstore. People could go to a movie, the theater, or a concert; they could partic-ipate in voluntary activities such as serving on the board of a charitable organization; they could be involved in sports—run a marathon, golf, work out, or go to a sporting event like a hockey or a football game. They could attend religious services, browse the Internet, or play a video game. They could play a board game, bowl, or simply watch television. Many activities, from restaurants to yard work to shopping in department and outlet stores, competed with book buying.

Competition

Since 1993, the number of independent retailers belonging to the American Booksellers Association had declined from 4,700 to 1,885. However, the independent bookstores had increased their market share by 2 percent in 2003, to18 percent of the $11 billion U.S. adult fiction and nonfiction category. Since 2000, they had reversed more than a decade of decline. Even though the number of independent stores was fewer, those that survived did better.

Some independents had decided to compete with the chains by supersizing their stores. They had anywhere from 30,000 to 70,000 square feet, which was significantly larger than the average 25,000-square-feet Barnes & Noble store. Some of the large stores also relied on restaurants and large cookbook selections. The restaurants might constitute 10 percent of revenue and 80 percent of staff. The Starbucks found inside a Barnes & Noble store could not compete with a full-service restaurant that was this big. The independents also had reading and dinner clubs. Some had health and well-being sections that sold lotions, candles, and quilted bags. Many independents were decked out as very comfortable places to with beautiful bookcases, fireplaces, luxurious couches, and large children's departments. These amenities catered to women who lingered in the stores and tended to buy more books than men. Competitive independents emphasized service, in-store events, and promoting local or little-known authors. Small stores (as small as 1,500 square feet) concentrated on just a few kinds of books, knew their customers well, and hand-picked every book they carried.

The main chains. The two main chains were Barnes & Noble and Borders. In 2003, Barnes & Noble had 653 stores. It opened about 30 to 35 stores that year, but it also closed stores (about 12 per year) and relocated stores (about six per year). Borders had 450 stores. Barnes & Noble began as B. Dalton; it was originally owned by Dayton-Hudson. Borders began as Walden Books; K-mart bought Walden Books in 1984.

Lenny Riggio, Barnes & Noble's founder, transformed the industry. Riggio grew up in a working-class Italian neighborhood in Brooklyn and had been too poor to attend college full time, so he worked during the day as a clerk in the New York University bookstore. In 1965, he created his own campus bookstore. During the next six years, he established four other bookstores on campuses in New York City. In 1971, he bought Barnes & Noble, then an unprofitable New York textbook seller, and in 1974, he opened a Manhattan Barnes & Noble annex where he aggressively marketed low-priced, remaindered books.

In 1986, when Riggio bought B. Dalton, he owned 142 college bookstores and 37 Barnes & Nobles stores. With the purchase of B. Dalton, Barnes & Noble became the largest bookseller in the United States.

By the late 1980s, both B. Dalton and Walden had more than 600 mall-based stores. In the early 1990s, Riggio decided to do something different. His main competitor at that time was Borders, a chain based in Ann Arbor, Michigan, which K-mart bought in 1992. Borders had pioneered a new concept—the superstore. Riggio decided to match Borders. His company was an aggressive second mover that acted faster than Borders and expanded more rapidly.

Riggio's father had been a professional boxer—the only one to defeat middleweight champion Rocky Graziano twice. In a 1982 letter to the *New York Times*, the elder Riggio wrote that to "come out a winner" in boxing you had to "hit your opponent more times than he hits you."[4] The younger Riggio said that he learned from his father to be quicker on his feet and more nimble than his opponents.

Superstores. The superstores also had a special atmosphere. They were meant to be a gathering place for people, a place where people would linger. They had comfortable places to sit, coffee to drink, and late-night hours. They tried to build a sense of community. Celebrity authors sold their books at in-store readings. Advertisements featured pictures of literary greats like Ernest Hemingway and Virginia Woolf.

The usual purchase at a superstore was about twice that of a purchase at a mall-based store. The premise was that the more time a person spent in a store, the more that person would buy. Barnes & Noble

4. Jeffrey Trachtenberg, "Title Role: Barnes & Noble Pushes Books from Ambitious Publisher: Itself," *The Wall Street Journal*, June 18, 2003, p. A1.

centrally acquired about 50,000 titles for each of its superstores, but local managers had the freedom to adapt selection to local tastes. The typical store had 175,000 titles packed into 30,000 square feet. In the mid 1990s, average sales per square foot were about $250.

Fierce competition. Competition between Borders and Barnes & Noble was fierce. Because Borders' chairman once ran Hickory Farms, Barnes & Noble executives referred to it as a company made up of "guys who sold meat." A Borders ad read, "Unlike faceless chains run by guys with bad ties, Borders is run by real book and music people."[5] Borders stressed its origins. It had started as a small used-book store in Ann Arbor, Michigan. Tom Borders had been a college English teacher. His brother Louis was an entrepreneur who developed the company's inventory system, which was later copied by Barnes & Noble.

Both Barnes & Noble and Borders were in a race to see which of them would expand most rapidly. Their top executives believed that about 35 percent of the prime markets for their superstores in the United States had not been covered. Their main fear was that Wal-Mart and other mass-market retailers would take away their business.

The number of superstores in the United States jumped to nearly 800 in the mid-1990s, and made up nearly 70 percent of the revenues of the two principal chains. Including their mall-based operations, super-stores captured about a quarter of the U.S. market. Barnes & Noble's market share was about 15 percent and Borders' was about 10 percent. The unknown factor was the role that Internet commerce would play. Internet bookselling was just getting started and the executives of Barnes & Noble and Borders did not know where it would lead (see Table 2.2). K-mart could not keep up with Barnes & Noble and had spun off Walden and Borders in 1995.

TABLE 2.2   Shares of adult books sold

	1993	1998
Bookstore chains	23.4%	25.3%
Independents	28.7	19.3
Other (includes mass merchants, discount stores, book clubs, & mail order)	47.9	53.3
E-commerce		1.9

Source: Ghemawat and Baird, "Leadership Online," Harvard Business School Case 9-198-063.

5. Pankaj Ghemawat and Bret Baird, "Leadership Online: Barnes and Noble vs. Amazon.com," Harvard Business School Case 9-198-063, April 2000.

Suppliers

Publishers brought out about 50,000 new titles each year, adding to the more than one million titles already in print. Barnes & Noble bought from more than 1,200 publishers and 50 wholesalers. It also had a list of titles that it self-published and sold under its own imprint.

The United States had thousands of publishers, but the top 20 accounted for nearly 90 percent of U.S. sales. Simon & Schuster, owned by Viacom, was the largest U.S. publisher, with about 11 percent of the market. The number of publishers, however, was declining as large media companies and global conglomerates swallowed up smaller companies. Publishers sold books in two ways—through wholesalers and by direct sales.

Wholesalers. The two largest wholesalers were Ingram Book Group and Baker & Taylor. Ingram sold more than a half million titles and had a 50 percent market share. Ingram did more than just distribute books. It distributed personal computer hardware and software and home videos, which were 90 percent of its business.

When publishers sold directly to retailers, the discounts were 44 percent to 55 percent off the list price. When they sold to wholesalers, the discounts were 2 percent to 3 percent higher. Because the average wholesaler had margins of about 1.5 percent, it had to be superefficient. To achieve higher levels of efficiency, Ingram upgraded its systems earlier than Baker & Taylor, but Baker & Taylor was catching up. Both companies invested heavily in warehousing and electronic ordering and inventorying. Ingram had very fast delivery times; it could get 90 percent of its books to retailers within 36 hours.

Direct sales. Wholesalers such as Ingram and Baker & Taylor generally supplied most of the books that independent booksellers sold. The publishers tried to supply the chains directly. Direct sales were as follows: retailers (35 percent); schools and colleges (21 percent), individuals (14 percent), and libraries and other institutions (6 percent). Under a consent order that the publishers signed, they agreed not to give chains like Borders and Barnes & Noble higher discounts than independent retailers, but the independents were still suspicious that the publishers favored the chains.

Profits. Before overhead and advertising, the profit for the publisher on a successful $25 novel that sold 30,000 copies was about $127,500 (see Table 2.3). The gross margins were about 17 percent. Overheads

TABLE 2.3   Typical division of the profits for a fairly successful
                       hardback novel

No. of copies sold	Revenue
30,000 copies sold at $25	$750,000
50,000 copies printed at $2 per book	-100,000
Shipping costs at $1 per book	- 50,000
Retailers get $10 per book	-300,000
Wholesalers get $2 per book	- 60,000
Author gets $3.75 per book	-112,500
Publisher's profit	$127,500
(before advertising and overhead)	

Source: Adapted from data found in Jeffrey Trachtenberg, "Title Role," *The Wall Street Journal*, June 18, 2003, p. A1.

and advertising ate into the margins and could destroy them. Celebrity authors like the Clintons could demand huge non-refundable advances against royalties in the millions of dollars, but the typical author got just a token advance and no more than 10 percent to 15 percent of each copy sold. Not all books, moreover, were successful. If 50,000 copies of a novel were printed, 30,000 copies might be sold. The 20,000 unsold copies would be shipped back to the publisher to be "remaindered" or destroyed. If they were remaindered, the publisher would distribute them to other channels to be sold at a deep discount.

Buying on consignment. Wholesalers and retailers bought books on consignment; they could return what they did not sell for full credit. This practice originated during the Great Depression when there was no other way for publishers to get their books on booksellers' shelves. In the 1990s, more than 30 percent of new hardcover books were returned because they did not sell. The publishers addressed this problem in a variety of ways. They might offer an additional discount of 3 percent to 5 percent if the retailer or wholesaler was willing to give up the return privilege. They might give rebates at the end of the year if the retailer or wholesaler returned a low percentage of books.

Publishers had also started to print fewer initial copies. On average, a first printing of a typical book now is 2,000 to 5,000 copies—about half what it was 20 years ago. If demand went up, a publisher would either reprint the book (improved manufacturing technology has reduced the time to produce reprints) or bring out a new edition. Also, publishers track sales better today than they did previously because they have point-of-sale data. They also make better forecasts about how well books will do, but they still make mistakes, and even an experienced publisher cannot always anticipate demand.

New entrants

The main new entrant into this industry is online booksellers. By 1997, it was estimated that there were several hundred of them operating on the Web. By 1998, they had captured nearly 2 percent of the adult book market. Still, Barnes & Noble was the undisputed champion of bookselling. It had more bookstores, the biggest market share, and the greatest potential for growth.

When Amazon.com opened online in July 1995, Barnes & Noble paid little attention. Its 1995 annual report did not even mention the Internet; instead, it focused on Barnes & Noble's commitment to continued expansion. The key competitive challenge the company faced was to open new stores quickly. Its goal was to expand at a pace of about 100 new stores per year.

Jeff Bezos. Barnes & Noble had to contend with Jeff Bezos. Bezos' founding of Amazon.com was the stuff of legend. A summa cum laude graduate of Princeton in 1986 with a degree in computer science, he had worked for a telecom startup and a hedge fund. Seeking to begin a business on his own, he examined 20 possibilities for Internet commerce before settling on bookselling. He believed that great opportunities presented themselves in books because the industry was highly fragmented.

Internet selling offered many advantages, including a large selection, high inventory turnover, high sales per square foot, and high sales per operating employee. It beat the typical brick-and-mortar stores on all these attributes.

Bezos moved from New York City and located his business in Seattle, Washington, to take advantage of the software talent and proximity to Ingram's large wholesale warehouse in Oregon. This location was one in which there were no state taxes on retail purchases, which made Internet sales more competitive with retail. No taxes compensated for the high shipping costs.

Amazon.com's return rate of books to their publishers was only 1 percent to 2 percent, something publishers found very attractive because they were left with fewer books to remainder. The company fulfilled 60 percent of its orders through Ingram, but still had to warehouse about 2,000 titles in Seattle.

Internet shopping. To carry out its operations, Amazon.com had to innovate and pioneer in the development of software for Internet shopping. Amazon.com spent vast amounts of money on R&D, out-spending Barnes & Noble.com by eight times in this category. Amazon.com created the look and feel of an Internet shopping site. It provided information about the books it sold, posted author interviews, offered free book reviews, and gave links to other sites and features. In 1999, Amazon.com obtained a patent for its one-click technology, which allowed customers to order from its Website with a simple click of the mouse. In contrast to a physical store, which opened and closed at fixed times, a person could shop at Amazon.com any time of the day.

Early successes. The venture capital firm Kleiner Perkins Caulfield & Byer gave Amazon.com $8 million to get started, and the business grew rapidly. In less than a year, Amazon.com had nearly $1 million in sales. Repeat customers provided more than 50 percent of the orders and the average transaction was for more than $50. Technical and business books made up a high percentage of Amazon.com's early orders. Thirty percent of its sales were international.

When the company went public in 1997, its market capitalization rose to $560 million on the first day. Suddenly Bezos was a multimillionaire, as he owned 42 percent of the stock. Investors had confidence in Amazon.com's business model even though the company did not make a profit and it was not clear when it would do so. Investors liked the cash flow. The typical customer paid Amazon.com with a credit card; Amazon.com then collected the sale price (minus a fee) within a few days from a credit card company. In the weeks that passed before the supplier was paid, Amazon.com had use of the customer's money.

A historic shift? Barnes & Noble's executives' concern was that Amazon.com's opening thrust was just the beginning of a historic shift toward buying more books online. Entry into online bookselling seemed relatively easy and Barnes & Noble's executives expected others to follow. These might include small booksellers that had loyal followings in special categories like science fiction and fantasy, publishers like Simon & Schuster, warehouses like Ingram, and mass-merchant retailers like Wal-Mart or Target.

Barnes & Noble Strikes Back

Barnes & Noble needed a strategy to deal with this phenomenon. Therefore, it launched its own Website in the spring of 1997, Barnes & Noble.com. The site featured personalized book recommendations and deep discounts every bit as good as Amazon.com's on most items. The company used its brand name to capture leadership in the general interest and fiction categories.

Delivery times and integration. Because of its warehouses and greater experience in shipping books, Barnes & Noble.com tried to beat Amazon.com's delivery times. It built two new warehouses—in Atlanta and Reno—that it added to its existing warehouse in New Jersey to ensure prompt distribution. It also built its own version of the one-click technology, which it called "express lane" ordering.

But Barnes & Noble did not seamlessly integrate brick-and-mortar operations with the Internet. It considered but rejected ideas such as putting Internet kiosks in bookstores so that customers could order online. It also considered but rejected the option of giving customers the choice of picking up the books they ordered at a local bookstore.

Barnes & Noble's concern was that if it moved in this direction, it would forfeit the tax advantages it enjoyed from selling over the Internet. The only connection Barnes & Noble made between its stores and its Internet site was to give away coupons to in-store shoppers to encourage them to purchase books online.

Who had the "biggest" bookstore? Barnes & Noble's executives were enraged when Amazon.com advertised that it was the "earth's biggest bookstore." Since 1970, the company's slogan had been that it was "the world's biggest bookstore." Barnes & Noble sued, arguing that Amazon.com was not a bookstore at all, but a book broker. Amazon.com, in turn, countersued. It sought an injunction against Barnes & Noble.com for using its one-click technology. Barnes & Noble, Amazon.com argued, had violated Amazon.com's patent. The companies settled these cases out of court.

In 1998, Amazon.com again went on the offensive. It ran an advertisement purporting to show that the number of Amazon.com's titles dwarfed those of Barnes & Noble. Barnes & Noble's retort was "Who's kidding who?" During 1998, Barnes & Noble increased the number of titles available on its online database to 8 million and the number of titles in its inventory to 750,000. This increase can be compared to the 4.7 million titles that Amazon.com then had in its database and the 300,000 titles it had in inventory.

Amazon.com's moves against the IPO. In 1999, Barnes & Noble had an IPO, which spun off Barnes & Noble.com as a separate company. Bertelsmann owned 36 percent of the new company, Barnes & Noble owned 36 percent, and the rest of the shares were sold to the public.

One month before the spin-off, Amazon.com took a number of aggressive steps to counter the IPO. Amazon.com added 1.5 million more titles to those it already listed; it introduced a personalized book recommendation service; and it started to sell bestsellers at a 50 percent discount. The 50 percent discount was especially galling to Barnes & Noble.com, because the company was forced to match the discount, which meant that it had to sell books at cost. Barnes & Noble found it hard to understand what Amazon.com was doing. The company's executives believed that Amazon.com had the most to lose from a price war, because Barnes & Noble sold more books than anyone else, and it could get the best deals from publishers.

Amazon.com's aggressive moves had their desired effect. The new company's stock climbed just 27 percent on the first day of the IPO, a huge disappointment in an era when stocks routinely doubled or tripled the initial asking price. Amazon.com was beating Barnes & Noble.com on the criterion that mattered most to Wall Street. The financial community was not much concerned about Amazon.com's lack of profits, nor did Barnes & Noble's overall market share particularly impress it. What mattered was "eyeballs," and on this measure Amazon.com dominated. Amazon.com had 8.4 million registered Internet customers to Barnes & Noble.com's 1.7 million. Its Internet market share was 75 percent to Barnes & Noble.com's 15 percent.

Industry data indicated that online sales were seriously damaging the revenues of the large chains. Barnes & Noble's CEO Riggio acknowledged that eventually the Internet would capture 2 percent to 5 percent of bookstore sales. With Barnes & Noble's growth in earnings less than predicted—10 percent to 15 percent a year rather than 20 percent to 25 percent—it was forced to cut back its new store openings by almost half in 1998 and 1999. Desperate to strike back at Amazon.com, it thought its only option was to go after Ingram. It made an offer to buy Ingram Book Group in 1998, only to be rebuffed because of antitrust scrutiny.

Amazon.com Reinvents Itself

The battle between Amazon.com and Barnes & Noble.com was intense. The two companies wore each other down. Perhaps the book-selling industry was too small for both of them. Amazon.com therefore came up with a new plan—to reinvent itself as a general merchandiser and Internet service provider.

A general merchandiser and Internet service provider. In June 1998, Amazon.com began to sell music online and quickly became the biggest online music seller; the company followed this move with video and DVD sales later in the same year. In both these cases, Amazon.com engaged in the full range of e-commerce activities: buying, warehousing, merchandising, shipping, and customer service. By the end of 1999, it had moved beyond books into other retail categories such as electronics, home improvement goods, and toys, while Barnes & Noble.com only sold media-related products and limited its increased consumer offerings to a few items such as music, posters, and prints. In 2000, Amazon.com added lawn and patio and kitchen products, cell phones, and wireless services to the array of products it sold.

Amazon.com also decided that in some of its initiatives it would not own the goods sold or take responsibility for order fulfillment. Like eBay or Yahoo!, it would be an e-commerce partner for individuals and for small and large businesses, earning fees for bringing people together and providing a technology for the marketing, distribution, and warehousing of their goods. In 1999, in partnership with Sotheby, Amazon.com launched an auction initiative oriented mostly toward higher end arts and antiques. In a few short years, Amazon.com morphed from an online bookstore to a purveyor of everything from CDs and palm pilots to power tools and waffle irons.

zShops. In 1999, Amazon.com created an area on its Website called zShops, where it facilitated transactions between customers and sellers. It signed agreements with dot.coms such as Drugstore.com, Living.com, Audible.com, and the online car-sales company Greenlight.com. Each would pay Amazon.com fees for the opportunity to be showcased on the company's Website. Unlike the launch of a new Amazon.com product category, which required spending on products and physical infrastructure, these deals cost Amazon.com virtually nothing, but the fees helped it move closer to profitability .

In theory, Amazon.com would not only be selling more products, but selling the attention of its customers to other Internet retailers. In this way, Amazon.com would become more like an Internet portal such as Yahoo! In comparison to Yahoo! and the other portals, however, Amazon.com claimed an advantage. Its customers were not just surfers and chatters; they were experienced online shoppers.

Regardless of how good this idea may have been, many of Amazon.com's partners quickly went out of business. They had promised to pay Amazon.com in rapidly falling stock rather than cash, so Amazon.com got little back from them. The net effect of these deals was losses and write-offs.

More deals. These losses and write-offs did not deter Amazon.com from pursuing its new strategy. In 2001, it signed deals with brick-and-mortar retailers such as Target, Circuit City, Virgin Records, and Borders; the company agreed to run all or part of their e-commerce operations. It would sell the retailers' products on Amazon.com, and in some cases warehouse products, distribute orders, and run the partner's Website. Unlike the dot.coms, these deals held the promise of real revenue, but in the end how much revenue would Amazon.com actually be able to earn?

Target, for instance, was doing anywhere from $50 million to $100 million in sales online each year. Amazon.com obtained a high single-digit percentage of that revenue, plus a per-item charge for warehousing and distributing Target's goods, and a fixed fee for letting Target use Amazon.com's technology to run Target.com. Amazon.com's cut of Target's online sales might reach 20 percent. Thus, if Target had $100 million in sales, Amazon.com would realize about $20 million in revenue.

Fifteen Target-sized deals, assuming operating margins of 20 percent, would signify about $300 million in revenue and $60 million in operating profits for Amazon.com. Factoring in interest payments from the company's heavy debt load and other expenses, these revenues and earnings would help Amazon.com move toward profitability, but they would not get it over the top. The revenues from these types of deals would leverage investments Amazon.com had made in e-commerce technology and in its distribution centers, which was a plus, but they would not bring Amazon.com to full profitability.

Difficult choices. Amazon.com still faced very difficult choices. Its main revenues and income continued to come from books and media like CDs and DVDs (see Table 2.4). Revenue and income from its other operations were not rising fast enough to make much of a dent on Amazon.com's lack of profits.

The gross margins in services were outstanding (more than 50 percent) and they far outstripped the profitability of Amazon.com's other businesses. However, they remained a small portion of what Amazon.com did; they provided just 7 percent of the company's revenues and 15 percent of its gross profits in 2002.

The single-store concept. In 2000, Amazon.com moved further in its efforts to reinvent itself as a general merchandiser and Internet service provider. It moved to "a single-store" concept, giving its third party sellers an equal level of access on its Internet site. Each of Amazon.com's sellers had a single page on the Amazon.com Website where they could display their goods.

Amazon.com also invested in five U.S. warehouses and made huge investments in technology that integrated its Website, customer service, payment processing, and warehouse operations.

The question Amazon.com faced was how it was going to leverage these investments quickly to reduce its debts and put it into the black. The company had to do all of this while at the same time protecting its bookselling business and moving into the entirely new territory of being an Internet service provider.

Amazon.com was evolving from a retailer to a commerce platform that supported third-party selling. This change meant that it would be

TABLE 2.4   Amazon.com's revenue and gross profit percentages

Revenue Percentages	1999	2000	2001	2002
Books, music, & DVD/video	80	61	54	49
Electronics, tools, and kitchen	9	18	18	28
International	10	14	21	17
Services (fees, etc. earned from partnering with 3rd party sellers)	1	7	7	7

Gross profit percentages	1999	2000	2001	2002
Books, music, & DVD/video	90	64	57	52
Electronics, tools, and kitchen	-7	10	9	
International	12	12	18	24
Services (fees, etc. earned from partnering with 3rd party sellers)	4	18	16	15

Source: Adapted from data in Stig Leschly, Michael Roberts, and William Sahlman, "Amazon.com 2002," Harvard Business School Case 9-803-098, February 2003.

a department store or mall and a service provider on the Web with some of the Web's best "real estate." It had four programs to help carry out functions for partner companies:

1. *Merchants@Amazon.com*—Large retailers such as J&R Electronics, Office Depot, Circuit City, and Toys "R" Us sold items on Amazon.com's Website, but they performed many e-commerce functions themselves.

2. *Merchants.com*—Amazon.com operated the websites of companies like Target for them. It also maintained the inventory, handled the distribution, and carried out most of the fulfillment functions for a fixed fee.

3. *Syndicated stores*—Amazon.com performed the functions discussed above as well as the buying, stocking, and pricing of products for such companies as Borders and Virgin Records. Here, Amazon.com shared a portion of the revenues it collected.

4. *Marketing deals*—Amazon.com promoted the products or services of companies like drugstore.com on its Website in exchange for a fee based on the number of customers it exposed or referred to these sites.

How profitable were these different models? How should Amazon.com promote them? A risk lay in the path Amazon.com had chosen. The company was highly dependent on brand recognition to bring customers to its site. Its customers, who were mostly wealthy and highly educated, identified Amazon.com with books. Would they no longer visit the site if Amazon.com was simply a place to buy charcoal grills and kitty litter?

Like retailers that overextend themselves, Amazon.com's one-stop shopping strategy might be misguided. Expanding beyond its core items—books, CDs, and videos—could obscure the Amazon.com brand at a time when its success demanded a clear image. Powerful brands had to stand for something simple. Amazon.com had succeeded because it represented books. Was it now ceding ground in this area to Barnes & Noble? Would a strategy in which Amazon.com was a purveyor of everything from books to socks actually work?

Bezos maintained that Amazon.com stood for high-quality customer service over the Web-and this service would attract customers regardless of what Amazon.com sold. Bezos wanted his customers to be "agnostic" about whether they bought from Amazon.com or not; his goal was to expand customer selection.

Amazon.com, however, had new competitors in bookselling. Search-engine giant Google developed a program called Google Print that allowed readers to search the content of books that publishers put on the Internet. The rivalry between Google and Amazon.com showed how barriers between once-separate markets such as Web searching, auctions, and retail were blurring. Google, Yahoo!, Amazon.com, and eBay were stepping into each other's territories (see Table 2.5).

A lack of focus. Barnes & Noble's CEO Riggio thought that Amazon.com's moves would not work in its favor. If Amazon.com became the Wal-Mart of the Internet and became known for selling music, videos, gifts, and greeting cards, holding auctions, and offering links to drug and pet stores, then Barnes & Noble.com's narrow focus—its commitment to books—would be an advantage. Staying focused on being what Barnes & Noble.com did best would earn it a larger market share of the book market among Web-centered customers.

Barnes & Noble, however, was hedging its bets too. Its stores also sold impulse items, which had higher margins than books—things like reading glasses, miniature nightlights, and Godiva chocolates. Barnes & Noble also tried to pioneer digital books, but consumers did not show much interest. Its latest initiative was to expand the number of titles it published on its own. This expansion put pressure on other publishers to lower costs. Barnes & Noble was publishing classics like *Moby Dick* to compete with the Modern Library. It published Spark Notes to compete with Cliff Notes. It had astrology, art, and how-to-do-it books that competed with Time Warner. It published a splashy best-seller called *Satisfaction: The Act of Female Orgasm*, with "Sex and the City" star Kim Cattrall and her husband Mark Levinson.

What to Do Next?

Amazon.com was looking for new categories in which it could expand. It recently began selling clothes, shoes, and other apparel. With an

TABLE 2.5   U.S. visitor traffic to the Web's biggest Internet companies (August 2004, ranked by number of visitors in millions)

1. Yahoo! sites	113.1
2. Time Warner network	112.1
3. Microsoft sites	111.0
4. Google sites	61.9
5. eBay	58.9
6. Ask Jeeves	38.9
7. Amazon.com sites	33.1

Source: comScore Networks (http://www.comscore.com).

increasing number of people throughout the world hooked up to the Internet, the possibilities of what it could sell were virtually limitless. Barnes & Noble, on the other hand, was digging in more deeply as a seller and publisher of books. The question for both companies was what to do next.

Questions for Discussion

1. What did Riggio mean when he said that books were sold based on emotion? What did he mean when he said that shopping was a recreational activity?
2. What accounts for Amazon.com having 17 times the market capitalization of Barnes & Noble despite the fact that it is not a profitable business and has never been one, while Barnes & Noble is a profitable business and nearly always has been one?
3. How attractive is the bookselling industry?
4. Assess the power and influence of *customers* vis à vis the booksellers.
    a. What had the booksellers done to increase store traffic?
    b. How were they fending off mass-market discounters like Wal-Mart?
5. How did booksellers stack up against *substitutes*?
6. Characterize the *competition* among booksellers.
    a. What role did independent bookstores play? Why were they not declining?
    b. What influence did Dayton-Hudson and K-mart have on the industry?
    c. Why did they give up on it?
7. How would you describe Leonard Riggio? What kind of competitor was he? How had his competition with Borders evolved? What role did the superstore play in industry evolution?
8. Characterize the *supply chain*.
    a. What was the role of publishers? How profitable were they?
    b. What was the role of wholesalers? How profitable were they?
    c. What was the role of consignment selling? Was this system antiquated? How could it be improved?
    d. How much power and influence did publishers and whole salers have? How could booksellers counter their power and influence?

9. Who were the main *new entrants* to the industry?
   a. How did Barnes & Noble originally respond? What did it later realize?
   b. How did Internet selling stack up against superstores?
   c. What were the challenges that Amazon.com as a startup had to overcome? How did it overcome these challenges?
10. How effective was Barnes & Nobles' response to the rise of Amazon.com?
    a. What actions did Barnes & Noble take? How did Amazon.com counter these actions?
    b. Who won the "battle" between the two companies?
11. Amazon.com's rationale for selling everything from tools and hardware to health and beauty products, toys and games, and electronics was that it would offer a total online buying experience. But what had it actually become? Was it still a bookseller? Was it still in the bookselling industry? Was it an Internet company, an online super-retailer, or something else?
12. How profitable wereAmazon.com's new initiatives? How aggressive would Amazon.com have to be in marketing them? To what extent would they detract from its core business? Draw up a plan for making Amazon.com profitable.
13. Do you believe that Amazon.com had overextended itself?
14. Assess Barnes & Noble's hedging strategies. Explain your answer. Did they make sense? Would they be effective? Why or why not?
15. In the long run, was it best for Barnes & Noble and Amazon.com to be more alike or more different? Should Barnes & Noble copy Amazon.com's Internet moves? Should Amazon.com buy brick-and-mortar bookstores? What do you think?
16. Will Barnes & Noble and Amazon.com be in the same industry five years from now? In what industry will Barnes & Noble be at that time? In what industry will Amazon.com be? How attractive will the industries be in which they will be competing?
17. What does this case say to you about industry evolution and the whole concept of what an industry is?

Exercises

1. Visit the Amazon.com and Barnes & Noble.com Websites. Go to a Barnes & Noble and a Borders store. Evaluate what and how merchandise is being sold. List ways of integrating the Internet with brick-and-mortar stores.
2. Based on your assessment of Amazon.com's customers, suppliers, competitors, etc., what is the competitive challenge that

Amazon.com faces from Barnes & Noble? Analyze the situation and give advice to management.

3. Based on your assessment of Barnes & Noble's customers, suppliers, competitors, and so forth, what is the competitive challenge that Barnes & Noble faces from Amazon.com? Analyze the situation and give advice to management.

Video

"Michael Porter on the Five Forces." Cambridge, MA: Harvard Business School, 1998.

Bibliography

Bahn, David, and Patrick Fischer. "Clicks and Mortar." Metropolitan State University of Minnesota. Unpublished manuscript: 2002.

Ghemawat, Pankaj, and Bret Baird. "Leadership Online: Barnes & Noble vs. Amazon.com (A)." Harvard Business School Case 9-798-063. April 2000.

Hof, Robert, and Heather Green. "How Amazon.com Cleared That Hurdle," *Business Week*. February 4, 2002:60.

Leschly, Stig, Michael Roberts, and William Sahlman. "Amazon.com.—2002." Harvard Business School Case 9-803-098. February 2003.

Louie, Dickson. "Barnesandnoble.com (B) and (C)." Harvard Business School Case 9-901-023 and 9-901-024. February 2001.

Norton, Rob. "Why the Bookstore Wars Are Good." *Fortune*. October 27, 1997:50.

Porter, Michael. "How Competitive Forces Shape Strategy," *Harvard Business Review*. March–April 1979:137.

Thomas, Cathy Booth. "Dell Wants Your Home." *Time*. October 6, 2003:48.

Trachtenberg, Jeffrey. "Title Role: Barnes & Noble Pushes Books from Ambitious Publisher: Itself." *The Wall Street Journal*. June 18, 2003:A1.

_____. "Plot Twist: To Compete with Book Chains, Some Think Big; Independent Sellers Gain with Size, Service; 'We Sell a Lot of Soap'; Eat, Then Buy the Cookbook." *The Wall Street Journal*. August 24, 2004:A1.

Vogelstein, Fred. "Mighty Amazon.com." *Fortune*. May 26, 2003:20.

Warner, Melanie. "Can Amazon.com Be Saved?" *Fortune*. November 26, 2001:156.

Wingfield, Nick, and Kevin Delaney. "Google Encroaches on Amazon as Rivalries Grow." *The Wall Street Journal*. October 7, 2004:B3.

Appendix

EXHIBIT 1   Amazon.com annual income statement (in millions of U.S. dollars except for per-share items)

	12 months ending 12/31/02	12 months ending 12/31/01	12 months ending 12/31/00	12 months ending 12/31/99	12 months ending 12/31/98
Total revenue	3,932.9	3,122.4	2,762.0	1,639.8	609.8
Cost of revenue	2,940.3	2,323.9	2,106.2	1,349.2	476.2
Gross profit	992.6	798.6	655.8	290.6	133.7
Selling/general/ admin. expenses, total	596.9	602.4	703.5	483.3	148.3
Total operating expense	3,868.8	3,534.7	3,625.9	2,245.6	718.9
Operating income	64.1	(412.3)	(863.9)	(605.8)	(109.1)
Interest expense, net nonoperating	(142.9)	(139.2)	(130.9)	(84.6)	(26.6)
Net income before taxes	(145.8)	(526.4)	(1,106.7)	(643.2)	(121.6)

Source: Yahoo! Finance (http://finance.yahoo.com).

EXHIBIT 2   Barnes & Noble annual income statement (in millions of U.S. dollars except for per-share items)

	52 weeks ending 02/01/03	52 weeks ending 02/02/02	52 weeks ending 02/03/01	52 weeks ending 01/29/00	52 weeks ending 01/30/99
Total revenue	5,269.3	4,870.4	4,375.8	3,486.0	3,005.6
Cost of revenue	3,855.8	3,560.0	3,169.7	2,483.7	2,142.7
Gross profit	1,413.5	1,310.4	1,206.1	1,002.3	862.9
Selling/general/ admin. expenses, total	965.1	904.3	813.0	651.1	580.6
Total operating expense	5,005.2	4,624.6	4,242.0	3,253.9	2,820.5
Operating income	264.1	245.8	133.8	232.1	185.1
Interest income, invest. nonoperating	(26.8)	(88.4)	(103.9)	(42.0)	(71.3)
Net income before taxes	199.3	109.3	(33.0)	218.6	156.6

Source: Yahoo! Finance (http://finance.yahoo.com).

EXHIBIT 3   Barnes & Noble.com annual income statement
            (in millions of U.S. dollars except for per-share items)

	12 months ending 12/31/02	12 months ending 12/31/01	12 months ending 12/31/00	12 months ending 12/31/99	12 months ending 12/31/98
Total revenue	422.8	404.6	320.1	193.7	61.8
Cost of revenue	327.3	313.4	261.8	159.9	47.6
Gross profit	95.6	91.2	58.3	33.8	14.3
Selling/general/ admin. expenses, total	98.0	138.4	175.5	119.9	82.4
Total operating expense	498.1	656.0	619.6	316.4	145.7
Operating income	(75.3)	(251.4)	(299.5)	(122.6)	(83.9)
Interest income (exp), net nonoperating	1.6	7.0	23.7	20.2	0.7
Net income before taxes	(73.7)	(244.4)	(275.7)	(102.4)	(83.1)

Source: Yahoo! Finance (http://finance.yahoo.com).

EXHIBIT 4   Borders annual income statement (in millions of U.S.
            dollars except for per-share items)

	52 weeks ending 01/26/03	52 weeks ending 01/27/02	52 weeks ending 01/28/01	52 weeks ending 01/23/00	52 weeks ending 01/24/99
Total revenue	3,513.0	3,413.2	3,297.1	2,968.4	2,595.0
Cost of revenue	2,552.1	2,474.6	2,380.4	2,127.6	1,859.4
Gross profit	934.0	913.3	890.8	840.8	735.6
Selling/general/ admin. expenses, total	745.2	744.8	736.2	659.2	557.6
Total operating expense	3,319.1	3,256.2	3,162.0	2,797.4	2,427.7
Operating income	193.9	157.0	135.1	171.0	167.3
Interest income (exp), net nonoperating	(12.6)	(14.4)	(13.1)	(16.6)	(16.2)
Net income before taxes	181.3	142.6	122.0	154.4	151.1

Source: Yahoo! Finance (http://finance.yahoo.com).

CASE 3

Strengths and Weaknesses
Dell versus Gateway[1]

During the second half of 1999 and most of 2000, Gateway's stock outperformed Dell's, but after 2000 Dell took the lead. The two companies had the same direct sales model, so what accounts for this difference? This case analyzes these companies' strengths and weaknesses.

Dell's and Gateway's Performance

Dell's rise to prominence over Gateway started in 1997. Before that, the two companies were close in sales and operating margins (see Table 3.1), but by 1999, the gap between them was wide.

Gateway's revenue slipped from $9.3 billion in 1999 to $4.2 billion in 2002, while Dell's grew from $18.2 billion to $31.2 billion (see

TABLE 3.1   Sales and operating margins for Dell and Gateway 1994–1999

	1994	1995	1996	1997	1998	1999
Dell sales ($ in billions)	2.8	3.5	5.3	7.8	12.3	18.2
Gateway sales ($ in billions)	2.7	3.7	5.0	6.3	7.7	9.0
Dell operating margin (percentage)	-1	7	7	9	11	11
Gateway operating margin (percentage)	5	7	7	5	6	7
Dell inventory turnover ratio*	11	9	10	24	41	52
Gateway inventory turnover ratio*	19	14	15	21	37	37

Source: Company records.
*Denotes the cost of goods divided by the company's average inventory.

---

1. This case was written by Alfred Marcus, University of Minnesota, Carlson School of Management. Copyright © 2005 by Marsh Publications LLC. All rights reserved.

Table 3.2). Gateway lost $1 billion in 2001 and $297.7 million in 2002, while Dell made $2.2 billion in 2001 and $1.3 billion in 2002.

Dell's challenge was to maintain its momentum despite its growth. Its market cap had surpassed that of the combined Hewlett Packard (HP) and Compaq companies (see Table 3.3). In 2003, Dell was more profitable than these firms, earning $2.38 billion, while they earned just $2.07 billion. Dell had more with just 39,100 employees, while the combined HP and Compaq had 141,000 employees.

Gateway's challenge was how to survive. It lost $394.7 million in 2003 and its revenue declined by 29.8 percent. It was in danger of being surpassed by Apple, which had more than three times Gateway's market cap.

The Personal Computer Industry

The personal computer (PC) industry was one of the largest in the world, with annual sales of $150 billion in 2002 and 125 million units shipped. Its 2002 sales were off by 4 percent; and for the first time since 1985 the PC industry was not growing.

TABLE 3.2   Gateway and Dell annual income statements 1999–2002

Gateway (in millions of U.S. dollars except for per-share items)	2002	2001	2000	1999
Total revenue	4,171.3	5,937.9	9,252.1	8,964.9
Cost of revenue	3,605.1	5,099.7	7,199.1	7,127.7
Gross profit	566.2	838.2	2,053.0	1,837.2
Selling/general/admin. expenses, total	994.4	2,022.1	1,547.7	1,241.6
Total operating expense	4,682.6	7,121.8	8,746.8	8,369.2
Operating income	(511.2)	(1,183.9)	505.3	595.7
Net income after taxes	(297.7)	(1,011.6)	250.5	427.9
Dell (in millions of U.S. dollars except for per-share items)	2002	2001	2000	1999
Total revenue	31,168	31,888	25,265	18,243
Cost of revenue	25,661	25,445	20,047	14,137
Gross profit	5,507	6,443	5,218	4,106
Selling/general/admin. expenses, total	2,784	3,193	2,387	1,788
Research & development	452	482	374	272
Total operating expense	29,379	29,225	23,002	16,197
Operating income	1,789	2,663	2,263	2,046
Net income after taxes	1,246	2,236	1,666	1,460

Source: Yahoo! Finance (http://finance.yahoo.com).

TABLE 3.3   Direct competitor comparison (September 2003)

	Dell	HP (plus Compaq)	Gateway	Apple
Market cap ($)	87.17B*	60.89B	1.95B	7.78B
Employees	39,100	141,000	11,500	10,211
Revenue growth (%)	13.60	25.10	-29.80	7.10
Revenue ($)	35.40B	56.59B	4.17B	5.74B
Gross margin (%)	18.25	26.60	14.19	27.52
Operating margins	8.45	3.16	-12.48	-0.88
Net income ($)	2.38B	2.07B	-394.7M**	-18.00M

Source: Yahoo! Finance (http://finance.yahoo.com).
*B=billions
**M=millions

The market for PCs had increased by 15 percent-plus per year in the 1990s. The decade ended in a frenzy as companies loaded up on new Y2K-ready machines, but as the 21st century unfolded, this growth abated.

In 2003 research showed that just 11 percent of customers wanted a new machine, the lowest percentage since 1995. Companies waited 41 months to replace their PCs, while individuals waited 60 months.

Conditions were so bad that Michael Dell, the 38-year-old founder and CEO of Dell, started to redefine his business as "computer systems and information technology (IT)." Ted Waitt, the 40-year-old founder and CEO of Gateway, suggested that his firm was in the "home entertainment industry." The industry had declined for many reasons, the foremost among them being an inability of technological innovation to spur additional demand, and intense competition among companies.

Technological saturation

Owners used to acquire new PCs to run the operating system and application upgrades that Microsoft introduced and the more powerful microprocessors Intel built. But the advantage of moving to faster and more powerful technology was losing its appeal. Despite a new Microsoft version of Windows XP and Intel's 3-GB Pentium 4, most customers were satisfied with their existing computers. Surveys showed that they believed the computers they currently owned were good enough to run most of the software they wanted to use. Most did not think that a $3,000 computer running XP with a 3-GB Pentium 4 was that much better than a $700 computer running the program with a 700-MHz Celeron.

With the advent of even cheaper computers, the competition was increasingly about price. A consumer could walk into a Wal-Mart and buy a cheap, no-frills product right off the shelf. Indeed, a growing number of consumers believed that a $300 Wal-Mart PC that operated software called "Lindows" was acceptable.

Without new technology that generated customer demand, the industry was likely to languish. User interest in new PCs and PC-related technology was waning. How could it be regained?

1. Apple was trying to attract interest among home users with its iMac. The company stressed the iMac's sleek design and its connectivity among pictures, music, and movies.

2. Microsoft, HP, and Sony were trying to attract interest among home users with home entertainment software. In 2002, HP brought out PCs with Microsoft's Windows XP Media Center edition. This software turned the PC into a home entertainment center, allowing it to function as a TV and to record video.

3. Microsoft was promoting a tablet PC, which looked like a laptop but had a screen that allowed it to work like a digital legal pad. The idea was that people would find situations, such as business meetings, where the tablet would be valuable.

4. Wireless computers were among the most recent developments. Intel had a new microprocessor that it sold under the Centrino label; it combined wireless with other functions. Microsoft programmers were working on wireless PCs.

IBM was creating new applications for business users. It launched a campaign called "Think Solutions" whose objective was to create a higher comfort level among PC users. It had an application that saved what users did to a special area on the hard drive so that the data would be easier to recover if the hard drive crashed. Another application enabled users to move between wired and wireless networks without having to change internal settings.

Innovations such as these would be valuable only if broadband became more ubiquitous. Longer battery life and the ability to switch computers on instantly were also needed. PCs so powerful they could understand the meaning of the spoken word and support three-dimensional visual interfaces were on the horizon. While important, however, these developments were not likely to spur a new wave of buying.

Intense competition

Meanwhile, competition in the industry was intense. With capacity high and demand low, no large PC maker other than Dell was making money. HP and Compaq's combined losses were $1 billion on $27 billion of PC sales in 1993. Gateway's losses were $1 billion on $4 billion in sales. IBM was doing no better than breaking even. It had not made money in years on PCs and it outsourced most of its manufacturing to a Taiwanese computer maker, Acer. IBM's profits came from consulting, not PCs. The company abandoned the consumer market in 1999, but still had a market share of 6 percent, because it sold PCs to business, not as stand-alone products but as a part of a package of services. In 2004, it sold its PC business to a Chinese company.

While the other large PC markers languished, Dell did well because it had the lowest cost structure in the industry. With this cost structure, Dell won market share. The winning formula was that high market share contributed to scale and scope economies, which drove down costs and made Dell even stronger.

Dell benefited from the economic slowdown in 2002–2003. Component prices dropped and the company passed the savings on to customers. Dell reasoned that it could make more money slashing prices than by raising them and selling less.

Dell pressed its rivals relentlessly. It kept pushing down costs and taking market share away from them. It increased its worldwide market share in PCs from 5 percent to 15 percent from 1998–2003 (see Table 3.4).

On the other hand, Gateway's sales declined almost 50 percent in 2001. The company laid off 4,600 workers and retreated from foreign markets.

Gateway was not the only company affected by Dell's dominance. Because neither HP nor Compaq could keep pace with Dell, they were forced to merge. Their combined world market share had slipped from 20 percent in 1998 to 14 percent in 2003.

Dell was the top-selling brand in the United States. The combined U.S. market share of HP/Compaq in PCs declined from what would have been 25 percent had they been the same company in 1997 to 18 percent in 2001, while Dell's increased from 10 percent to 25 percent. In an increasingly zero-sum game, Dell gained while its competitors lost.

TABLE 3.4   Global PC market shares in June 2003

Dell	HP/Compaq	IBM	NEC	Toshiba	Others
15%	14%	6%	3%	3%	59%

Source: V. K. Rangan and Marie Bell, "Dell: New Horizons," Harvard Business School Case 9-502-022, October 2002.

Gateway still had about 8 percent of the U.S. market in 2001, up from 5.4 percent in 1994. It sold over 70 percent of its computers to home users and to small- and medium-sized businesses, while Dell sold over 70 percent of its computers to large businesses and other commercial establishments.

Dell's aim was to get even bigger; it wanted to *double* its revenues in five years, but its top executives were hard-pressed to know how they could accomplish this feat.

Capabilities and Competencies

Like Gateway, Dell relied on the direct model; its machines were made to order and delivered directly to customers without a middleman (see Figure 3.1). Customers obtained the exact devices they wanted, and they paid Dell weeks before Dell had to pay its suppliers.

Dell perfected this system over a period of 20 years. When Michael Dell began to sell computers out of his University of Texas dorm room in 1984, he realized that he could eliminate a high proportion of the selling costs by circumventing the dealer and selling directly to customers. If the parts to the average computer cost $600 and the average price was $3,000, he could squeeze inefficiency out of the system.

Michael Dell believed that he could sell customers low-priced, built-to-order machines, taking orders and delivering products one-at-a-time. This system provided a cost advantage because it did away with the reseller and retailer markup and eliminated inventory risks.

Born of necessity, these principles became the central tenets in Dell's business model. Eliminating alternative channels to customers, Dell concentrated on its suppliers and customers. The company's pur-

FIGURE 3.1   The direct model

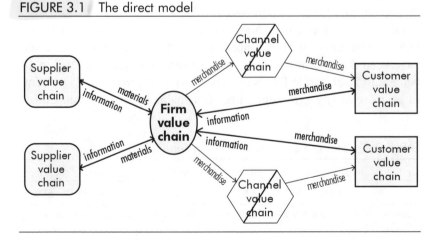

pose was to maximize value to the parties with whom it directly interacted. These direct relationships with the company's customers and suppliers resulted in valuable information that was the basis for mass customization and just-in-time manufacturing.

Dell won with superior capabilities for coordinating resources in the supply chain and putting them to productive use. A number of key capabilities accounted for how Dell did business (see Figure 3.2); its relationships to suppliers, fast inventory movement, performance metrics, its understanding of customers' needs, its ability to forecast demand, and its ability to be a technology advisor to its customers. These capabilities were very similar to those possessed by Gateway and set both companies apart from HP/Compaq, IBM, and other PC companies that relied mainly on resellers.

Relationships with suppliers. At the inception of the PC industry, companies had to create all the components themselves—disk drives, memory chips, and application software. As the industry matured, specialized firms produced these components. This specialization allowed Dell and Gateway to leverage investments other companies had made and focus on delivering solutions to its customers. Dell and Gateway evaluated what suppliers made (monitors, hard drives, etc.) and picked from the best of the lot. By operating in this way, Dell and Gateway had fewer areas and people to manage, which meant fewer things could go wrong.

With its suppliers, Dell and Gateway had two tasks: to set quality objectives, and to build data linkages. These companies shared information and plans with their suppliers freely in a real time. They assured their suppliers they would be with them over the long term. They stitched together their businesses by treating the suppliers as if they were almost part of their companies. Dell and Gateway followed the rule that they should have as few suppliers as possible, but have the strongest possible relationships with their suppliers. Virtual integration allowed companies that were once small companies like Dell and Gateway to best a large company in PCs like IBM that had much greater resources.[2] Dell was the leader in perfecting the direct model.

2. Dell and Gateway were virtually and not vertically integrated; they bought goods and services from suppliers outside themselves and sold them to customers outside themselves. They had arm's length relations with their customers and suppliers based on price. The challenge was to go beyond price in coordinating these relations. Dell and Gateway wished to create the type of coordination that might otherwise only be possible if all parties were employees of the organizations and obeying a single command.

FIGURE 3.2   Dell's core competence and its constituent capabilities

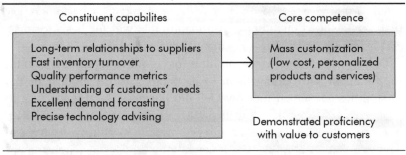

Constituent capabilites

Long-term relationships to suppliers
Fast inventory turnover
Quality performance metrics
Understanding of customers' needs
Excellent demand forcasting
Precise technology advising

Core competence

Mass customization
(low cost, personalized
products and services)

Demonstrated proficiency
with value to customers

Therefore, it makes sense to examine what Dell did in greater detail (Figure 3.2).

Fast inventory movement. Dell worked with suppliers to reduce inventory and increase speed. The company believed that holding assets as inventory and having accounts receivable were unnecessary business risks. Holding inventory in the computer industry was risky because the cost of materials declined rapidly and goods quickly became obsolete. Moreover, a company became vulnerable to product transitions and getting stuck with obsolete product. Therefore, a company had to keep its inventory moving as quickly as possible.

Performance metrics. Dell increased the velocity of inventory movement by using information and performance metrics to speed execution and drive operations. Inventory velocity was one of a handful of key performance measures that Dell watched closely. Other critical measures that it watched were margins, average selling price, and overhead.

Dell closely examined gross margins by customer segment and focused on segments it could profitably serve through scale economies. It also kept very close tabs on its profit-and-loss statements, dividing the numbers by product, customer segment, and geography. It cut its market into finer and finer segments to maximize value to customers.

Dell ran its operations by the numbers. It relied on performance metrics to fix problems before they occurred. The company used these metrics to ensure quality and prevent quality breakdowns that might otherwise slow the flow of goods and materials.

Keeping track of customers. Dell built only in response to a customer's order, thus avoiding typical industry stop-and-start cycles in which companies stuffed channels to get rid of excess inventory and meet short-term financial objectives. Ninety percent of Dell's sales were to businesses and government institutions. Seventy percent were to very large customers that bought more than $1 million in PCs per year. But no customer represented more than 1 percent to 2 percent of revenues, so the flow of goods to customers was relatively even. One week one customer bought, and the following week another customer bought.

Other companies with channels between themselves and their customers were at a disadvantage. Since they were not close to their customers, they had poorer information about demand, which resulted in them having more stop-and-start cycles, more inventory, higher costs, and more risk.

Dell originally did not pursue the consumer market because it was hard to control and predict. Its executives did not think they could reach their profit objectives in this segment. It let competitors like Gateway serve this market with machines, which tended to have rock-bottom prices and zero margins. Consumers buying their second or third machines, wanting more powerful ones, and needing less hand-holding came to Dell. Its average selling price to consumers increased while that of the industry as a whole went down.

Forecasting. Direct selling allowed Dell to keep track of a customer's total PC needs. Forecasting was the key. The company forecast segment by segment to keep its costs down and maintain a tight linkage to customers. For example, account managers regularly led customers through a discussion of their needs. They communicated with staff in every department of a customer's business, asking employees to designate which needs were certain and which contingent, and when customers' needs were contingent on some event, and what the event was, so the company could follow up. Dell fed this information back to customers, which extended the value of what it provided; the customer now had a better understanding of what its IT costs would be.

Dell also added value to its customers by loading their software in its factories and putting an asset tag with the customers' logos on their machines. In this way, it kept an electronic register of the customers' assets and in effect functioned for them as an IT department. It gave other companies' employees the same access to Dell's internal online support tools as the company's own technical support teams had.

For its largest customers, Dell developed customized intranet sites called "Premier Pages." These sites existed securely within the customers' firewalls, and they gave Dell's customers, as well as Dell, direct access to purchasing and technical information about the PCs the customers had purchased.

In a company like Boeing that owned 100,000 Dell PCs, Dell embedded its employees in the firm. It had 30 of its employees permanently stationed on the company's premises.

Being a technology advisor. Dell was a technology "selector" and "navigator" for its customers. It talked to them about "relevant" technology rather than the most powerful technology. It ran forums to ensure the free flow of information. Platinum Councils, for example, were regional meetings for its largest customers. These meetings were held every six-to-nine months for information executives and technicians. At these meetings, Dell's senior technologists shared their views on where technology was heading and laid out roadmaps of the company's product plans over the next two years. All of Dell's senior executives from around the company participated, each spending time with the customer.

The purpose of these meetings was for Dell to play more of an advisory role, trying to help its customers understand what new technology really meant. Dell's approach was to put the customer in control, and to take existing technology and apply it in useful ways to meet customers' needs.

Dell was not trying to invent new technology itself, but rather was using existing *or* new technology to improve the customer experience; this service meant delivering the latest relevant technology, making it easy to use, and keeping costs down.

A core competence in mass customization. Dell's core competence in mass customization (low-cost, personalized products and services) was based on the capabilities described above. Alone, none of the capabilities was sufficient to enable Dell to reach its goals; it was the company's ability to merge, align, harmonize, and forge these capabilities that explained Dell's success. Together, these capabilities were larger than the sum of their separate parts.

Dell developed and refined its capabilities in historical accretions that rivals could not master. The company learned from its mistakes. For instance, it tried to sell its computers in retail outlets, but quickly pulled back when it realized that it was not meeting its profit goals.

A hard road to travel. From Dell's perspective, Gateway was a more dangerous opponent. Its business model was very similar. HP, on the other hand, had a long road to travel to catch up to Dell. Just half of HP's PC business went directly from the factory floor to customers.

Michael Dell was not convinced HP could ever achieve its goal of reducing the overhead it required to build a PC by more than 40 percent. He felt that CEO Carly Fiorina's hope that the combined company (HP and Compaq) could drastically reduce costs was largely an illusion.[3] HP competed with its own resellers, companies like Ingram, and with retail chains on which it relied, like Best Buy. As long as HP continued to sell devices through resellers and retail, it would face channel conflict. Conflict would exist between selling direct to consumers and to resellers who sold to consumers.

Dell's intent was to continue to perfect the direct model and apply it to a large number of other product categories. No matter what customers wanted, Dell's goal was to flexibly and quickly provide them with a low-cost, customized product. The customer got a very good deal—a good price, not necessarily a rock-bottom one. The customer also got a feeling of being in control; it had choices that Dell respected by tailoring products to meet the customer's individual needs. The whole user experience was less stressful than it would have been had Dell carried it out under different terms.

Gateway's Relationships with Individual Consumers

The PC industry was split between companies that sold through middlemen such as HP/Compaq and IBM, and those that sold directly, such as Dell and Gateway. Dell and Gateway both relied on the direct model and had virtually no inventory, low distribution expenses, and direct contact with the customer, which provided them with many opportunities to extend and grow their businesses. However, Dell mainly sold to large, institutional customers, while Gateway mainly sold to individual consumers.

The home consumer. Unlike Dell, Gateway's specialty was home computing. The company had not succeeded in the global arena, an arena where Gateway executives did not think it could excel. Further, its frequent attempts to enter the business market also did not go well.

---

3. Cutting costs was the major reason that Fiorina argued persistently and forcefully for the merger between HP and Compaq despite the strong and persistent opposition of a board member from the founding Hewlett family.

Gateway's base was the home consumer and the small businessperson. But Dell had become much more aggressive in this market as well. Dell and Gateway were going head to head, with Gateway holding the lead but Dell catching up fast. Like corporations, home shoppers needed help setting up, managing, and operating PCs and networks. Gateway focused on this niche. Like Dell, it had started in the PC business by selling standard PCs over the phone; it did so more efficiently than its rivals could through stores. Like Dell, Gateway had a distinctive CEO in ponytailed Ted Waitt, who often appeared in company ads and other promotions. Waitt was hopeful and resilient despite the company's setbacks. A college dropout, he took a job handling mail-order PC sales in Des Moines, and then started Gateway in 1986 backed by a $10,000 loan guaranteed by his grandmother. He located the company in a farmhouse near his Sioux City, South Dakota, home. By January 1988, Gateway had entered the national market with an ad in *Computer Shopper* that read "Computers from Iowa?"

Responding to the sub-$1,000 PC. In 2001, when Dell slashed prices, it put Gateway in great jeopardy. Gateway, however, had faced a similar crisis earlier in its history. In 1997, it had great trouble dealing with the economics of the sub-$1,000 PC, so it took a number of steps to build its capabilities in order to deal with this phenomenon. These steps are discussed below.

1. Gateway spent $190 million to acquire Advanced Logic Research, an Irvine, California, company, to enable it to enter the higher-margin corporate market, but Gateway was not able to attract many corporate customers. It lost $107 million in the third quarter of 1997.

2. Gateway started to build country stores. Ultimately, it had almost 300 of these stores in the United Sates and abroad. The purpose of having the stores was to give prospective customers a chance to "kick the tires" before buying. These stores had only Gateway products. Because they carried no inventory, they were much less expensive to operate than conventional computer stores. Gateway found that consumer purchases in the stores were nearly $2,000 more than they were over the phone or on the Internet. Gateway later tested a "store within a store" concept at a number of OfficeMax locations, which it abandoned when they did not work out.

3. Waitt hired 43-year-old Jeff Weitzen, a former AT&T executive, to

be his second in command and heir apparent. Then, he moved the company's headquarters out of the Corn Belt to San Diego, California, so that he could recruit people who would be more innovative. There he brought in 10 other new people to be part of the top-management team.

4. The new management team then took a number of steps to turn the company around. It stopped calling Gateway a computer company and started referring to it as an "experience" company. The experience Gateway was marketing was a combination of computing, content, and communications. It wanted a full "relationship" with its customers; it was not just looking for a "transaction."

The "hexagon." To realize this vision, the new Gateway team developed what it called its "hexagon" strategy in 1999. Gateway would have a number of distinct but related businesses—systems, peripherals, software, warranties and financing, training, Internet access, portals and content, and financing. It would not rely on hardware alone. All of the businesses except peripherals had better profit margins than hardware (see Table 3.5). By selling more of these products and services, Gateway could sell more PCs for less and still make more money on each sale. From Internet access, portal ads, financing, warranties, and training, the company would obtain recurring income that would show up regardless of how many PCs it sold.

The PC maker for the Internet generation. Gateway branded itself as the "PC maker for the Internet generation." In an Internet-dominated world, the Gateway management team saw the PC as a way to sell Web and other higher-margin services. It started to rethink the company's hardware offerings and began to sell Internet appliances that directly connected to America Online (AOL). It offered the following appliances: a kitchen countertop device, a wireless Web pad, and a desktop machine for e-mail access. Gateway also had been working on a TV

TABLE 3.5   Gateway's products in 1999

	Desk-tops	Lap-tops	Servers	Periph-erals	Soft-ware	Warranties, Financing	Training	ISP & portal
Revenue (in millions of $)	6,507	1,148	280	363	219	70	36	23
Operating margin (%)	6.5	6.8	9.8	4.5	28.5	44.5	8.5	35.7

Source: Company reports.

service with AOL that would deliver interactive entertainment and shopping.

Because Gateway sold directly to customers, it was easy for Gateway to sell extra software or peripherals. A high percentage of Gateway's customers bought additional software bundles at an average price of $100 or more.

But beyond PC sales, financing was Gateway's biggest source of income. The "Your:)Ware" package, introduced in 1998, allowed consumers to pay less in monthly installments for a PC bundled with software, Internet access, in-home repair, and the industry's first trade-in option.

Gateway was also the only PC maker with a major training program. At one time the company had as many as 5,000 classroom seats in its stores. Its goal was to be a trusted Internet guide, to help people install computers, set up networks, and to train people. Its Web-based courses too were highly profitable; the margins were as high as 90 percent.

Gateway was also the first PC company to have its own ISP. It partnered with AOL to operate its access service. Its portal, Gateway.net, was comanaged by AOL, and was modeled after well-known portals such as Yahoo. Gateway expected to make money from advertising and other services.

A temporary revival. The changes discussed above temporarily helped to revitalize Gateway and keep it going. Revenues went up from about $6 billion to over $9 billion in 2000, and employment grew from 12,000 to 19,000, but in 2001, revenue collapsed by almost 50 percent and the company was faced with massive layoffs.

Gateway's response was somewhat similar to Dell's when its initiative of selling through retail outlets failed. After entering the retail space in the early 1990s and stumbling, Dell also realized that it had to have new faces in its top-management team. After retreating from retail, Dell was led by a triumvirate of Michael Dell, Mort Topfer, a Motorola veteran, and former Bain & Company consultant, Kevin Rollins. The new management team helped to craft and continues to carry out the strategy that has made Dell the world's largest PC maker. But Ted Waitt was not having the same type of long-term success with the new strategy that his top-management team introduced. This strategy gave the company a temporary pickup and created considerable excitement among analysts, but the excitement faded when Gateway failed to permanently deliver on its promise.

The convergence of computers and electronics

Gateway was taking new initiatives in the consumer market, where it rubbed shoulders with Dell. In 2002, it unveiled this new strategy.[4] Since the PC was becoming an integral part of the home-entertainment landscape, the company would position itself in a broader segment than PCs alone; it would take full advantage of the convergence of consumer electronics and computers and start to sell products in this category.

The first product Gateway marketed under this strategy was a 42-inch, flat-panel plasma television. By keeping the prices significantly lower than those of comparable products, Gateway was able to make this product a success; it gained a double-digit market share within a year.

Gateway's advantage over Dell in selling to individual consumers was that it owned about 175 Gateway Country Stores throughout the United States, and had close relations with Asian manufacturers. The stores allowed Gateway to demonstrate to consumers what the Asian manufacturers' products could do in their homes. Gateway's strategy was to grow by showing people all the ways they could use PCs and related PC products in their homes.

Dell, however, was not sitting still and ceding this market to Gateway. It recognized that the home market was different than the business market and that its approach had to be different. It too began to emphasize the multimedia, home-entertainment experience. During the 2002 Christmas season, Dell ran a series of commercials that explained to consumers how they could expand the range of "fun" things they could do with their home PCs. Dell's aim was for consumer PCs to be 20 percent of the company's sales—up from 15 percent in 2002.

Dell forays into consumer electronics. In September 2003, Dell announced that it would sell products such as flat-panel televisions. Michael Dell claimed that by introducing high-performing consumer electronics products that closely integrated with the computer, Dell delivered what consumers wanted most—content and experience—at better value than they could obtain from competitors.

Dell's move followed Gateway's success with the 42-inch plasma television. Gateway was successful with its $2,999 plasma TV, but it was not clear it could continue to advance now that Dell had entered the picture. In addition to televisions, Dell's slate of consumer elec-

---

4. In 2002, Waitt's company was hurting and he had no choice but to cut costs drastically. Though the company was losing money, it was able to build up a $1 billion cash reserve.

tronics included a digital music player, an online music service, and a home entertainment projector. At the heart of Dell's strategy was a belief that the digital home was about to become a reality, with the personal computer at the center running movies, music, and many other devices around the house.

Gateway's pullback. Dell's offensive hurt Gateway. In 2003–2004, Gateway closed all of its Country Stores because they were losing money. The company acquired e-Machines. It sold this brand as a super low-priced computer in retail outlets such as Best Buy and CompUSA. It also sold notebook PCs and the Gateway brand as a premium-priced computer in these outlets.

The former head of e-Machines, Wayne Inouye, became Gateway's CEO. In 2004, after Gateway had sold big-screen TVs, DVD recorders, and digital cameras for four years, Inouye announced that the company was retreating from the consumer electronics market and returning to its roots of marketing PCs. He reshuffled Gateway's management and laid off many veteran Gateway executives. He announced that the company would shrink from more than 11,000 to less than 2,000 employees, most of the layoffs being a result of closing the Country Stores. Gateway would go from the highest overhead in the industry, 26 percent of sales, to less than Dell's 9.5 percent overhead.

Inouye signaled to Wall Street that he would be running Gateway in a very different way. He would be going back to the company's origins by simplifying processes, achieving cost reductions, and improving customer support and satisfaction. Inouye aimed to consolidate component suppliers, boost quality, and make sure that the company was able to fill its retail orders on time. He wanted to revitalize the original model that had made Gateway and Dell so successful and so efficient. The big difference this time around for Gateway was that it would not just be selling PCs on the Internet. Its computers would be sold retail in the United States and throughout the world.

Inouye had great hopes for global sales, a market that Gateway had failed to penetrate previously. He believed that in global markets, where discretionary spending by households was much lower than in the United States, the supercheap e-Machine would be a big hit.

This gamble was huge. Gateway, in Inouye's opinion, could not engage in multitasking. A resolute focus on the low-cost global market was the only way the money losing company could return to profitability. When Gateway bought e-Machines for $290 million in stock and cash it was a consistently profitable business with $1 billion in annual sales. e-Machines had just 138 full-time employees. Inouye's goal was to become the leading seller of home PCs (in 2004, HP had 60 percent of the U.S. market and Gateway had 30 percent). He wanted Gateway to grow into a $10 billion concern in just three to five years.

Transferring Dell's Strengths to Other Lines of Business

Unlike Gateway, Dell continued to rely exclusively on the direct model. It refused to deal with resellers and retailers. Its strategy was to transfer its strengths with the direct model to other lines of business. It took its distinct competence in mass customization and extended it to a host of additional devices and services. From servers to storage and printers and handheld devices, Dell attempted to bring the same value to customers. It made the decision to move into other devices and services because exclusively selling more PCs, with prices declining so rapidly, no longer made sense.

Reproducing the model. Dell's executives believed they had to move in the direction of trying to reproduce their model in a variety of product categories. Customers increasingly were combining their bids for a range of IT products, from desktops and handheld devices to networking and storage, and were seeking to buy these items from the same vendor. They were asking companies like Dell and the combined HP/Compaq to bundle the PC with other products and services. Dell therefore could no longer afford to be just a PC company; it had to be an all-purpose seller of whatever IT needs its customers had.

On average, Dell's market share across a range of computer-related products such as software, peripherals, and networking was just 3 percent, so it had plenty of room to grow, even if tech spending as a whole did not increase. Under these circumstances, Dell's growth would have to come at the expense of competitors, both old ones like Gateway, the merged HP/Compaq, and new ones like Cisco and 3Com in networking and switches.

Tearing relationships apart. The moves Dell made antagonized some of its traditional partners. For example, with Dell inaugurating its own printer and ink cartridge business in affiliation with Lexmark, it antagonized HP to the point where HP no longer was willing to supply Dell. Similarly, Cisco and 3Com decided not to ally themselves with Dell any longer, as they perceived that a collaborator had become an antagonist. HP managers found consolation in the fact that Dell might be overreaching itself. They compared Dell's moves to Napoleon's invasion of Russia: Napoleon was doomed to failure and the same would be true of Dell. The combined HP/Compaq was a much larger company than Dell. It had more than three times the number of employees and almost twice the revenues. It also had highly profitable products such as printers where its overall market share was greater than 50 percent. Nevertheless, surveys of business customers showed that they perceived Dell as being just as capable as HP/Compaq of providing them with a range of bundled IT products and a total package of services.

Consulting. In this arena, both Dell and HP had to contend with IBM, the largest service provider in the industry. Its hugely profitable consulting business, IBM Global Services, was active at the high end of the market. The competition here was fierce with IBM fighting off the likes of Accenture (formerly Andersen Consulting) and EDS. A main reason for the HP/Compaq deal was that Compaq had previously acquired Digital, a company that had the capability to stand up to the IBM consulting stalwarts. The combination of HP and Compaq created a service business that could compete with IBM and take sales away from Dell. Dell, in contrast, was a total novice in consulting. It was a machine assembler that had no real experience in this area and whose business model could not be easily applied to consulting.

IBM continued to sell a wide range of hardware, but its main business was service; it had a horde of consultants who advised customers on how to use computer technology. Dell often partnered with EDS, but it was unable to fully service large corporations.

Hardware. Rather than going forward with the full-service, consulting model, Dell emphasized hardware markets, which it expected to fuel its growth. It assumed that it would be able to get higher margins from hardware businesses than from consulting. Dell was pushing into products that were PC related, and it gained sizable markets in products that were increasingly becoming commoditylike in nature.

PDAs and switches. One example was personal digital assistants (PDAs). Although a new entrant to the handheld PDA market, Dell quickly commanded a 5 percent market share (see Table 3.6). Its ability to deliver a well-priced, made-to-order device to customers was difficult for other device makers to equal.

Another example was switches. Dell began to sell a product that Cisco and 3Com long had dominated—the black boxes that connect computer networks. With a lucrative $17 billion market that had operating margins of up to 50 percent, switches constituted a perfect opportunity for Dell. IT managers considered them overpriced, so Dell had the opportunity to come in on the low end and steal market share.

Servers and workstations. Other markets Dell entered and in which it started to compete more aggressively were servers and workstations.

The worldwide server market totaled about $69 billion. In entry-level servers, Dell made rapid inroads. From a 10 percent market share in the United States in 1997, it gained over 29 percent of this market by 2003 (see Table 3.7). During this time, the combined market share of HP/Compaq fell from 40 percent in 1997 to 28 percent in 2003.

Dell made this advance because its prices were significantly lower than those of its competitors. Dell's entry-level server, the PowerVault for instance, sold for $9,999 in 2001, or 7 cents a megabyte (MB). In contrast, the Compaq TaskSmart server sold for $34,710 or 21 cents a MB. Dell, however, was not competing in the area of midrange servers. In this arena, HP/Compaq shared market leadership with Sun. Both had 38 percent of the U.S. market in 2001.

The worldwide workstation market was worth about $9 billion in 2001, a decline of almost 10 percent from 1999 levels. In this market, Dell had taken the lead from HP/Compaq. It had built a market share of about 44 percent in Windows NT workstations compared to an

TABLE 3.6   World handheld PDA market shares in June 2002

Palm	HP/Compaq	Sony	Dell	Others
38%	15%	11%	5%	31%

Source: Adapted from Rangan and Bell, "Dell: New Horizons," Harvard Business School Case 9-502-022, October 2000.

TABLE 3.7   Market shares in servers in June 2002

Dell	HP/Compaq	IBM	Sun	Fujitsu	Others
29%	28%	20%	16%	5%	1%

Source: Adapted from Rangan and Bell, "Dell: New Horizons," Harvard Business School Case 9-502-022, October 2000.

HP/Compaq share of about 30 percent, with IBM holding about 14 percent of this market. In all workstations (Windows and non-Windows), Dell commanded 30 percent of the market compared to the HP/Compaq's share of about 24 percent and IBM's share of 13 percent.

To understand how far Dell had come, we need only note that in 1997, Dell's share of the world marketplace in Windows NT workstations had been 7 percent in comparison to HP/Compaq's share of 75 percent. At that time, Dell had just about 3 percent of the entire workstation market in comparison to HP/Compaq's share of nearly 45 percent.

Dell's rapid progress in these markets showed how effective it could be in entering domains where it previously had not been active. As computer-related products became commodities, Dell—with its low cost structure—was in a good position to gain market share.

Storage. Internet infrastructure needs were pushing the increasing demand for storage, which began skyrocketing in 2000 at the rate of 23 percent per year. Industry sales were $32 billion that year. EMC was the leader in external storage while Dell was a weak player. Commanding the sixth largest market share, Dell had just $1 billion in sales, but its sales were growing at a rate of more than 25 percent per year. In 2001, Dell signed an agreement with EMC to be a marketing channel for EMC's low-priced line of products, which were geared toward medium- and small-size businesses and government accounts.

International. Compared to its main competitors, Dell was the weakest in the international arena. While it had manufacturing facilities abroad, it did not have the market share of HP/Compaq or IBM in most regions (see Table 3.8). In the global market, resellers were much more important than domestically. Gateway hoped to make inroads globally with its supercheap e-Machines which it would sell in retail channels, where it would not have to compete with Dell.

What to Do Next?

In this new environment, Dell and Gateway executives would have to make a number of important decisions. As they made their next moves, the companies' capabilities and competencies certainly would be tested.

TABLE 3.8 Global market share of Dell and major competitors in international markets (2000)

	Western Europe	Asia/Pacific	Japan	Latin America	Rest of the world
HP/Compaq (%)	25.2	10.3	6.5	24.7	13.4
IBM (%)	7.9	7.6	9.8	6.0	5.4
Dell (%)	9.8	3.7	4.2	3.3	3.6
Total units sold	29,741	19,976	14,129	7,761	7,594

Source: Adapted from Rankan and Bell, "Dell: New Horizons," Harvard Business School Case 9-502-022, October 2000.

Questions for Discussion

1. What does mass customization mean? What does virtual integration mean? What does channel conflict mean?

2. Why would it be difficult for HP or any other competitor for that matter to copy Dell's model? Do you agree with Michael Dell that HP and other competitors will continue to have a hard time replicating Dell's model? Why or why not?

3. How do you explain the period of time, the second half of 1999 and most of 2000, when Gateway's stock outperformed Dell's?

4. Why did Dell's performance start to pull away from Gateway's in 1997?

5. Which markets are most suited for application of Dell's model? Hardware? Consulting? Storage? International? The home market? If you choose hardware, which devices and systems should Dell emphasize? Why?

6. Dell aims to double its revenues in five years. Draw up a concrete plan with projections in the various markets in which it competes that show how Dell will reach this goal. Is the goal realistic or a real stretch?

7. What is the likelihood for the PC market to rebound? On what would such a rebound depend?

8. Which markets are most suited for the application of Gateway's strengths? Which are least suited for the application of its strengths? How would you steer the company? Is it moving in the right or wrong direction? Would a move back to South Dakota help or hurt Gateway?

9. Which key capabilities is Dell missing given the markets in which it is competing? What does it have to do to acquire these capabilities? Which capabilities can it discard because it no longer needs them to remain competitive?

10. Which key capabilities does Gateway need? What capabilities does it need to acquire in order to be competitive? Which can it discard because it no longer needs them?

Exercises

1. Visit the Dell and Gateway Websites. Evaluate what and how merchandise is being sold on these companies' Websites and in the computer stores where Gateway products are found.
2. Can Gateway build the resources, capabilities, and competencies to challenge Dell? As a management consultant, what would you tell Gateway to do?
3. Does Dell have the resources, capabilities, and competencies to maintain an advantage in the long run? What should Dell do to counter the moves that competitors such as Gateway might make?

Video

"Your Computer, Your Way: Dell and the Direct Sales Model." Films for the Humanities and Social Sciences, #10070, 1999.

Bibliography

Anders, George. "The Carly Chronicles." *Fast Company*. February 2, 2003:66.

Banham, Russ. "Does Dell Stack Up?" *CFO-IT*. Fall 2003:39

Brull, Steven V. "Gateway's Big Gamble." *Business Week*. June 5, 2000:26.

Coyne, Kevin, Stephen Gorman, Stephen Hall, and Patricia Clifford. "Is Your Core Competence a Mirage?" *The McKinsey Quarterly*. Number 1 (1997):40.

Dell, Michael. "The Power of Virtual Integration: An Interview," *Harvard Business Review*. March–April 1998:73.

_____. "Direct from Dell: An Interview." *Technology Review*. August 2001:40.

Frei, Frances, Youngme Moon, and Hanna Rodriguez-Farrar. "Gateway: Moving Beyond the Box," Harvard Business School Case 1-601-038, May 2002.

Jones, Kathryn. "The Dell Way," *Business 2.0*. February 2003:60.

Kirkpatrick, David. "The PC's New Tricks." *Fortune*. October 28, 2002:103.

McWilliams, Gary. "Gateway CEO Presses Restart: Back to PCs." *The Wall Street Journal*. September 13, 2004:B1.

Park, Andrew. "Why You Don't Know About Dell. *Business Week*. November 3, 2003:76.

Prahalad, C.K., and Gary Hamel. "The Core Competence of the Corporation," *Harvard Business Review*. May-June 1990:79.

Rangan, V. K., and Marie Bell. "Dell-New Horizons." Harvard Business School Case 9-502-022, October 2002.

Rivkin, Jan. "Matching Dell: Teaching Note." Harvard Business School Case 5-700-084, March 2001.

Serwer, Andy, and Julia Boorstin. "Dell Does Domination." *Fortune*. January 21, 2002:70.

Thomas, Cathy Booth. "Dell Wants Your Home." *Time*. October 6, 2003:48.

CASE 4

Positioning
Best Buy versus Circuit City[1]

In 1996, Best Buy surpassed Circuit City in becoming the largest electronics retailer in the United States. From 1999–2003, it dominated its archrival in returns to shareholders. Best Buy had a tremendous string of successes, but with the downturn in the U.S. economy in the early 2000s, it was not obvious what either Best Buy or Circuit City should do next. Electronics retailing was a volatile business in which it was hard to do consistently well. Though Best Buy's returns had been better than those of Circuit City, the pattern of these returns was erratic, with large swings up and down.

Both Best Buy and its indefatigable competitor, Circuit City, had taken their lumps; both had made mistakes. Perhaps Best Buy's biggest mistake had been the purchase of the Musicland Group (Sam Goody, Media Play, and On Cue stores). These stores did not fit with Best Buy's business model. The company could not turn them around and make them profitable. Neither Best Buy nor Circuit City had a good sense of what the future of the competition between them would be, and neither company was certain what actions they should take.

The Recent Performance of Best Buy and Circuit City

The second-quarter 2003 performance of the two companies was not good (see Table 4.1). Best Buy narrowed its first-quarter losses with revenue gains derived from stronger consumer confidence after the U.S. invasion of Iraq, but still reported a net loss of $25 million. Circuit City had a net loss of $43.9 million.

---

1. This case was written by Alfred Marcus, University of Minnesota, Carlson School of Management. Copyright © 2005 by Marsh Publications LLC. All rights reserved.

TABLE 4.1   A comparison of second quarter 2003 and 2002
performance of Best Buy and Circuit City

	Second quarter earnings ($)		Second quarter revenues ($)		Same store sales compared
	2003	2002	2003	2002	2002 & 2003
Best Buy	-25 mill	-333 mill	4.67 bill	4.2 bill	+2.2%
Cir City	-43.9 mill	28 mill	1.93 bill	2.12 bill	-10.0%

Source: Company reports.

Best Buy's $333 million loss in the second quarter of 2002 was because of a $308 million charge associated with Musicland, the mall-based entertainment software and music retailer it had acquired a few years earlier. In 2003, the company sold Musicland to a Florida-based private investment firm.

Best Buy's sales grew by 11 percent from the second quarter in 2002 because it opened 79 new stores and enjoyed growing demand for digital products. Its same-store sales expanded by 2.2 percent, while those of Circuit City contracted by 10 percent.

Circuit City's losses were attributable to remodeling and relocation costs that doubled from one year to the next. The company was hurt by the loss of CarMax, which had provided $18.4 million in added earnings a year earlier. CarMax was spun off as an independent entity in 2002.

Circuit City's new strategy was to concentrate on its retail electronics business. In February 2003, it dismissed 3,900 of 16,000 commissioned sales staff and hired 2,100 hourly workers. This move made its selling practices similar to those of Best Buy, which had relied on salaried employees for in-store sales assistance and information since 1989.

With Best Buy's sale of Musicland and Circuit City's spin-off of CarMax, the two retailers were becoming indistinguishable. The way they did business was not that different; their attention was not diverted by other endeavors. The companies were going head to head in the one area they knew best. They mainly had each other to worry about, though at the low end of the market, large general-purpose discount retailers such as Wal-Mart and Target cut into their sales and at the high end, high-quality specialty retailers such as Ultimate Electronics and the Good Guys cut into their profits. Around the corner, they also had to be concerned about e-retailers like Amazon.com, which offered similar products. A comparison of the two companies' 1999–2003 annual income statements can be found in the appendix.

The Evolution of Best Buy

Best Buy had gone through a series of changes since 1983 when it adopted the name Best Buy and became a discount retailer. The ferociously competitive environment in consumer electronics fueled each change. To avoid extinction and survive in a world in which only the fittest prevailed, the company continually fine tuned a philosophy of offering the best value for the money. Some of its competitors might be able to match its low cost (Wal-Mart and Target). Other competitors might be able to equal it on differentiation (Ultimate Electronics and the Good Guys) but none could do both (see Figure 4.1). They could not combine these elements in an attractive value-for-the-money package in the same way that Best Buy did.

Early on, Best Buy's top executives realized that price slashing by itself was not going to lead to success; in fact, continuous price wars could be disastrous in an industry as competitive as consumer electronics. Budget-minded consumers came to expect low prices, but that was not all they were looking for. They wanted knowledgeable service, fast checkout, interesting selection, and an exciting in-store atmosphere.

FIGURE 4.1   An attractive value-for-the-money package

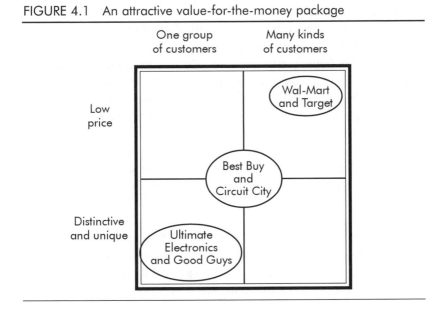

Consumers sought an enthralling experience, which would lead them to come back again and again.

As the percentage of retail sales based on discounts rose (from 8 percent in 1971 to 78 percent in 2002), low prices were less relevant. Discounting was so common that customers were desensitized to it; it no longer translated into brisk business growth. While discounting was necessary, it was not sufficient by itself to attract customers. Customers were looking for something more—a high-tech environment and a riveting shopping experience.

Brad Anderson—the new CEO. Brad Anderson, celebrated for his outgoing, optimistic personality, had taken over from Best Buy's founder and Chairman Richard Schulze as CEO of the company in the summer of 2002. His goals were clear: to increase the share of business Best Buy was getting from existing customers and to improve efficiency. These were the same aims that had motivated the company for many years.

Anderson's belief was that customers would not be won over with low prices alone. The company had to renew its emphasis on exciting products. Digital technology currently was hot; it had the potential to really take off. Anderson thought that the market was at a very early stage, given that only about 4 percent of U.S. households had a digital TV, and ESPN was the first channel to come online with high-definition, digital images.

Anderson also wanted the company to offer additional services. He was thinking about a new customer loyalty program, a more customized Website, and in-home computer repair. He wanted to initiate an advertising campaign that would call attention to the helpful information that sales associates provided. Another initiative on the drawing board was a joint venture with a company called Black Box to install data, voice, video, and audio cables in new houses.

Anderson was afraid of lethargy; he had to keep the momentum going. Best Buy had gone through prior makeovers. A history of these makeovers is illustrative of the kind of dynamism the company showed over the years.

Concept one: 1983–1989. The first transformation Best Buy underwent was from a high-quality audio electronics store called "Sound of Music" to Best Buy. The name change signified the new format under which the company would operate—as a superstore with more floor space, greater product selection, and better prices. Some of the new products the company added at the time were video equipment, microwave ovens, major appliances, and cameras. With higher volume sales, it achieved economies of scale in such areas as advertising and distribution, and gained greater clout over suppliers.

Concept two: 1990–1995. The new concept toward which Best Buy moved was to combine the best of the specialty retailer it had been (Sound of Music) with the best of the mass-merchant retailer it had become. It became fixated on creating a unique shopping experience to differentiate itself from its competitors.

The company conducted a survey from which it concluded that customers did not want to be pressured into buying. They wanted an enjoyable shopping experience. They wanted to be able to see, touch, and feel the merchandise, as well as find a broad assortment, trusted brands, and guaranteed low price.

Best Buy undertook a major innovation by creating a low-pressure selling environment that relied on salaried workers instead of a commissioned sales force. This decision was a defining moment in the company's history; the contrast with the high pressure Circuit City sales environment was striking.

In addition to low-priced products, Best Buy decided to bring back value products in select categories. Thus, it sold what it called "commodity" and "myth" items. Commodities, such as modestly priced PCs and household appliances, yielded sales volume; they appealed to a customer's intellect. Myth items, such as plasma TVs and camcorders, resulted in higher profits; they appealed to a customer's emotions. Together, these items increased interest in the stores and upped the traffic level.

In these ways, Best Buy reached its goal of being recognized as a "fun place to shop." It accomplished the transformation quickly and under the radar of competitors who could not and did not respond.

But these innovations created their own problems. Some vendors were concerned about poor representation of their premium brands in a discount store; they therefore removed products or refused to let Best Buy sell them. Best Buy's relationships with vendors such as Amana, GE, Harmon Kardon, Mitsubishi, Magnavox, and Sony deteriorated.

But the store format, which combined excitement, low prices, and high value, was so successful that the vendors came back because they needed Best Buy as much as Best Buy needed them. From 1990–1995,

Best Buy also benefited from selling PCs, which were a great draw. PCs increased store traffic, and although their profitability was low, they accounted for as much as 35 percent of the company's sales.

Concept three: 1996–2001. This concept too became stale. Sales were booming and Best Buy surpassed Circuit City, becoming the largest specialty retailer in the United .States in 1996, but its profits were depressed; they were at a five-year low. The company had to place renewed emphasis on profitability. This challenge prompted another reinvention.

Best Buy pushed harder on both sides of the hybrid paradigm—commodity and myth items. VCRs now were a commodity, but flat-screen TVs, car stereos, and camcorders were myths.[2] By upgrading the product mix with profitable categories and enhancing the in-store environment with more interactive opportunities and fun, hands-on experiences, Best Buy enhanced profitability while maintaining strong sales growth.

The stores introduced all kinds of demonstration areas—surround sound systems, CD listening posts, and places to try video games. There was a new store layout and displays featuring upscale products from companies like Braun, Oster, and Cuisinart. Best Buy sold high-end condiments along with gourmet housewares. The stores were advertised as bright, no-hassle, fun places to shop.

Best Buy divided its customers into the following four categories.

1. *Value-driven shoppers.* The largest group (32%), were price conscious. They checked ads, waited for prices to come down, did comparison shopping, and bargained over warranties.
2. *Techno-savvy entertainment consumers.* The next largest group (26%) wanted to buy what was newest and had the most features. Price was not the main consideration.
3. *Older customers.* These shoppers (23%) required considerable handholding. They were intimidated by new technology and needed assistance in making their purchases. Service was more important to them than price.
4. *Pragmatic buyers.* This final group (19%) looked for trusted brands and reliable service. They did not have the time for or interest in a prolonged shopping experience.

---

2. Appliances were in the middle. Best Buy had to win back big appliance makers such as Amana and GE that had refused to let the company sell their upscale brands.

Under concept three, the company tried to appeal to all four gourps. It took the following initiatives:

1. It expanded the appliance department and sold more appliances because they were more profitable than other items.
2. It improved inventory management to ensure that items in high demand were available and that highly profitable myth items were prominently displayed.
3. It simplified the stores so that staff would need less time to find and retrieve requested items.
4. It achieved tighter relationships and greater clout with vendors to guarantee that the most up-to-date products were available at low cost.
5. It reduced shrinkage (employee theft), which at 1 percent was high given the company's low margins.
6. It enhanced employee development and training so that staff would be more knowledgeable about products and product features.
7. It introduced an extended service plan, which it sold at a 30 percent discount from Circuit City's price.

The last action struck a hard blow at Circuit City, because 75 percent of its profits were from service plans and warranties.

The current makeover

What should Best Buy do next? It could not stand still. It had two decisions to make: (1) what to sell and (2) how to sell it.

What to sell. With, about 60 percent of U.S. households owning PCs, it was hard to get additional PC sales (see Table 4.2). PCs were just a replacement business.

TABLE 4.2   Store revenue by product category as a percentage of total store revenue

Product category	Percentage of total revenue fiscal 2003	Percentage of total revenue fiscal 2002	Percentage of total revenue fiscal 2001
Consumer electronics	34	33	33
Home office (includes PCs)	30	31	34
Entertainment software	22	22	19
Appliances	6	6	7
Other	8	8	7
Total	100	100	100

Source: Company reports.

Consumers were buying faster Internet download speeds from cable, telephone, and satellite companies. Sales for non-PC devices were growing. These devices included DVDs, MP3 players, Palmlike personal digital assistants, digital and Internet cameras, satellite TV and radio, and Sony's PlayStation 2, Nintendo Gamecube, and Microsoft's Xbox.

Sales of DVDs started slowly in 1997, but picked up rapidly. DVD sales more than tripled to 712,000 units in 1998 and more than quadrupled to 3.2 million units in 1999. They peaked at 9 million units in 2000. Their growing popularity was connected to declining prices; prices were down from about $600 in 1997 to as little as $100 in 2001.

How to sell it. Best Buy also had to update its stores. It believed that the stores had to be updated every four to seven years for the company to maintain profitability. The design had to accommodate large (45,000-square-feet) and small (30,000-square-feet) spaces. The layout had to be flexible and efficient so that new as well as old technology could fit in.

Usually, Best Buy rolled out a new store design in a particular market and diffused it to the rest of the country. Seattle was the current market in which it concentrated. The city was the last significant domestic market the company had yet to penetrate. The late entry was not deliberate. Best Buy had been late in Seattle for logistical reasons. It needed a distribution center west of Oklahoma, which it completed in central California in 2000. To compete in the Pacific Northwest, it added 450,000 square feet to the 600,000-square-foot California distribution facility (see Table 4.3).

In the Seattle rollout, Best Buy continued to work with the philosophy to which it had long adhered: Keep the overt pressure on customers to a minimum and use store design and layout to entice cus-

TABLE 4.3 Best Buy's distribution centers

Location	Square footage	Owned or leased
Findlay, Ohio	1,024,000	Leased
Staunton, Virginia	725,000	Leased
Dublin, Georgia	742,000	Owned
Dinuba, California	1,050,000	Owned
Ardmore, Oklahoma	565,000	Leased
Bloomington, Minnesota	425,000	Leased
Edina, Minnesota (entertainment software)	326,000	Leased
Franklin, Indiana (entertainment software)	715,000	Owned

Source: Company reports.

tomers to buy. To accomplish this goal, the Seattle stores had very wide center aisles and bright overhead signs with slogans like "Fulfillment" and "Simplicity."

The new Seattle stores put fast-growing, high-margin digital goods—such as cameras and DVDs—in the front and center. Destination goods like computers, home theater, and music were placed against the walls. The purpose was for shoppers to move from the center to the edges and thus come into contact with the entire retail space.

The wide center lane was a big change. Best Buy had long depended on an aisle winding around the sides of its stores, which tended to push shoppers to the right. The problem was that 75 percent of store traffic never made it to the left of the store. The wide center aisle allowed for better circulation to both sides and a clearer view of all departments.

Product categories changed position in the new design. To make room for the display of DVD movies, Best Buy gave less space to its top-drawing music.

The company aimed to attract customers with solutions, not just products. Thus, the entertainment center was placed next to TV sets, and both were across the aisle from the satellite service display. Printer paper was found in the computer department close to digital imaging equipment.

The back right-hand corner of the stores had appliances. They were placed between computers and televisions to attract young families. The back left was reserved for car audio and music. This space was meant to keep Best Buy's core young male shoppers happy. Products of varying qualities and price were found near each other. The idea was to appeal to both a shopper's intellect and emotions by offering many options for different tastes.

The new layout was meant to be helpful to buyers based on what Best Buy knew about their shopping habits. The stores had a single queue that fed multiple registers as in airport ticketing lines. Consumers were able complete complex purchases, such as arranging appliance delivery and Internet service, at separate transaction centers.

The store itself was a way for the company to differentiate itself from its competitors. In the cutthroat world of consumer retailing, store design was an important distinguishing feature. If Best Buy succeeded in Seattle, it planned to spread the new design to other cities in the United States and abroad to Canada, Europe, South America, and to additional global markets.

Based on experience Best Buy obtained from its "lab" stores in cities like Seattle, the company was setting out a new policy of "customer centricity" that it intended to roll out in other stores throughout the country in 2005. CEO Brad Anderson maintained that the purpose of the new policy was to get employees to engage more deeply with customers by empowering them to deliver tailored products, solutions, and services in the company's stores, on its Website, through its call centers, and via its in-home services.

Customer centricity was aimed at five segments, with each store adapting to serve one or more of the dominant customer segments shopping at a store. These segments were as follows:

1. Affluent professionals who want the best in technology and entertainment and who demand excellent service.
2. Active, young males who seek the latest technology and equipment.
3. Practical family men who want technologies that improve their lives.
4. Busy suburban moms who desire to enrich their children's lives.
5. Small business owners who aim to use the technology to enhance the productivity of their businesses.

The test of customer centricity in Best Buy's lab stores showed sales gains of 7 percent in comparison to similar stores. However, these sales gains came at a price. Gross profits increased by 50 percent but selling, general, and administrative expenses grew by 240 percent. Best Buy expected these costs to go down as it learned how to implement the model better.

Circuit City's Responses

In the face of the changes Best Buy was making, Circuit City did not stand still. Alan McCollough became Circuit City's CEO and chairman of the board in the year 2000. He joined the company in 1987 as general manager of corporate operations and worked his way up, holding a series of different posts in the firm. In 1999, Best Buy outperformed Circuit City on almost all key retail measures such as sales per square foot, sales growth, and new store openings. The first two decisions McCollough made were to drop major appliances, which faced stiff competition and price-cutting from Home Depot and Sears, and remodel or rebuild all the company's 618 stores.

Exiting appliances

In 2000, Circuit City left the appliance business. The exit from appliances allowed the company to close eight distribution centers and eight service centers. The exit costs exceeded $70 million over three years. With the company's exit from appliances, it would have the space to expand its selection of home electronics (see Table 4.4). A typical Circuit City store had 15,000 square feet for sales. That number was supposed to go up to 23,000. Without appliances, the amount of space left for electronics would increase by 70 percent.

Appliances had accounted for about 14 percent of Circuit City's annual sales, but they were unprofitable and largely responsible for the company not meeting its profit goals. McCollough hoped to compensate for the lost appliance sales offering greater sales of computer peripherals, video games and equipment, music, and movies.

These moves were essential because Best Buy already had overhauled stores to emphasize increasingly popular digital products like DVDs. The old design of Circuit City stores made shopping for such products difficult. McCollough was going to change the situation even if doing so meant some trial and error. He did not believe that the company would get it right the first time, but that it had to make the effort because without a more satisfying customer experience, Circuit City would not survive.

Remodeling and rebuilding the stores

Circuit City operated 626 stores throughout the United States. As it was established in virtually the nation's entire top 100 markets, geographic expansion was unlikely. The company's top priorities had to be remodeling and rebuilding its existing stores.

The only other option was relocation and Circuit City did relocate stores. When trade began to shift away from a store site, the company moved the store to a better location. The purpose of upgrading existing stores was to eliminate extra warehouse space and put more products

TABLE 4.4   Circuit City's intended remake: The approximate square footage of the average store

	Before	After
Warehouse/inventory	18,000	10,000
Home electronics	13,000	23,000
Home appliances	2,000	none

in customers' immediate sight. In a Best Buy store, shoppers had an easier time choosing what they wanted and checking out than they did in a Circuit City store. Most of Best Buy's merchandise was on the shopping floor, while Circuit City shoppers often had to ask a salesperson to bring out merchandise they wanted. The gap between the two chains was greatest during the holidays, when customers did not have the patience to deal with a salesperson, and often left a Circuit City store without buying anything.

The company conducted several remodeling tests and developed a framework for evaluating store sites and determining an optimal approach. Remodeled stores had less space for warehousing and inventory and more space for displaying home electronic products. They had a brighter, more contemporary look, and an open, easily navigable floor plan conducive to browsing.

The remodeled stores in the Baltimore-Washington, D.C., and Chicago markets did not have the gray, serious, reserved, and almost foreboding presence they previously had; they were brighter, warmer, and more open.

In 2003, Circuit City completed the first large-scale phase of the remodeling initiative with changes in the video department and full-store lighting upgrades in 299 stores. Changing the video department allowed the company to better showcase this category, as consumer interest was growing in digital televisions and other new display technologies, including flat-panel plasma and LCD televisions.

McCollough insisted that the company should proceed as fast as it could, even though its actions were risky. He did not think it would be a good idea to "dribble out" the changes. He believed that delay would leave Circuit City without a future.

The CEO was mindful of the demise of other retail chains. He believed that success in retail was fleeting and victory by any chain was not permanent. McCollough maintained that the company's future depended on implementing tangible changes that made the customer's experience more satisfying quickly.

The per-store cost for remodeling efforts was expected to be $2.5 million, or about $1.5 billion for all 618 stores. Because the changes were not being made after years of experimentation, mistakes were inevitable and the costs were likely to rise.

Circuit City also tried to change its image. It developed a new logo. It revamped the red, black, and chrome design scheme found in most of its stores, and it introduced hardwood floors and bright new signs.

It improved the way products were placed adjacent to each other so that customers could better compare features and benefits across product categories and shop for related accessories and peripherals that were in convenient proximity. Shopping carts, baskets, and cash register checkouts at the front of the store created a more comfortable environment for pulling merchandise off the shelves.

The prototype for Circuit City's new stores was its store in Jacksonville, Florida. This store had wider aisles, a more expansive space for displaying merchandise, and more items that customers could manipulate, touch, feel, and pick up on their own. Customers had more reasons for using a shopping cart or basket and buying more.

At the end of April 2003, 17 percent of the company's stores had been fully remodeled, relocated, or newly constructed within the prior three years. The process was turning out to be longer, more complex, and more expensive than anticipated. If these changes were going to pay off, they would have to result in truly superior sales and profits.

Low price and differentiation

Circuit City's advertising generally featured the company's low-price guarantee, called "Price Match Plus," and focused on differentiating elements in the service offered such as the "no-hassle" return policy and the Website's express pickup feature. In most cases, if customers found a lower advertised price, including Circuit City's own sale price, within 30 days, Circuit City would refund the difference plus 10 percent to these customers. Customers who ordered on the Web, but picked up their product at the store using the express pickup feature, automatically received the lower of the Web price or the in-store price.

Broad assortment plus a high level of service. Circuit City offered a broad assortment of items plus a high level of service. The strategy was to emphasize an extensive selection of products, including the newest technologies, at a wide range of prices. For each major product category, the company had a balanced mix of startup and midlevel items along with full-featured, high-end technology that carried premium prices. The percentage of merchandise sales represented by different product categories in 2003 and 2002 is found in Table 4.5.

Some of the service features that Circuit City incorporated into its product mix were convenient credit options, factory-authorized product repairs, home delivery and home installation, onsite installation for

TABLE 4.5   Circuit City's merchandise sales in different product
categories (percent)

	2003	2002
Video	40	40
Audio	14	15
Information technology	33	34
Entertainment	13	11
Total	100	100

Source: Company reports.

automotive electronics, and no-hassle exchange. No-hassle exchange
meant that every Circuit City purchase, whether made at a store or on
the company's Website, could be returned or exchanged at any of the
company's 600-plus stores.

Most of the company's merchandise was supplied directly to the
stores from one of its seven distribution centers, which were strategically located in different parts of the United States, and from a centrally located, automated software entertainment distribution center.
During fiscal 2003, Circuit City's 10 largest suppliers accounted for
about 59 percent of the merchandise purchased. The largest suppliers
were Hewlett Packard, Panasonic, Thomson Multimedia, JVC,
Toshiba, Hitachi LTD, Apex Digital, eMachines, and Universal Music
and Video.

In 2003, the company created alliances with a number of key manufacturers to provide unique product offerings not available from other
retailers. For example, Circuit City partnered with Sharp to be the
exclusive national retailer for its award-winning line of ultrathin laptop computers.

The company also offered a comprehensive CityadvantageSM
Protection Plan that provided product protection beyond a manufacturer's warranties. The protection plan options included replacement protection, which reimbursed a customer for the original price of a defec-
tive electronic product that was uneconomical to repair. The total
extended revenue from this warranty plan was declining partially due
to the sales mix shift, which included more products, such as entertainment software, for which warranty contracts were not sold.

Complete Web integration. Circuit City's consumer online business
was another special features. Customers had a choice of placing their
orders directly on www.circuitcity.com or using the telephone. The

online business provided extensive product selection, including more than 300,000 music and movie titles; in-depth product and technology information features, such as convenient side-by-side comparisons; and more than 75,000 customer ratings and reviews.

Internet customers could check the inventory at any Circuit City store, in addition to the in-stock availability of the items sold on the company's Website. Delivery options included shipment to anywhere in the United States and express pickup at any of the more than 600 Circuit City stores. Products purchased through the Website could be serviced through, exchanged at, or returned to any store.

In addition to Circuit City's own Website, the company partnered with Amazon.com to increase selection and convenience for Amazon.com's consumer electronics shoppers. The partnership gave Amazon.com's customers the privilege of immediate in-store pickup at Circuit City stores. In cases where Amazon.com and Circuit City offered the same items, customers had a choice between Amazon.com's shipping options or immediate pickup at a Circuit City store. Items offered exclusively by Circuit City were available either in-store or by shipment from Circuit City's distribution channel. Amazon.com delivered its own products.

This arrangement was the first example of Amazon.com offering a pickup option on its Website. Amazon.com had deals with other retailers—Toys "R" Us Inc. and Borders Group Inc.—to jointly sell products online, but without a pickup option. Unlike Borders, which merged its Website into Amazon.com's, Circuit City continued to operate its own separate online store in addition to selling through Amazon.com. The alliance provided advantages to both companies, which were otherwise competitors. Circuit City was looking for cheap ways to bring in new customers as it carried out its massive renovation. Amazon.com would be able to win new revenue without having to directly maintain the Circuit City inventory. And with direct pickup, Amazon.com's customers also would be able to eliminate waiting and shipping charges.

Move to a salaried workforce

Circuit City's trained product specialists were in place to represent the high level of service that the company wanted to provide. These specialists were trained using comprehensive online courses. In 2003, the company set up a certification program for the specialists. This program established minimum proficiency levels and measured each specialist's knowledge and customer service skills.

As of 2003, the company had 39,432 hourly and salaried employees. In early February 2003, Circuit City changed from a dual pay structure, which included both commission and hourly pay for its sales force, to a single hourly pay structure. Circuit City's executives realized they could no longer afford to pay large commissions to their sales staff, while its rivals paid less for hourly help.

Unfortunately, the sales staff was miffed by this change, which was not handled particularly well; the sales staff complained bitterly that Circuit City gave them no warning. Employees referred to the day of their layoff as "Bloody Wednesday." On that day, they waited to hear their fates. Some expected that their commissions would be cut. Others believed that underperforming sales personnel would be fired. Few anticipated that so many employees would be fired for little or no reason. The commissions they earned were too high at a time when the company was seeking to drastically lower costs.

The employees that survived made less than $14 to $18 an hour, including commissions, or $29,100 to $37,400 a year for full-time work. The cuts were supposed to save Circuit City $130 million in labor costs. Before the restructuring, Circuit City had treated top-earning sales professionals fairly well. They were asked to join the President's Club and were eligible for prizes such as weekend vacations. Now dismissed sales staff simply received a letter saying they were being cut for financial reasons—without even a letter of recommendation.

A buyout offer

In 2003, the Mexican financier Carlos Slim Helu made a proposal to acquire the shares in Circuit City that he did not already own (he had a 9.2% stake) for $8 apiece, or about $1.5 billion, but the company spurned his offer. The purpose of the offer was to combine the consumer-electronics retailer with the computer superstore CompUSA which the Mexican financier already owned. Apparently, Slim believed that if the two companies were combined, the possibility of synergy increased, as did the likelihood of Circuit City having more clout with vendors, which could help with cutting costs. CompUSA had about 220 retail stores; the Mexican financier bought the company for nearly $1 billion in the year 2000, and it was supposed to be a profitable business.

What to Do Next?

During the 1990s, Circuit City had been hurt by management missteps and the company was slow to respond to changes in the retailing environment. It was now refurbishing its stores and changing the way it did business in the hope that it could make a comeback.

A decade ago, Circuit City's annual revenue was double that of its arch foe Best Buy, but the approach to its business that it used at that time did not stand the test of time. In 2003, Best Buy's revenues of $19.6 billion were more than twice that of Circuit City's.

Best Buy had gained dominance over Circuit City, but would this dominance continue? It appeared that the only constant in consumer electronics was change.

All consumer-electronic retailers were experiencing decline in traffic, and the attractiveness of product categories was shifting. The shift at the start of the 21st century was to wireless and digital satellite system products and to more complex technologies such as digital imaging and flat-plasma, big-screen televisions.

In this new environment, would Best Buy continue to prevail? What new surprises would Best Buy and Circuit City face? What did they have to do to improve their positions vis à vis each other?

Questions for Discussion

1. What is the threat that Wal-Mart and Target pose to Best Buy and Circuit City? What is the threat Ultimate Electronics and the Good Guys pose to these companies? What can the two companies do about this threat?

2. What does "best value for the money" mean in the context of this industry? What role do commodity and myth products play in this strategy? What role does product mix and store design play? How important is service to this strategy? In what ways is it the same and in what ways does it differ from a combined low-cost/differentiated strategy?

3. Is it in Circuit City's interest to further differentiate itself from Best Buy or to become more like Best Buy? What about Best Buy: Should it try to be more different or more like Circuit City?

4. Do you agree that discounting has reached its limits as a strategy in retail? Explain.

5. Be specific: Which products should Best Buy feature in its stores

today? Why? Which products should Circuit City feature and why?

6. What explains Best Buy's relative dynamism? Why was Circuit City so lethargic in its responses to Best Buy's initiatives? Has Circuit City overcome this lethargy under its current CEO? Is Circuit City's restructuring something that should be of concern to Best Buy? How should Best Buy react to Circuit City's recent initiatives?

7. Is it appropriate to say that Best Buy has moved via concepts one, two, and three from a differentiated to a low cost to a combined low-cost/differentiated strategy? In comparison to the earlier changes Best Buy made, does concept three lack boldness and imagination, or does Best Buy simply need to fine-tune its formula?

8. Is store layout really that important to profitability? Is Best Buy putting too much emphasis on it?

9. Is Circuit City stuck—running a race to make its stores look more like those of Best Buy? Can it ever win this race? Is there a better way for Circuit City to catch up with Best Buy? What might an alternative strategy look like?

10. Wouldn't a combination of Circuit City and CompUSA be in Circuit City's best interest? Why did Circuit City reject this offer?

Exercises

1. Visit the Best Buy and Circuit City Websites and go to their stores. Walk around the stores. Get a good feel for how they carry out their business. Find out how Best Buy matches up to Circuit City with respect to Circuit City's:

   * Low-price guarantee
   * No-hassle return policy
   * Website pickup feature
   * Product selection
   * Credit terms, delivery, and home installation
   * Unique products
   * Warranties

2. Give advice to management. What does Circuit City have to do to catch up to Best Buy? How should it distinguish itself from Best Buy?

3. As a management consultant, your role is to think through what Best Buy should do next. How should it reinvent itself again to

ensure that it will maintain an advantage over competitors like Circuit City?

Video

"Michael Porter on Competitive Strategy" (see Porter's discussion of positioning), Harvard Business School Video Series, 1988.

Bibliography

Berner, Robert, and Sheridan Prasso. *"A Porsche You Can Boot Up," Business Week* May 13, 2002:12.

Chakravarthy, Balaji, and V. K. Rangan. "Best Buy." Harvard Business School Case 9-598-016, October 1997.

"Consumer Electronics: Industry Outlook." *Retail Forward*. July 2003.

Folpe, Jane. "Hold Off the Dirges—Circuit City Still Thrives." *Fortune*. May 15, 2000.

Haeberle, Matthew. "Checkmating the Opposition." *Chain Store Age*. October 2001.

Levy, Melissa. "Best Buy Unveils New Store Format in Tech-savvy Seattle." Minneapolis *Star Tribune*. November 18, 2001:B18.

_____. "Best Buy CEO Marks End of First Year at Helm." *Minneapolis Star Tribune*. June 24, 2003:B24.

Mahmood, Takai, and Richard Rosenbloom. "Circuit City in 1995." *Harvard Business Review*. April 1996.

Patterson, Gregory A., and Steve Alexander. "Non-PC devices Will Drive Electronics Market in 2001" *Minneapolis Star Tribune*. January 14, 2001:14.

Ramstad, Evan. "Circuit City's CEO Gambles to Galvanize the Chain—Decision to Drop Major Appliances, Overhaul Stores Aimed at Keeping Up." *The Wall Street Journal*. September 18, 2000:B4.

Schulze, Richard. "Why Best Buy Is Best in Class." (Interview) *Business Week Online*. April 8, 2002:0,4.

Appendix

EXHIBIT 1   Best Buy's annual income statement (in millions of U.S. dollars except for per-share items)

	52 weeks ending 03/31/03	52 weeks ending 03/02/02	52 weeks ending 03/03/01	52 weeks ending 02/26/00	52 weeks ending 02/27/99
Total revenue	20,946.0	17,711.0	15,189.0	12,494.0	10,064.6
Cost of revenue	15,710.0	13,941.0	12,177.0	10,100.6	8,250.1
Gross profit	5,236.0	3,770.0	3,012.0	2,393.4	1,814.5
Selling/general/ admin. expenses, total	4,226.0	2,862.0	2,401.0	1,854.2	1,463.3
Total operating expense	19,936.0	16,811.0	14,578.0	11,954.8	9,713.4
Operating income	1,010.0	900.0	611.0	539.3	351.2
Provision for income taxes	392.0	356.0	248.0	215.5	135.4
Net income after taxes	622.0	570.0	401.0	347.1	216.3
Accounting change	(82.0)	0.0	0.0	—	—
Discontinued operations	(441.0)	0.0	(5.0)	—	—
Net income	99.0	570.0	396.0	347.1	216.3

EXHIBIT 2   Circuit City annual income statement (in millions of U.S. dollars except for per-share items)

	12 months ending 02/28/03	12 months ending 02/28/02	12 months ending 02/28/01	12 months ending 02/29/00	12 months ending 02/28/99
Total revenue	9,953.5	9,518.2	10,330.0	10,599.4	9,344.2
Cost of revenue	7,603.2	7,180.3	7,836.1	7,977.2	7,060.2
Gross profit	2,350.3	2,338.0	2,493.9	2,622.2	2,284.0
Selling/general/ admin. expenses, total	2,286.7	2,207.6	2,305.6	2,081.4	1,882.4
Total operating expense	9,886.5	9,311.8	10,144.1	10,072.5	8,964.5
Operating income	67.0	206.4	185.9	527.0	379.6
Provision for income taxes	25.5	78.4	70.6	200.2	144.6
Net income after taxes	41.6	128.0	115.2	326.7	235.0
Equity in affiliates	—	—	—	0.9	(18.1)
Discontinued operations	64.5	90.8	45.6	(130.2)	(68.5)
Net income	106.1	218.8	160.8	197.3	148.4

CASE 5

Repositioning
Charles Schwab versus Morgan Stanley[1]

The financial services industry had gone through an extraordinary transformation. The Financial Modernization Act in 1999 permitted banks to offer a broad range of services including investment banking, brokerage services, and insurance. This act made de jure what already was a fact. The boundaries between brokerages, banks, insurance companies, finance companies, and credit card issuers had been blurred. Commercial and investment banking, brokerage, and insurance industries were competing in the same space. Salomon Smith Barney was now part of the megabank, Citicorp. Old standbys such as Morgan Stanley and Goldman Sachs continued to rely on a highly differentiated full-service model. They handsomely compensated commissioned brokers who provided specialized investment products and services for wealthy clients. Online brokers such as TD Waterhouse, eTrade, Siebert and Company, Ameritrade, and Datek had entered the industry. They used an ultra low-cost model that yielded very low margins. Charles Schwab, which had pioneered in the discount broker niche, had trouble keeping up. Schwab was trying to find its way in this new environment. The financial services industry in which Charles Schwab and Morgan Stanley participated also faced a difficult environment characterized by scandals, an uncertain economy, and waning trust. In his 2002 letter to shareholders, Phillip Purcell, CEO of Morgan Stanley, wrote:

> As we look back at 2002, it was a most difficult year. We began the year with the memory of 9/11 still fresh in our minds. In the months that fol-

---

1. This case was written by Alfred Marcus, University of Minnesota, Carlson School of Management. Copyright © 2005 by Marsh Publications LLC. All rights reserved.

lowed, we had to contend with the continued decline in equity markets and a highly publicized investigation of Wall Street research and investment banking practices. (Phillip Purcell, letter to shareholders, December 2002)

This case examines the environment in which Charles Schwab and Morgan Stanley operated, the positions they staked out, and the choices they faced.

The Performance of Charles Schwab and Morgan Stanley

Charles Schwab had a great run during the bull market of the 1990s. At the height of the Internet economy—the half-dozen months between June and December of 1998—its stock price rose by 158 percent. It was the most highly capitalized firm in the industry. Its $25.5 billion valuation edged out Merrill Lynch's $25.4 billion. However, its ascendancy was short-lived. By October 2003, Morgan Stanley was the most highly capitalized firm in the industry, Merrill Lynch was a close second, and Charles Schwab was far behind.

After the stock market bubble burst in 2000, the industry in which Morgan Stanley and Charles Schwab participated suffered. Between 2000–2002, Morgan Stanley's revenues fell by 28 percent, its profits were down by 42 percent, and it had to reduce its workforce by over 8 percent. In the same period, Schwab's revenues dropped by 29 percent, its profits fell by 86 percent, and it had to lay off more than 15 percent of its employees.

Firms such as Merrill Lynch, Goldman Sachs, and eTrade experienced similar declines (see Table 5.1). The issues that all firms in the financial services industry faced were corporate scandals and a declin-

TABLE 5.1   The performance of Morgan Stanley and Charles Schwab in comparison to other companies in their industry (Oct. 14, 2003)

	Morgan Stanley	Merrill Lynch	Goldman Sachs	Charles Schwab	Etrade
Market cap ($)	58.78B*	55.06B	41.92B	18.24B	3.87B
Employees	55,726	50,900	18,421	16,700	3,500
Revenue ($)	32.42B	28.25B	22.85B	4.48B	1.90B
Net income ($)	3.50B	2.90B	2.54B	117.00M**	85.21M

Source: Yahoo! Finance (http://finance.yahoo.com).
*B=billion
**M=million.

ing economy. (For additional information on the performance of Schwab and Morgan Stanley, see Appendix A.)

Corporate scandals

In his 2002 letter to shareholders, Phillip Purcell, CEO of Morgan Stanley, wrote:

> Equity prices have gone through the most severe and prolonged decline since the 1930s . . . In 2002, our company faced challenging financial markets and poor business conditions for the third year in a row. We also had to contend with the harsh regulatory environment that came in the wake of scandals at a number of companies. (Phillip Purcell, letter to shareholders, December 2002)

The scandals plaguing corporate America (see Appendix B) were having a profound effect on the financial services industry in which Morgan Stanley and Charles Schwab participated, more so on Morgan Stanley, a full-service firm encompassing investment banking as well as institutional and retail sales, than Schwab, which focused mainly on the retail customer.

Role of research analysts. The role played by research analysts, who worked for full-service firms like Morgan Stanley, was under intense scrutiny. These analysts were supposed to be doing independent and objective research, identifying stocks that were "good" buys, which the firm's brokers sold to their clients. These analysts' obligation was to provide impartial, unbiased assessments of the companies they analyzed so that clients could make better investment decisions. But the analysts in many firms were assuming another role—supporting the activities of their firms' investment banking units. They often issued favorable reports on companies whose underwriting business their firms were trying to obtain, even in cases when they did not have good reasons to be favorably disposed toward these companies.

The analysts were motivated by the fact that their compensation was tied to how much investment banking business they helped their firms generate. In addition, they reported directly to the investment banking side of their firms, a relationship that increased the pressure on them to issue positive ratings on companies with whom the investment bankers might do business.

Analysts gave good ratings to stocks that did not deserve a good grade because such ratings might attract investment-banking business; but if they issued a positive recommendation on a stock that did not deserve a good grade, that recommendation misled investors who might buy the stock. A "Chinese Wall" that separated investment banking from the selling of stocks was supposed to exist, but in many firms it had been breached and conflicts of interest were prevalent.

During the heyday of the Internet economy, sell ratings accounted for less than 4 percent of the recommendations analysts made. When the market turned sour, buy ratings continued to consistently outnumber sell ratings, adding to the suspicion that analysts were afraid to offend the companies they followed. They were not willing to issue negative ratings out of fear that their firms might not obtain lucrative investment-banking deals. If they issued anything but a positive rating, the top managers of firms they followed might retaliate by blacklisting their company (see Appendix C: "Analysts Accused of Misleading Investors").

New rules. On May 10, 2002, the SEC and NASD approved new rules that stated the following:

1. A firm could not offer favorable research ratings in exchange for future business considerations.
2. The rating systems that firms used had to be clearly defined.
3. No research analyst could be supervised by a firm's investment-banking division.
4. Investment bankers could not discuss pending research reports with analysts before the reports were distributed.
5. An analyst's compensation could not be directly tied to investment-banking transactions.
6. Compensation indirectly related to investment-banking deals had to be disclosed.

Fines. Ten of the largest U.S. securities firms, in addition, agreed to pay $1.4 billion to settle SEC charges relating to conflicts of interest. J. P. Morgan was part of the settlement, as was Merrill Lynch, CSFB, Salomon Smith Barney, Goldman Sachs, UBS Warburg, Piper Jaffray, Lehman Brothers, Bear Stearns, and Chase. These companies agreed not to seek insurance repayments or tax deductions for $487.5 million of the settlement charges, and to put a "buyer beware"-type sticker on their research, which would state whether their firms also had investment-banking relations with the companies they analyzed.

Other rules that the ten companies would have to follow included: (1) separating supervisory from reporting structures for investment banking and research; (2) compensating analysts only for the quality of their research, not their contribution to investment banking; and (3) not allowing analysts to accompany investment bankers when they talked to prospective clients.

Restoring public trust and confidence. Morgan Stanley had been somewhat more defiant than the other firms that were party to the settlement. Nonetheless, it still had serious issues with which to deal. The company had to decide if it should do anything more to restore public trust and confidence.

Part of the problem was that the ambition that drove people to engage in questionable and illegal acts might be part of the psychological makeup of a desirable investment-bank employee. The drive to secure business was a welcome trait, but it had to be tempered by a respect for the rules and an understanding of conflicts of interest.

Charles Schwab: Exploiting the scandals. Charles Schwab knew exactly what to do about the scandals—exploit them. Since its founding as a discount brokerage company in the 1970s, the company practice had been to fight the major Wall Street players. In the 1970s, it opposed this group by taking advantage of the end of fixed-rate commissions. In 2002, its goal was to do the same—use the uneasiness of investors to make inroads on the established players' positions. Schwab would try to capture the most profitable customers of Morgan Stanley, Merrill Lynch, and other large brokers by projecting its "clean" image.

Clients blamed bad advice for their troubled financial performance and their loss of trillions of dollars. They were especially upset with the research the financial-services industry had done because it misled them. Schwab used this dissatisfaction to launch an aggressive marketing campaign that suggested its rivals were responsible for their clients' losses, but that Schwab operated by different rules, making the company less likely to be guilty of such offenses.

Schwab owed nothing to corporate clients, because it did not engage in investment banking. Therefore, it could give its clients a truly unbiased research option. It offered them a new rating system that relied on an in-house computer model that graded stocks on an *A* to *F* scale based on 24 objective measures, such as a company's free cash flow and sales growth. In its ads, Schwab maintained that its advice, unlike that of its rivals, was neutral and unbiased. Moreover, it claimed that

its top 30 selections also were performing very well; they beat the
Standard & Poor's 500-stock index by 4.6 percent in 2001.

The economy

Ultimately, a revival of the financial services industry depended not
only on what happened with regard to these scandals but also on how
well the economy did. The economy's health and that of the stock market were closely connected.

A recession. At the start of the 21st century, the U.S. economy was
mired in its seventh recession since 1960. Signs of a recovery clearly
were at hand, but as long as the economic slump persisted, corporate
earnings were depressed, which kept stock prices from advancing and
held the financial services industry back (see Figure 5.1).

A key question was whether the slow and gradual comeback that
seemed to be taking place in the U.S. economy was genuine. Morgan
Stanley's chief economist, Stephen Roach, known for his pessimism,
was not sure. He argued that the world was facing "its toughest array
of . . . problems since the end of the Second World War." On the plus
side, there was strong consumer spending, a positive housing market,
and indications that manufacturing might revive.

Consumer spending. Since 1995, about 60 percent of the cumulative
growth of the world economy's output had come from the United
States, which was more than the U.S. share of global Gross Domestic

FIGURE 5.1   U.S. economic performance: 1960–2002
(annual growth in real GDP, in percents)

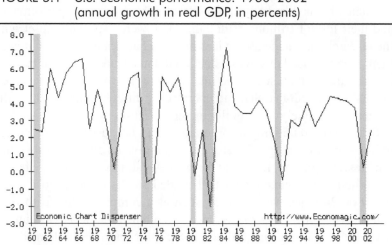

Source: Economagic.com home page (http://www.economagic.com).

FIGURE 5.2   U.S. stock market performance: 1960–2002
(Dow Jones Industrial Average close)
(percentage change from same period last year)

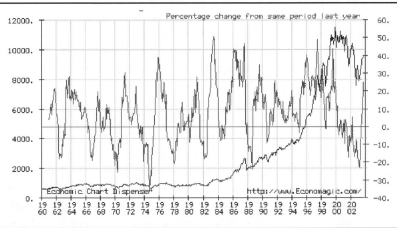

Source: Economagic.com home page (http://www.economagic.com).

Product (GDP). America's disproportionate contribution to global growth reflected the strength of consumer spending, which grew an average of 3.7 percent a year since 1995, twice the increase in other developed nations. Global prosperity depended heavily on U.S. demand, but what if that demand plummeted? The indebtedness of the U.S. consumer was a danger to the world economy, because it lowered the likelihood that people would continue to spend at the same levels they had in the past.[2]

Investors in other countries. The U.S. economy depended on investors in other countries investing in the United States, but private investors abroad were starting to reduce the amount they invested in America. Asia's central banks—mainly in Japan and China—continued to buy U.S. bonds to keep their currencies weak in relation to the dollar. Weak currencies supported Asian exports to the United States, but they posed a threat of their own: they lead to the loss of U.S. manufacturing jobs.[3]

---

2. The United States had to borrow large sums from foreigners to maintain its rate of spending. Foreign borrowing was more than 5 percent of U.S. GDP, a historically high level. In the 1980s, the United States was the world's largest creditor nation. By 2003, it had become the world's largest debtor nation. If foreigners were reluctant to offer credit, U.S. consumer spending might go down.

3. The United States was rapidly losing manufacturing jobs—more than 16 percent of all its manufacturing jobs or 3 million since the start of the recession in 2000. Bush administration officials might pressure Asian governments to strengthen their currency versus the dollar. The flow of dollars from abroad into the United States might slow, which would dampen U.S. consumption.

Decline in the dollar. Because the dollar was in decline, the likelihood was lower that foreign investors would continue to find the United States an attractive place to put their money. From 2002–2003, the dollar was falling at a rate of 8 percent against the currencies of the U.S.'s trading partners. In comparison to the Euro, the decline was 20 percent, but there was virtually no drop versus the Asian currencies because they were being propped up by their governments to preserve jobs and economic growth.[4]

The federal deficit. If consumer indebtedness continued to grow at a rate two times faster than consumer income, consumers would be limited in how much they could spend. Businesses and government were in no position to pick up the slack. After the stock market fell in 2000, business investment was down, and the federal government's budget surplus of more than 2 percent of GDP in 2000 had shifted to a deficit of more than 4 percent of GDP in 2003 because of tax cuts and the war in Iraq.

Consumption spending would have to come from elsewhere.[5] However, for more than a decade, Japan had not coped well with the aftermath of an economic collapse, and Europe had suffered from macroeconomic policies designed to fight inflation. Their people were reluctant to spend heavily.[6]

Risks to investors. These conditions had not augured well for the U.S. economy and American stock markets (see Table 5.2). They were risks that had to be honestly and forthrightly described to prospective investors, but they were not the kinds of risks that investors would be able to easily understand. Investors' horizons were typically short. Most looked at what took place yesterday, not what was likely to happen tomorrow. They still were hoping that the stock market might rebound to its late 1990 levels.

---

4. In the 1980s, the dollar had declined more than 55 percent against both the Deutschmark and the Yen. Currently, the dollar might have to fall even farther, but the decline had to be more evenly distributed because if the entire decline took place against the Euro, the European economy would suffer great harm. Moreover, a fall of the dollar had to be managed; a free fall might have disastrous repercussions. There also were questions about whether the leaders of the world's governments could coordinate their actions as effectively as they did in the 1980s.

5. In the early 1980s, similar conditions prevailed; foreign borrowing was over 3 percent of U.S. GDP. It came down without a global recession because of a controlled drop in the dollar and a prosperous Germany and Japan.

6. They had rigid economic systems that did not encourage growth, and the populations of these nations were aging.

TABLE 5.2   U.S. economic performance: 2001–2003

Year	GNP growth (%)	CPI (%)	Unemp. rate (%)	S&P yearly return (%)
2001	1.2	1.5	4.8	-16.1
2002	2.4	2.4	5.8	-23.0

Source: Economic Report of the President, 2003, and Survey of Current Business.

Describing these types of problems to investors would not stimulate the type of investment boom that Wall Street firms so desperately needed. All industry firms did well in a bull market (like that of the 1990s). All would do poorly in a bear market. There were many complicated imponderables in the industry, making it difficult to predict what was likely to take place in the next five years.

The period that started in 2000 could lead in many directions (see Appendix D). The 2003–2007 period could be most like the 1990s. The economy could show steady growth rates with inflation under control, declining unemployment rates, and growing market confidence. A second possibility was that this period would be most like the 1980s, when there was more variability in GDP, inflation, and unemployment, but the trends generally were positive, and the market had some very good years. A third possibility was that this period would be most like the 1970s, a troubled time when inflation and unemployment grew and the stock market had no momentum. Key factors that would affect these outcomes included:

• Changes in real wealth domestically and globally;
• Changes in inflation and interest rates;
• Positive or negative supply shocks (for example, energy supply disruptions and price changes);
• Changes in productivity;
• The fiscal and monetary policies in the United States and abroad;
• Changes in the balance of payments and exchange rates; and
• Changes in business confidence.

How these factors would interact was subject to much speculation.

Looking ahead, investors could expect a great deal of uncertainty. Though the primary factors driving market performance were corporate profits and economic growth, investors had many macroeconomic and other variables to consider, including the weakening dollar, global terrorism, oil prices, and international politics.

Communicating this uncertainty to investors and providing them with the tools to protect as well as grow their assets was the responsibility of the people who worked on the retail side of the financial services industry. But how should these people respond to these challenges?

What did investors want?

What did it mean to be a responsible advisor under these circumstances? Given the uncertainty, what did investors want from their financial advisors—more handholding or less? If more, what type of handholding did they need? The model that Charles Schwab used when working with clients was very different from Morgan Stanley's model.

The discount model. When Schwab became a discount broker, it tried to break with the investment banks full-service model. The company not only reduced commissions, but it eliminated advice. Schwab gave clients the ability to make decisions on their own. Its sales force was not comprised of brokers who earned commissions from passing on tips to clients and completing transactions for them. Schwab's sales force was salaried, taking its orders directly from clients. The beauty of this discount model was that it lowered Schwab's costs. A salaried sales force was less expensive to maintain than the advisors in a traditional brokerage firm.

Schwab did not anticipate the advent of online brokers, who outflanked Schwab and knocked even more of the costs out of the system. Schwab responded aggressively. It continued to be a powerful online force, but it also went after the full-service brokers and tried to attract their most profitable accounts, targeting the businesses of high-net-worth individuals.

High-net-worth individuals. How could Schwab enter this business rapidly? It did not want the overhead associated with hiring a large staff of full-service financial advisors. Instead, it created a virtual organization, setting up a referral service to rapidly create a presence among high-net-worth individuals. Schwab had lists of affiliated professional account managers to whom it referred high-net-worth clients in need of more handholding than Schwab typically provided. These affiliated account managers provided full-service advice to so-called preferred clients.

The affiliated account managers were not Schwab employees.

*Look at J part of paper to see if part of Grp stratd has Stat.

Charles Schwab versus Morgan Stanley   101

Rather these people used Schwab's technological infrastructure as a platform to carry out trades, maintain their accounts, and do their bookkeeping. For the services Schwab rendered, the company charged a fee; it also received a fee for referring a client.

The acquisition of U.S. Trust. The affiliated account manager model described above made great sense. It allowed Schwab to expand rapidly and to take advantage of the varied talents and abilities of the many independent advisors. But this model also had its limits, so in 2000 Schwab bought a full-service investment firm—U.S. Trust—for $2.7 billion. This acquisition would allow Schwab to be in an even better position to compete with organizations like Morgan Stanley that catered to the very wealthy, known as the "bulge bracket."

Under pressure from the extreme discount brokerages that opened on the Internet, Schwab was moving toward a business model that was more like that of the full-service brokers (see Figure 5.3). With the acquisition of U.S. Trust, Schwab was able to provide services like those of Morgan Stanley. However, a new dilemma accompanied the acquisition. Schwab had to decide how to better integrate the work of U.S. Trust's full-service advisors with that of the independent advice givers to whom it had previously referred its best clients.

FIGURE 5.3   Different business models in financial services

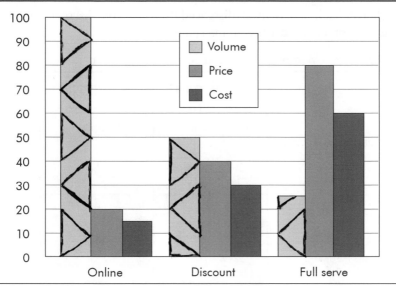

Source: Alfred Marcus, *Management Strategy*, McGraw Hill, 2005.

The acquisition of Dean Witter. Full-service brokers like Morgan Stanley had not been standing still while Schwab was making these changes. Just as Schwab invaded their turf, they encroached on Schwab's space. The most dramatic example was Morgan Stanley's purchase of Dean Witter, a downscale but huge brokerage firm once owned by Sears and aimed at the average American.

Morgan Stanley bought Dean Witter in 1997 and in the process obtained over 10,000 brokers whose clients, for the most part, were not the high-net-worth individuals to whom Morgan Stanley traditionally had catered. The gilt-edged crowd that earlier had been drawn to Morgan Stanley now saw their firm appealing to a different clientele.

With the acquisition of Dean Witter, Morgan Stanley's culture of exclusivity had to make way for a more common touch. Thus, the merger of the two organizations was a major challenge and gigantic headache for Morgan Stanley.

Morgan Stanley had a dual approach to its business, one model for the extremely affluent, the traditional Morgan Stanley model, and another for those with more moderate means, the traditional Dean Witter model.

With the merger, Morgan Stanley came to compete more directly with Schwab (see Figure 5.4). The two organizations, though they came from different directions, were now going after the same groups. Morgan Stanley was BMW moving downscale, while Schwab was Toyota moving upscale. As Morgan Stanley distanced itself from Goldman Sachs and Schwab distanced itself from the discount brokers, the two companies clashed in the same space.

FIGURE 5.4   Morgan Stanley and Schwab begin to collide

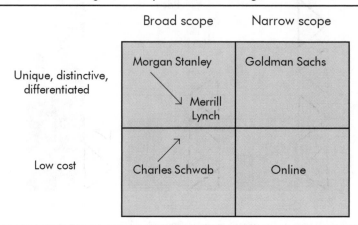

With the burst of the stock market bubble, the entire industry was under duress. The two companies were not only competing in the same space but they were competing for a smaller pie. In these circumstances, they were scrutinizing their prior business models and asking how much room they had for innovation.

Morgan Stanley's business model

Morgan Stanley's business model differed substantially from Schwab's. Morgan Stanley was vertically integrated. It both produced financial products and sold them. In 2004, Morgan Stanley was the global leader in underwriting. It also had its own mutual funds, including the Van Kampen line, which it sold to clients. Morgan Stanley traded its money to boost earnings and provided trading services to hedge funds. It also had its Discover credit card business. The company netted healthy earnings from bond trading and earned billions of dollars in fees when clients refinanced debt.

Schwab engaged in none of these activities. Nonetheless, in one area Morgan Stanley directly competed with Schwab. Its brokerage unit that once had been owned by Sears and had been dubbed the "socks and stocks" unit was a direct competitor. Phillip Purcell, Morgan Stanley's current CEO, had come from the brokerage side of the business. A former McKinsey and Company consultant, Purcell was hired by Sears in 1978 to build Dean Witter. As CEO of Morgan Stanley, Purcell had established trust with the powerful investment bankers in the firm by delegating to them considerable authority. The company's star-studded investment bankers had substantial autonomy.

An investment bank. Indeed, Morgan Stanley was first and foremost an investment bank, which put it in touch with some of the richest people in the world. It dealt with underwriting, mergers and acquisitions, and it earned much of its revenues and profits from providing these services to high-level corporate clients.

The company was the only member of the 1960s' elite underwriters, which included First Boston, Kuhn Loeb, and Dillon Read, to survive intact. Its main competitors on the underwriting side of the business were Goldman Sachs and Merrill Lynch. Morgan Stanley was also active in fixed-income investments, institutional sales, and research. These activities were far removed from those in which Schwab engaged.

Dividing up customers. Morgan Stanley divided up its customers according to how much wealth the customers had to manage.

1. At the bottom rung, Morgan Stanley had what it called people in the *wealth-seeding* phase. These individuals might have anywhere from $100,000 to $1 million to invest. For the most part, they would buy domestic securities and mutual funds.

2. People Morgan Stanley referred to as being in the *wealth-building* phase were in the middle. They might have anywhere from $1 million to $5 million to invest. Morgan Stanley was competing with other full-service firms and trust companies to service them. Their needs were greater than the *wealth seeders* because they were likely to have issues regarding retirement, the education of their children, and intergenerational transfers. Besides helping these people manage their overall assets and selling them domestic securities and mutual funds, Morgan Stanley would handle their international securities, real estate, and other commodity needs.

3. Finally at the top, were those Morgan Stanley referred to as being in the *wealth-realization* stage. They might have anywhere from $5 million to more than $1 billion in assets to manage. Managing the assets of these people was very complex. The competition was intense for doing so and included firms like Goldman Sachs and select private Swiss banks. The products Morgan Stanley offered were extensive, and in addition to those offered to *wealth seeders* and *wealth builders*, they might include coinvestment opportunities, restricted securities, hedging, and other rarefied options.

The experience and training to work with high-net-worth individuals. Morgan Stanley had the experience and training to serve high-net-worth individuals. Its brokers had credibility with wealthy clients. The company had proprietary investment products and high-end services such as restricted stock sales and asset allocation that Schwab had not been able to provide. The professionals Morgan Stanley hired were an elite group. They had worked with the bulge-bracket investment crowd for years. They knew these people intimately and in a way that Schwab's salaried sales force had never really known them.

Morgan Stanley account representatives came mainly from Ivy League schools. Many of them had advanced degrees such as an MBA, or high-level certification as financial planners. They had built long-lasting relationships with some of the richest people in the world and did business in a first-class way.

A big part of their clientele consisted of individuals with substantial inherited wealth, as well as entrepreneurs and business owners. In many instances, Morgan Stanley's account representatives managed this wealth through "change-of-circumstance events" such as deaths, liquidations, or the sales of businesses. The sums involved often exceeded $1 billion.

A team approach. The model for working with the client or the client's family was that a whole team from Morgan Stanley assisted the company's representative and contact person in helping the client. The Morgan Stanley team might have expertise in such disparate areas as business development, asset allocation, money management, and traditional securities brokerage activities, including equity, fixed income, restricted stocks, hedging, and monetization. The Morgan Stanley team was able to offer a wide variety of products from the entire company to such a client.

Merging with Dean Witter. Morgan Stanley had always catered to individual investors, but these investors had not constituted a high percentage of its business until the 1997 acquisition of Dean Witter. With the acquisition in place, Morgan Stanley had 260 elite professionals in its private client service (PVS) division and it obtained more than 10,000 new brokers and 4 million retail customers from Dean Witter.

The inherited Dean Witter account representatives were less focused on the very wealthy. Dean Witter had branch offices throughout the United States. Along with the company's Discover credit-card business, which Morgan Stanley also bought, Dean Witter was the personification of Middle America. It recruited its account executives (AEs) from the communities it served by means of career nights, through newspaper ads, and from other referrals of this nature. It also competed vigorously to attract experienced and successful brokers from other firms. These people often were self-starters who had built their practices from scratch, often starting by cold calling.

Dean Witter tried to entice this entrepreneurial group with bonuses and other forms of compensation, often amounting to millions of dollars stretched over long periods of time. A full 20 percent of Dean Witter's account executives came to the company in this manner.

Morgan Stanley's aim in merging with Dean Witter was to bring these account executives and their clients into the company's fold.

Morgan Stanley's underwriting capability needed a strong retail arm. After the merger, the firm almost had the same number of brokers as Merrill Lynch (see Table 5.3).

In a league with Merrill Lynch. The Dean Witter merger, along with the 1996 acquisition of Van Kampen, brought distribution channels to Morgan Stanley that put it more in the league of a Merrill Lynch and gave it a leg up on Goldman Sachs. Having strong distribution channels was considered a major requirement for effective underwriting in the future.

The Morgan Stanley/Dean Witter merger was premised on the fact that each unit would take a distinct approach, both of which could survive in the same firm. Unlike the private-client advisers at Morgan Stanley, Dean Witter AEs did not have discretionary authority over client accounts. The Morgan Stanley representatives could manage their clients' assets either in pooled vehicles or separate accounts using sophisticated products customized to a specific client's needs.

Dean Witter account executives. Dean Witter's account executives were not as well trained as Morgan Stanley's private-client advisors. However, Dean Witter had established an extensive training program for its brokers in 1989 in conjunction with the University of Pennsylvania's Wharton School. But only 300 of the 10,000 AEs that Morgan Stanley brought on board had entirely completed the program and were fully versed in such things as asset allocation and portfolio theory. Moreover, very few of these AEs knew how to use the special-

TABLE 5.3   Competitive landscape: U.S. full-service brokerage

Rank	Company	No. of U.S. brokers
1	Merrill Lynch	15,147
2	Morgan Stanley Dean Witter	13,191
3	Salomon Smith Barney	12,927
4	UBS Paine Webber	8,801
5	Edward Jones	8,595
6	Wachovia Securities	7,595
7	A.G. Edwards	7,267
8	Prudential Securities	5,384
9	RBC Dain Rauscher	2,100
10	Legg Mason	1,322
11	Raymond James Financial	1,213
12	Wells Fargo Investments	1,100

Source: SIA Yearbook 2002–2003. Numbers as of January 1, 2002.

ized software packages that Dean Witter gave them, packages that relied on these techniques. Therefore, the assets of Dean Witter's very wealthy clients were collected into accounts that were externally managed.

Dean Witter representatives were often criticized for the narrowness of their product offerings. The two companies thought that the merger might correct this limitation, as Dean Witter brokers would be able to sell Van Kampen and Morgan Stanley's other products.[7] A very high percentage of the typical sales of a Morgan Stanley AE was in-house products such as the company's own mutual funds.

By 2004, there were indications that the merger had not worked as planned. The former Dean Witter brokers had trouble attracting clients outside the wealth seeder category. Merrill Lynch was doing better than Morgan Stanley. It cut the ranks of its brokers much more heavily than it had during the 2000–2001 recession, and its annual revenue per broker by 2004 was much higher, $712,000, compared to Morgan Stanley's $451,000. Morgan Stanley settled a complaint with the SEC that its brokers were favoring Morgan Stanley affiliated mutual funds, even when these funds performed poorly, because of the higher fees the brokers earned when they sold the funds. With the economy still uncertain and people continuing to look for investment opportunities outside stocks and bonds, Morgan Stanley was unsure of what to do next with its brokers.

Schwab's business model

Meanwhile discount brokers like Charles Schwab had increased their share of the $15 trillion of U.S. assets under management in 2000 (see Table 5.4). From next to nothing in 1995, they captured about 10 percent of this market by 2000. Full-service brokers such as Morgan Stanley continued to control about 30 percent of the market. The share of banks went down from close to 45 percent to under 30 percent. The remaining 30 percent of the market was divided between mutual funds and insurance firms.

A category of one. Schwab traditionally referred to itself as "a category of one." Its view of the industry was that of a constellation, not a

---

7. Most of Dean Witter's account executives sold products that Dean Witter had developed. Morgan Stanley's earnings on the sales of its own products were greater than its earnings on the products of other firms. Schwab portrayed this fact as a liability. A Morgan Stanley representative had an incentive to sell the company's products whether they were the best ones for a client or not.

TABLE 5.4   Market share of the $15 trillion of U.S. assets under management in 2000

Full-service brokerages	Banks	Mutual funds	Discount brokers	Insurance companies
30%	30%	20%	10%	10%

Source: RBC Dain Rauscher.

continuum; the industry had room for many players. No company or segment dominated. Merrill Lynch was the largest full-service broker. In 2000, it was managing about $1.5 billion in assets. The largest discount broker was Schwab, which was managing about $600 million in assets. But both faced substantial competition, and not only from Morgan Stanley. Among full-time brokers, a client could choose from such firms as Edward Jones, AG Edwards, Prudential, and UBS Paine Webber. Among discount brokers, a client could choose from such firms as Brown and Brown (owned by J. P. Morgan Chase), Datek, Muriel Siebert, TD Waterhouse, and Quick and Reilly. Even more extreme discount brokers such as Scottrade.com, Firsttrade.com, Buy and Hold, and Portfoliobuilder had emerged. They offered trades for as little as $4 a transaction.

A brokerage company had to be precise about who its customers were. Three-quarters of U.S. households had less than $100,000 to invest; only 2 percent had more than $1 million to invest. The most attractive clients were those in the bulge bracket who had lots of money to invest (see Table 5.5).

Dividing its customers. Schwab divided its customers into three main groups.

1. *Self-directed* investors were generation X people (21–35 years old) with investments under $100,000.
2. *Validators* were baby boomers (36–55 years old) with investments between $100,000 and $1 million.

TABLE 5.5   Households with money to invest: 1999

Investments	All U.S. households
$1-$100K**	75% (86 M*)
$100K-$500K	19% (22 M)
$500K-$1 M	4% (4 M)
+$1 M	2% (2.6 M)

Source: RBC Dain Rauscher.
*M=millions.
**K=thousands.

3. *Delegators* were mature investors (>56 years old) with investments above $1 million.

Schwab believed that self-directed investors were looking for unbiased information and tools and wanted to manage their money by themselves; validators made their own decisions but were looking for some consulting help; and delegators basically wanted someone else to help manage their money for them. Schwab had something to offer each category, but its focus was on the validators, because it believed this group was most likely to be the affluent group of the future.

The future affluent. Schwab understood that the future affluent, most of whom were likely to arise from the validator group, shared a number of characteristics: higher education, higher-paying managerial or professional jobs and/or business ownership, and the possibility of accumulating significant assets over a lifetime of work. Compared to other groups in the population, this group was self-directed. The people of whom it was comprised had upbeat outlooks and a higher than average tolerance for risk. They were sociable and optimistic about technology, read a lot and worked hard, valued marriage and were less likely to be divorced. They tried to take good physical care of themselves; a very high percentage belonged to health clubs. A high percentage also lived in cities with populations of more than 2 million on both the East and West Coasts.

Though people in the future affluent group preferred established brands to new ones, they were hungry for convenience and looking for innovation. Schwab believed that they were more likely to want to be active participants in the management of their own money. They were seeking collaborative advice from a financial services provider and were looking for ways to aggregate their financial transactions. Many of these people already had accounts with Schwab, but they also had accounts with other brokers. Schwab was looking for ways to manage more of this group's money.

Putting customers in control. Schwab had gone through a number of business redesigns to appeal to the validators and to follow them as they aged. Schwab tried to meet this group's financial needs at each stage of the life cycle. The company's goal was to provide high-quality service at an affordable price that was designed to empower these investors with the information and tools they needed to make good, informed decisions. The investor bore ultimate responsibility for these decisions. Schwab was the enabler; it provided people in this group with the ability to make and execute good decisions on their own.

Schwab's advertising and marketing emphasized putting customers in control of their investments. Schwab portrayed itself as the trusted, neutral company from whom people in this group could receive advice and act on it. This image was credible because Schwab brokers were not paid a commission and their incentive was not to churn an account or to actively manage clients' accounts for them for the sake of commissions.

Schwab made it easy to interact with this group. It had a number of different distribution methods besides the telephone and the Internet. An investor could have direct personal contact with a Schwab representative, and Schwab had branch offices in nearly every part of the United States. Most new accounts were initiated in the branch offices.

Technology. Schwab pioneered in technologies that made it easier and more convenient for average investors to manage their accounts via the telephone and the Internet. Schwab developed its own in-house system for clearing trades, an automated voice-response telephone brokerage system, as well as a method for seamless integration with Quicken personal money management software, a software product that people in this group often used. Schwab was the leader in online trading. Despite the fact that it generally charged more for trades than such competitors as Etrade, Datek, and TD Waterhouse, Schwab had the largest market share in online trading.

Following its customers. Schwab built its business on an understanding of how members of its core group of customers were changing (see Table 5.6). When Schwab saw its clients moving to mutual funds, it rushed to fill this breach. In 1980, investors held over $135 billion in assets in mutual funds; by 1991, they had $716 billion in these funds. The problem was that they had a dizzying array of choices: By 1991 there were 361 fund companies and more than 3,400 funds. Investors were paying load fees on some funds in addition to brokerage fees.

Schwab set out to change the system for the benefit of its clients by offering a comprehensive approach where customers could buy a smorgasbord of funds without a load or transaction fee. Instead, the mutual fund companies paid Schwab for marketing their funds.

The switchboard. Schwab brought customers and mutual fund companies together by means of a business model that it referred to as a

TABLE 5.6   Schwab's business redesigns

	1980s low cost	1988 differentiate	1992 low cost	1997 low cost	2002 differentiate
Customer	Do-it-yourself investor	Financial planners	Mutual funds	Regional brokers	Bulge bracket
Value capture	Commissions	Fees, referrals	Fees	Fees	Fees, advice
Differentiation/control	Brand/branches	Technical partner	Switchboard	Technical referral	Independent
Scope	Discount broker	Back office	Discount funds	Discount insurance	Objective research
Definition	Discount broker	Service provider	Switchboard	2nd gen. switchboard	Almost full service

Source: Adapted from Adrian Slywotzky, David Morrison, and Bob Andelman, *The Profit Zone,* Crown Business, 1997.

switchboard. The company made all a customer's funds accessible via a single contact, and set up a system in which it tracked all transactions on a single account statement. Schwab did all the account servicing and maintained regular contact with the customer.

In 1997, Schwab repeated this formula with insurance. Thus, in 1992 and 1997, the company innovated as a low-cost provider in both mutual funds and insurance by means of the switchboard method. It claimed that it was the trusted intermediary who brought customers and investment service providers together. Schwab was independent of any single mutual fund company or insurance provider. Because it had few products of its own, it was not dedicated to directing its clients to its own offerings.

A referral service. When Schwab realized that its clients wanted more advice than its branch office assistants could provide, it set up a referral service to small- and medium-sized, independent financial advisors for whom it performed back-office transaction processing and accounting activities for a fee. This move enabled Schwab to establish in essence 6,000 branch offices without being directly responsible for the overhead. Using Schwab's proprietary software, this virtual sales force was able to interact with Schwab offices from anywhere in the United States or abroad without a hitch.

With the acquisition of U.S. Trust, Schwab was trying to follow its customer base, the future affluent. By the year 2000, more than 10 percent of the company's customers had over $1 million in investable assets and they therefore needed more intensive advice and assistance.

More intensive advice. The newly affluent, Schwab reasoned, still wanted a high degree of control. People in this category wanted independence. They were still willing to embrace technology, but they wanted a higher level of counsel because they had more responsibilities as their finances became more complicated. Providing this advice was what Schwab had to do. Doing so was good for the company because it would make Schwab less dependent on revenue from individual trades for its growth.

The need for growth. Schwab's appetite for growth was large. To continue to be a low-cost provider required growth and the scale economies that came with it. The technological infrastructure that was at the base of Schwab's business was expensive to maintain.

The company therefore aimed to add up to $125 billion assets per year, boost its revenue per employee to $300,000, and increase its profitability by continuing to emphasize cost cutting while at the same time expanding the number of clients it served. All the while, investors worried about the economy, and Schwab was rubbing up against some of the biggest and toughest competitors in the business such as Morgan Stanley.

Schwab still faced the problem of integrating U.S. Trust. By 2004, U.S. Trust's pretax profits had fallen by almost 60 percent since Schwab had purchased it. Banks such as Citicorp and J. P. Morgan Chase offered more investment vehicles. Schwab had little experience in hedge funds, private equity funds, and other exotic investments that well-healed clients were seeking. The U.S. Trust's annual fee of 1.25 percent of the amount a client invested was higher than many competitors. Investors were clamoring to know what they were getting in return.

The Schwab culture and the U.S. Trust culture were continually at war. For instance, Schwab referred to the people with whom it did business as customers, while U.S. Trust insisted that they be called clients. Schwab considered the U.S. Trust staffers overpaid. The company cut their bonuses. As a result, many left the firm, taking their clients with them. Remaining staff resented the heavy pressure Schwab was putting on them to boost earnings Schwab expected U.S. Trust to increase earnings 30 percent per year, which was double U.S. Trust's usual growth. Schwab was disappointed in U.S. Trust's technology and its infrastructure. In 2001, the government fined U.S. Trust $10 million for lax recordkeeping, one of the biggest fines ever in the industry for this offense. David Pottruck, Schwab's CEO, fired Jeff Mauer, U.S. Trust's CEO, but in 2004, the Schwab board ousted Pottruck and replaced him with Schwab founder, Charles Schwab.

The company still was uncertain where to turn. It was trying to find its direction in a period different than anything it had experienced in the past. It was weighing its options. Should it become more of a full service firm like Morgan Stanley or should it return to its roots and compete more vigorously than ever with the online brokers? To protect its discount name, it decided to lower what it charged customers with more than $1 million in assets for a trade. It also lowered its rate for investors who traded more than 30 times a year, but these rates still were not competitive with extreme discount brokers.

Moreover, the customized investment advice for which Schwab charged $125 a quarter was given free by such rivals such Fidelity, Etrade, and Vanguard. Schwab no longer had a unique niche either as a low cost company or a specialized service provider. How should it reorient itself in an intensely competitive industry where customers had so many choices?

What to Do Next?

The Schwab model for doing business was very different from the Morgan Stanley model, but increasingly the two companies were competing against each other for a similar group of customers. Two disparate firms with very different traditions—Charles Schwab and Morgan Stanley—were now going head to head in some areas. Their management had to decide how to best do so in a period when the credibility of their industry was under question and the future of the economy was uncertain.

Questions for Discussion

1. Why did Schwab do so well during the bull market of the 1990s? As it was not tainted by decline like Morgan Stanley, why was its decline steeper than Morgan Stanley's?

2. Why were investment banks like Morgan Stanley mired in scandal? What were their analysts accused of doing? Why was this behavior wrong?

3. What kinds of new rules were firms like Morgan Stanley now subject to? If the separation between investment banking and research

under the new rules had to be near complete, how were investment banks going to pay for research?

4. Was Schwab's attempt to project a "clean image" likely to lure customers away from full-service firms like Morgan Stanley? How could Morgan Stanley counter Schwab's image?

5. As an investment advisor, how would you explain economic conditions to your clients? What would you tell them about the risks they face?

6. Given the uncertain economic conditions, which business model is more attractive—that of Schwab or that of Morgan Stanley?

7. Why did Schwab buy U.S. Trust? What was it trying to accomplish with this purchase? What problems did this acquisition pose?

8. Why did Morgan Stanley buy Dean Witter? What was it trying to accomplish with this purchase? What problems did this acquisition pose?

9. Why was Morgan Stanley so interested in acquiring a strong retail arm? How did this give it a leg up on Goldman Sachs?

10. Why was Schwab so interested in the bulge bracket? Why did it feel it had to have a strong foothold in this market?

11. To what extent does Schwab's empowerment model make sense? What if your brain surgeon told you that he operated under a philosophy of putting his patients in control. Would you trust the brain surgeon?

Exercises

1. Visit the Websites of Charles Schwab and Morgan Stanley. Try to learn more about the companies, the products and services they offer, their overall image, and recent developments from these Websites.

2. Assess the threat that a competitor like Schwab poses to Morgan Stanley. How should Morgan Stanley respond to this threat?

3. Assess the threat that a competitor like Morgan Stanley poses to Charles Schwab. How should Charles Schwab respond?

Video

"The Charles Schwab Corporation: A Presentation by David Pottruck," Cambridge, MA: Harvard Business School.

Bibliography

Applegate, Lynda, F. W. McFarlan, and Jamie Ladge. "Charles Schwab in 2002." Harvard Business School Case 9-803-670, February 2003.

Bond, Gregory. "Edward Jones." Harvard Business School Case 9-700-009, June 2000.

Craig, Susanne, and Ken Brown. "Schwab Ousts Pottruck as CEO; Founder Returns to Take the Helm." *The Wall Street Journal*. July 21, 2004:A1.

Cullen, Terri. "As Schwab Returns to Its Discount Roots, Small Investores Face Shifting Choices." *The Wall Street Journal*. August 4, 2004:D1.

Darst, David, AnnKelsy Rusher, and Catherine Connelly. "Morgan Stanley Dean Witter Private Client Services." Harvard Business School Case, 9-899-107, December 1999.

Davis, Ann. "Will Morgan Stanley Do a Transforming Deal?" *The Wall Street Journal*. October 8, 2004:C1.

Elkind, Peter, Mary Danehy, Jessica Sung, and Julie Schlosser. "Where Mary Meeker Went Wrong." *Fortune*. May 14, 2001.

Esperson, Tom. "Charles Schwab: A Category of One." Harvard Business School Case 9-700-043, December 2000.

Frank, Robert. "U.S. Trust Feels Effects of Switch: Schwab Unit Was Perceived as Ousted CEO's Deal; Shake-Up Is Likely in Offing." *The Wall Street Journal*. July 21, 2004: A8.

Frank, Robert, and Susanne Craig. "White-Shoe Shuffle: Banker to the Rich, U.S. Trust Stumbles After Sale to Schwab; The Discount Broker's Style Irked 151-Year-Old Firm; Profits Fell as Staffers Quit; Protest Over Colored Smocks." *The Wall Street Journal*. September 15, 2004: A1.

"Leadership and Luck." *Economist*. September 20, 2003 (Special section).

Lee, Louise, and Emily Thornton. "Schwab vs. Wall Street." *Business Week*. June 3, 2003.

Mandaro, Laura. "The Pitch by Schwab: Advice Free of Conflicts." *American Banker*. May 15, 2002.

McGeehan, Patrick, and Landon Thomas. "No Worry Even Now at Morgan Stanley." *New York Times*. April 2, 2003:1(Section 3).

Smith, Randall. "Merrill Places Bet on Its Brokers." *The Wall Street Journal*. February 18, 2004:C1.

Vogelstein, Fred, and Ellen Florian. "Can Schwab Get Its Mojo Back." *Fortune*. September 17, 2001.

Appendix A

EXHIBIT 1   Morgan Stanley annual income statement (in millions of U.S. dollars except for per-share items)

	12 months ending 11/30/02	12 months ending 11/30/01	12 months ending 11/30/00	12 months ending 11/30/99	12 months ending 11/30/98
Revenue	31,779	43,358	44,593	34,343	30,760
Other revenue, total	636	516	513	244	282
Total revenue	32,415	43,874	45,106	34,587	31,042
Cost of revenue	24,487	34,612	33,049	24,140	23,642
Gross profit	7,292	8,746	11,544	10,203	7,118
Selling/general/ admin. expenses, total	1,133	1,277	1,582	1,221	1,411
Unusual expense (income)	235	0	0	—	0
Other operating expenses, total	1,840	2,251	1,956	1,498	1,289
Total operating expense	27,695	38,140	36,587	26,859	26,342
Operating income	4,720	5,734	8,519	7,728	4,700
Net income after taxes	3,075	3,660	5,484	4,791	3,393

Source: Yahoo! Finance (http://finance.yahoo.com)

EXHIBIT 2   Charles Schwab annual income statement (in millions of U.S. dollars except for per-share items)

	12 months ending 12/31/02	12 months ending 12/31/01	12 months ending 12/31/00	12 months ending 12/31/99	12 months ending 12/31/98
Revenue	3,992	4,214	5,684	4,415	3,119
Other revenue, total	143	139	104	71	59
Total revenue	4,135	4,353	5,788	4,486	3,178
Cost of revenue	1,947	2,023	2,591	1,989	1,462
Gross profit	2,045	2,191	3,093	2,427	1,658
Selling/general/ admin. expeneses, total	211	246	332	248	160
Unusual expense (income)	434	419	69	0	0
Other operating expenses, total	1,054	1,126	1,257	970	720
Total operating expense	3,967	4,218	4,557	3,388	2,500
Operating income	168	135	1,231	1,099	678
Net income after taxes	97	78	718	666	410

Source: Yahoo! Finance (http://finance.yahoo.com)

Appendix B.   Analysts accused of misleading investors

Jack Grubman. Jack Grubman was a star Salomon Smith Barney telecommunications analyst against whom investors filed claims maintaining that he misled them to secure lucrative investment banking deals. Grubman was accused of being nothing more than a cheerleader for stocks his firm took public. As a person who had intimate ties with the top-management team and the boards of companies like WorldCom, he should have known that these firms had poor earnings outlooks, but he did not reveal what he knew to unsuspecting investors. Indeed, he rated WorldCom a "buy" until a day before it declared bankruptcy.

WorldCom was not the only example. As long as Salomon Smith Barney generated profitable investment-banking fees, Grubman remained bullish on companies such as Qwest, XO, and Winstar even as their finances disintegrated. Grubman only reversed an AT&T sell rating when his firm won AT&T's investment-banking business.

Grubman's 1999 compensation for landing billions of dollars in underwriting fees for Salomon Smith Barney was $20 million. In one of his e-mails, Grubman was caught by the attorney general of New York admitting that he wanted to "downgrade" stocks "months ago" but did not do so because of the "huge pushback from banking."[1]

Citicorp faced fines of more than $400 million for the misdeeds of Salomon Smith Barney. In 2002, it fired Grubman, though he was able to retain his $32 million severance package. The SEC then barred Grubman from working in the financial services industry for life and made him pay a $15 million fine.

Henry Blodget. A lawsuit filed against Henry Blodget of Merrill Lynch alleged that to enhance Merrill Lynch's investment-banking relationships with the company Excite@Home, Blodget issued reports with positive ratings that were misleading because they were inconsistent with his private assessments of the company. In e-mails subpoenaed from Merrill, he called Excite@Home "junk" and a "piece of crap."

Merrill Lynch found other instances in which Blodget privately derided the companies he praised in public. For instance, Blodget had a code for the stocks he personally disliked but nevertheless hyped to the investing community. In his e-mails, he referred to them as POS or "piece of —."[2]

---

1. Elkind, Danehy, Sung, and Schlosser, "Where Mary Meeker Went Wrong," *Fortune*, May 14, 2001.

2. Ibid.

Merrill Lynch was charged with fraud for the research Blodget did on such stocks as GoTo.com and InfoSpace, and for the exaggerated statements he made about other stocks. The company had to pay $400 million in a settlement with the state of New York. The National Association of Securities Dealers fined Blodget $2 million; he was required to pay another $2 million for ill-gotten gains; and he was barred for life from the brokerage business.

Mary Meeker. Morgan Stanley's tech stock analyst, Mary Meeker, was neither fined nor barred from working in the industry, but she too was accused of misleading investors. She kept the ratings of Internet stocks high even as evidence mounted that these firms did not deserve such ratings. She did not downgrade Priceline, Amazon.com, Yahoo, and other Internet stocks even when they declined 85 percent to 97 percent from their peak. Her purpose appears to have been to keep the Internet companies from defecting from Morgan Stanley's investment banking operations.

As long as high-tech firms pulled in positive ratings from investment analysts like Meeker, they were likely to do deals with Morgan Stanley's investment bankers. Morgan Stanley's investment bankers helped launch dozens of Internet companies. In 1999, in the midst of the Internet boom, Meeker earned more than $15 million a year.

Meeker covered such companies as Microsoft and Compaq. Her reputation, however, rose when she brought Netscape to the attention of Morgan Stanley investment bankers who handled Netscape's Initial Public Offering (IPO). In 1995, Meeker issued a widely sought after and read report on the Internet. She continued to stick by companies she supported like Netscape even as their value declined. In 1997, when Netscape lost 20 percent, she upgraded the company from a "buy" to a "strong buy." In 1999, she helped Morgan Stanley execute 27 Internet IPOs, despite her growing reservations about many of these companies. Attorney General Eliot Spitzer of New York State subpoenaed all of Meeker's e-mails, but he found no evidence that Meeker was consistently criticizing companies in private that she publicly recommended.

Frank Quattrone. Meeker's former mentor at Morgan Stanley, Frank Quattrone, faced obstruction of justice charges for destroying documents the SEC had been seeking from Credit Suisse First Boston (CSFB). Quattrone earned more than $200 million after joining CSFB, and he helped bring in more than $5 billion in underwriting and merger advice. The SEC accused him of "spinning," or allocating "hot" IPO shares to corporate executives who then steered their investment-banking business to CSFB. The maximum penalties for the charges against him were ten years for obstructing a grand jury investigation, five   years for obstructing an SEC investigation, and ten years for witness tampering.

Quattrone was only the seventh major figure in Wall Street's history to face a jail sentence. The first trial against Quattrone ended in October 2003 in a hung jury. In the second trial, he was convicted. Quattrone's firm, CFSB, was charged with issuing fraudulent and misleading research on numerous stocks and failing to disclose its analysts' ownership stake in other stocks.

Appendix C.   Past U.S. economic performance

EXHIBIT 1   U.S. economic performance: 1990–1997

1990s	GNP growth (%)	CPI (%)	Unemp. rate (%)	S&P yearly return (%)
1990	1.8	5.4	5.6	8.4
1991	-.5	4.2	6.8	22.7
1992	3.1	3.0	7.5	10.6
1993	2.7	3.0	6.9	12.9
1994	4.0	2.6	6.1	.5
1995	2.7	2.8	5.6	38.7
1996	3.6	2.9	5.4	26.3
1997	4.4	2.3	4.9	26.9

Source: Economic Report of the President, 2003, and Survey of Current Business.

EXHIBIT 2   U.S. economic performance: 1980-1987

1980s	GNP growth (%)	CPI (%)	Unemp. rate (%)	S&P yearly return (%)
1980	-.2	13.5	7.1	19.5
1981	2.4	10.3	7.6	-2.1
1982	-.2	6.1	9.7	27.7
1983	4.3	3.2	9.6	17.5
1984	7.3	4.3	7.5	15.2
1985	3.8	3.5	7.2	22.9
1986	3.4	1.9	7.0	33.9
1987	4.2	3.7	6.2	-3.3

Source: Economic Report of the President, 2003, and Survey of Current Business.

EXHIBIT 3   U.S. economic performance: 1970–1977

1970s	GNP growth (%)	CPI* (%)	Unemp. rate (%)	S&P yearly return (%)
1970	.2	5.8	4.8	17.1
1971	3.3	4.3	5.7	11.8
1972	5.4	3.3	5.4	14.9
1973	.6	6.2	4.9	-14.0
1974	-.4	11.1	5.5	-16.5
1975	5.6	13.5	8.0	36.6
1976	4.6	10.3	7.4	5.3
1977	5.5	6.1	7.0	-8.1

Source: Economic Report of the President, 2003, and Survey of Current Business.
*CPI=Consumer Price Index.

CASE 6

Mergers, Acquisitions, and Divestitures
Time Warner versus Disney[1]

This case concerns why the Time Warner (TW) merger with AOL and the Walt Disney Company (Disney) merger with ABC have not worked as planned to date, and what the management of these two companies can do to reverse the situation. It provides background on the entertainment industry in which TW and Disney participate. Movie studios and broadcast networks are key parts of this industry. The model toward which all of the companies in the industry are converging is to have both production and distribution media and entertainment holdings. This case analyzes this model, investigates why it has not worked as intended, and discusses what TW and Disney can do to turn the situation around.

The Recent Performance of Time Warner and Disney

In October 2003, TW was slightly bigger than Disney in market cap and revenue, and it was growing at a faster rate than its rival (see Table 6.1). However, it was burdened by huge losses in goodwill that it had incurred when America Online (AOL) acquired the company.[2] Instead of realizing the benefits of combining a new economy powerhouse—AOL—and an old economy powerhouse—TW—the merger resulted in a loss of more than $200 billion of market capitalization from the

---

1. This case was written by Alfred Marcus, University of Minnesota, Carlson School of Management. Copyright © 2005 by Marsh Publications LLC. All rights reserved.

2. Goodwill is defined as the excess that a company like AOL pays over the fair value of the net assets of a company it acquires like TW. AOL paid for TW by issuing TW shareholders AOL stock that was grossly overvalued. AOL officially paid $147 billion for TW. At the time of the acquisition, it recorded $130 billion in goodwill. When the stock market bubble burst, TW took a huge goodwill impairment charge that went straight to the bottom line and resulted in immense losses for 2002, from which TW was just beginning to emerge in 2003.

TABLE 6.1   A comparison of Time Warner and Disney in 2003

	Time Warner	Disney
Market cap (billions $)	72.94	47.08
Employees	91,250	112,000
Revenue growth	10.00%	0.20%
Revenue (billions $)	40.96B	25.33B
Gross margin	41.49%	8.85%
EBITA* (billions $)	-39.11B	2.38B

Source: Yahoo! Finance (http://finance.yahoo.com).
*Earnings before interest, taxes, amortization, and depreciation (EBITA) are especially useful when one company takes over another and can use the additional funds to cover the loan payments.

combined firm. Disney's financial problems were not as acute as those of TW, but since the company merged with Capital Cities/ABC, its performance had been a disappointment.

Additional information about the financial performance of these two companies can be found in Appendix A.

The Entertainment Industry

The entertainment industry in which TW and Disney compete is one in which merger, acquisition, and divestiture activity is very common. In 1988, the industry was much more fragmented than today. It consisted of many companies, such as:

• Warner, which had $3.4 billion in revenues in movies and TV production,
• Time, which had $4.2 billion in revenues in publishing and cable,
• Disney, which had $2.9 billion in revenues in cartoons and theme parks,
• Capital Cities/ABC, which had $4.4 billion in revenues in a broadcast network and in TV and radio stations,
• Paramount, which had $3.2 billion in revenues in movies and publishing,
• Viacom, which had $.6 billion in revenues in TV syndication and cable, and
• News Corp., which had $3.5 billion in revenues in tabloids and a production studio (20th Century Fox) and was just starting to build its TV network, Fox.

By 2001, five vertically integrated companies (revenues in parentheses) had emerged as dominant in this industry:

Time Warner ($36.2 billion)

Disney ($25.1 billion)

Viacom ($20.4 billion)

Vivendi (Universal, $16.3 billion)

News Corp. ($13.4 billion)

Only one large company remained, Sony (Columbia pictures, $19 billion in revenues), which concentrated solely on producing films. Because it was foreign, Sony was not permitted to own a U.S. broadcast network.

And only one large company remained that had only a broadcast network—GE, which owned NBC ($5.8 billion in revenues). NBC was dependent on competitors' studio's for its top-rated TV shows because it did not have a production studio of its own. But that soon changed when GE bought Universal Studio from Vivendi in 2003.

Between 1985–2003, a vast amount of merger and acquisition activity took place in this industry:

1. Time Warner merged (1991), bought Turner (1995), built the Warner (WB) network, and was acquired by AOL (2001).
2. Disney bought Capital Cities/ABC (1995).
3. Viacom bought Paramount (and Blockbuster) (1993), built UPN, and then bought CBS (1999).
4. News Corp. bought the 20th Century Fox studio (1985) and built the Fox network.
5. Vivendi, the French water utility, bought Seagram (2001), which had purchased Universal (MCA)/Polygram from Philips, bringing together the content of Universal with Canal+, one of Europe's largest pay-TV providers.
6. GE (NBC) bought Universal Studios from Vivendi (2003).

GE saw Vivendi's difficulties as an opportunity it could not pass up.[3] It purchased a well-established and successful production studio from a company that was desperate to sell.[4] In a deal valued at about $14 bil-

---

3. Vivendi was trying to sell its entertainment assets to undo the damage caused by prior acquisitions. It had created an entertainment empire but had not managed it well, and high debt was forcing it to sell off its holdings. Vivendi was unloading all its entertainment assets except Universal Music.

4. The new company—NBC Universal—would be much more diverse than NBC had been. NBC earned 90 percent of its revenue from advertising, while advertising would consist of just 50 percent of NBC Universal's revenue. TV production, movies, and theme parks would be 40 percent and subscriber fees from cable, 10 percent. The new company would be jointly owned— 80 percent by NBC and 20 percent by Vivendi.

lion, GE acquired Vivendi's film, television, and theme park assets. Through this acquisition, GE was taking steps similar to those taken by other firms in the industry. It was combining production—Universal— with distribution—NBC.[5] The only company that did not conform to this pattern after GE purchased Vivendi was Sony.[6]

Owning content and distribution. With the Vivendi acquisition, virtually all of the major entertainment companies were conforming to the same pattern. The studios were the entertainment companies' factories for generating content, and the broadcast networks and cable channels were the way they distributed this content.

The business model Disney pioneered had content distributed through many channels (see Figure 6.1). Bringing together content

FIGURE 6.1   Disney's model of combining production
            and distribution

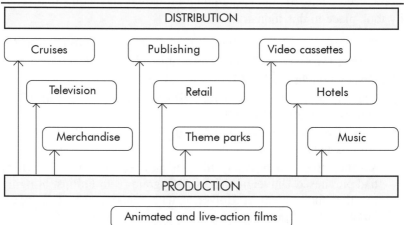

Source: Author's adaptation of Exhibit 10.4, p. 208 in Adrian Slywotzky and David Morrison, *The Profit Zone*, New York: Three Lives Press, 2001, Mercier Management Consulting.

5. Before government regulation took hold in the 1950s and put an end to this practice, all the large Hollywood studios had combined production and distribution. Only in the late 1980s were the studios again allowed to do so.

6. The consolidation of production and distribution at NBC Universal was supposed to create $400 million to $500 million in savings. This sum was large in a company that would have about $13.1 billion in revenues in 2003. Analysts, however, were skeptical about whether the deal would work. Would the approach to management practiced by a large conglomerate best known for its airline engines, power systems, and household appliance divisions be compatible with a movie studio and a chain of theme parks? The theme park business had been in decline since 9/11, and in every market in which Universal's theme parks competed with those of Disney, they were behind. Analysts thought GE should sell the theme parks, but because of the weakness of the business and the low price they would likely fetch, GE's executives were reluctant to do so (see Appendix B).

production and distribution was a rationale for mergers and acquisitions. Combining the two reduced the risks of generating hits, and it provided outlets for creative work. For every hit the studios produced, they had dozens of flops. The networks therefore could cut costs when they owned and/or supplied more of their own prime-time programming. They had more bargaining power as well. If a producer threatened to pull a "hit" show from a network, the network could fall back on its own shows. If Warner threatened to pull "ER" from NBC, NBC now could rely on Universal.

Though networks were likely to be more understanding of their own production units, they had their limits. A network's production company could not force a network to air an unpopular show. Paramount, for example, could not force CBS/UPN to carry a show that did not have the potential for a strong audience.

"Hot" networks, moreover, like NBC, had bargaining power; they could demand a high price for the shows they aired.[7] Even with consolidation, production companies would continue to offer shows to the highest bidder and networks would be in the market for the best shows regardless of who made them. Relationships between production and distribution units would remain open.

Why then was it so important for companies to own production and distribution? Another reason had to do with the convergence of the entertainment, computing, telecom, and information industries, which created a hierarchy with creative content like story ideas and compelling characters, the scarcest commodity, at the bottom of a pyramid that fed many distribution channels.

Each revolution in distribution and transmission provided companies

---

7. NBC had been the dominant U.S. broadcast network (see Appendix C: Exhibit 4), but it was slipping. For instance, in the October 2003 rating sweeps, which determine the prices networks can charge for advertising until the next sweeps in February, NBC had 5.71 million prime-time viewers in the key 18–49 age category compared to CBS's 5.34 million, ABC's 4.74 million, and Fox's 4.01 million. Each network, however, (except for CBS, which increased its share by 2 percent) was losing viewers. Fox was down 14 percent, NBC 10 percent, and ABC 7 percent from the previous year. CBS had the lead in overall viewers (all age categories). For the week of 11/17/03 to 11/23/03, CBS had six top-ten shows, NBC had four, and ABC had one. Being the most popular network among older viewers made up for CBS's relative weakness in the 18–49-year-old age category. But in 2004, NBC—now joined together with Universal—started to slip. As it fell, it suffered through serious declines in total viewers and viewers aged 18–49, for whom advertisers paid a premium. In the key Thursday evening time slots that historically had the most viewers, its bulwark shows were not drawing the same audience that they once had. Between Sept. 20 and Oct. 10, 2004, CBS drew an audience of 5.4 million people between 18 and 49 years old, up 11 percent from the previous year; ABC drew an audience of 5.1 million people between 18 and 49 years old, up 3 percent from the previous year; and NBC drew an audience of 5.0 million people between 18 and 49 years old, down 16 percent from the previous year.

with more outlets for their creative content. The evolution had been from broad mass audiences (TV networks), the aggregation of specific audiences (children, news, movies, comedy) on cable, to catering to individual interests via direct satellite services (15% of U.S. homes) and digital cable (>250 stations), to markets of one and entertainment on demand on the Internet. Truly interactive TV would enable viewers to see cartoons, watch movies on demand, and build their own newscasts.

NBC, CBS, and ABC, the broadcast networks that tried to cater to mass audiences, had lost ground to media that targeted individual groups, a trend that was likely to continue. The Internet, some believed, would be the ultimate distribution channel, consolidating and personalizing the delivery of many different types of content.

Were the mergers really working?

The rationale for consolidation existed (see Table 6.2), but was the theory really working in practice? Many analysts believed that it was not. They viewed companies such as TW and Disney as agglomerations of separate properties that underperformed pure-play firms and should be broken up. The separate production and distribution companies that TW and Disney had agglomerated would be worth more if they were sold and managed as separate businesses than if they were retained under the TW and Disney umbrellas. The top-management teams at TW and Disney did not add enough value to justify their oversight and control of the companies under their jurisdiction.

An analysis of the portfolio. Each company had its share of so-called stars, question marks, cash cows, and dogs, with different expected values if sold as separate entities (see Table 6.3).

TW's stars were its cable channels and systems, which together had estimated revenues of about $16 billion in 2003 and EBITA of $5.3 billion. Disney's star, its cable networks, had estimated revenues of about $16.5 billion in 2003 and EBITA of $2.1 billion. These cable channels and systems were "stars" because TW and ESPN were dominant in cable networks and TW was a top cable system (see Appendix D). For both TW and Disney, the stars were on the distribution side of the business. Also on the distribution side, TW and Disney had dogs or near dogs; TW's was AOL and Disney's were ABC and consumer products.

No real stars existed on the creative or production side of either TW or Disney. Film entertainment was probably a question mark for both companies. The dominant U.S. film studios were Disney and Warner.

TABLE 6.2   The rationale for consolidation: Combining production and distribution

	TW production	Disney production
Film entertainment	Warner Bros., New Line Cinema Hanna Barbarra, Castle Rock Entertainment. (Past hits include *Harry Potter* and *Lord of the Rings*). Television shows include "ER," "Friends," "Drew Carey Show," "West Wing."	Walt Disney Pictures, Hollywood Pictures, Touchstone, Miramax, Buena Vista. (Past hits include *Snow White, Good Morning Vietnam, Who Framed Roger Rabbit, Lion King, Pretty Women, Pulp Fiction*). Walt Disney Television. (Shows include "Sunday Movie," "Golden Girls," "Siskel & Ebert," "Regis and Kathie Lee").
Music	Warner Bros., Elektra, Atlantic, Rhino, Sire	Buena Vista Music Group. (Labels include Hollywood Records, Mammoth Records, Lyric Records.)
Publishing	*Time, People, Sports Illustrated, Fortune, Life, Entertainment Weekly, Golf, Ski, Popular Science, Field and Stream*. (86 magazines and >268 million readers), Little Brown, Warner Books, Book-of-the-Month Club.	Disney Press, Hyperion, *Los Angeles Magazine, Women's Wear Daily*

	TW distribution	Disney distribution
Cable channels and systems	HBO: "Sopranos," "Sex and the City." CNN, TBS, TNT, Cinemax, Time Warner Cable *(Roadrunner)*.	ESPN, Disney Channel, Toon Disney, SoapNet.
Broadcasting network	WB (Past hits include "Dawson's Creek").	ABC (Past hits include "Who Wants to Be a Millionaire"? "Monday Night Football," "Home Improvement"), 21 radio stations, and 10 TV stations.
Recreation and shopping	Sports franchises & Six Flags amusement parks	Disneyland, Walt Disney World, Disneyland Paris, Disney Vacation Club, Disney Cruise Lines, Mighty Ducks, Disney Stores.
Internet	AOL (CompuServe, Netscape)	Joint venture with Infoseek (GO network)

TABLE 6.3   Portfolio analysis (based on October 2002–October 2003 performance)

	Revenue ($ billions)	% change	EBITA	Estimated value ($ billions)
Creative content				
Film entertainment				
Time Warner	10.6	6	1.3	16+
Disney	7.0	4.5	.54	6–7
Publishing				
Time Warner	5.5	2	1.1	12–13
Music				
Time Warner	4.3	2	.5	1–2
Distribution				
Cable channels				
Time Warner (Turner, HBO, etc.)	8.5	11	2.3	16+
Disney cable (ESPN, A&E, History, etc.)	16.5	13.9	2.1	19–20
Disney broadcast (ABC, etc.)	5.4	6.5	.1	6–7
Cable systems				
Time Warner	7.8	10	3.0	16–17
Internet				
Time Warner (AOL)	8.5	-6	1.6	7–8
Shopping				
Disney	2.4	-3	.35	4–5
Theme parks				
Disney	6.5	.6	1	14–15
Total estimated value of Time Warner				70+
Total estimated value of Disney				53+

Source: Morgan Stanley Report.

Between them, they typically captured more than 45 percent of the market at any point in time (see Appendix E: Exhibit 6), and their revenue was growing, but profits were not that good due to high production costs and the risk that audiences would find a movie unappealing.

Publishing was TW's cash cow, but there was not much growth in print media and it was not that profitable. Disney's theme parks and its other recreational holdings were profitable cash cows, but after 9/11 and the slowdown in travel, little real growth took place in either of these areas.

The music divisions were dogs because of piracy. They experienced little growth and weak profitability. Music was a high-risk business because of Internet downloading. Sales were off by as much as 30 percent. The Bronfman group, nevertheless, had offered about $2.5 billion in cash for Warner music.[8] For TW, the sale sped up its efforts to cut its debt.[9]

The Disney-ABC merger

When Walt Disney Company merged with Capital Cities ABC in 1995, it was the biggest media merger ever. Though Disney paid handsomely for Capital Cities (22 times Capital Cities' 1995 estimated earnings), initially both companies' stock prices leapt. Since the merger, however, the earnings of the combined company had dropped (see Appendix A). Growth was slow and operating income, net income, and earnings per share declined. The stock price plunged, and many key executives left.

Postmerger problems. Postmerger culture differences were at the heart of the merged companies' problem. Disney was top-down and hierarchical. Capital Cities ABC had been decentralized. Michael Eisner, Disney's CEO and chair of its board, put an end to all that. Eisner was considered insular and arrogant. His plodding centralized decision making was not appropriate to the needs of the rapidly changing entertainment business. Eisner did not delegate well; he did not grant autonomy to the company's separate divisions. The synergy department that he created was artificial. The internal transfer-pricing mechanism that the company initiated was cumbersome. Eisner abandoned his "gong-show" method of managing creativity because people resented having their ideas heartily dismissed when they were asked to brainstorm for new concepts.

After the merger, Disney lost 75 of its top-level managers, who decided that the environment was not one in which they wanted to work. The company's president, Frank Wells, on whom Eisner relied, died in a helicopter crash in 1994. Jeffrey Katzenberg, who had been very successful as head of the animated film division, left the merged company for Dreamworks, Steven Spielberg's independent film production company, when he was not offered Wells' position.

---

8. TW shed its music division when an investor group led by former Seagram CEO Edgar Bronfman, Jr. was TW's choice to buy Warner Music Group. Bronfman beat out EMI, thus providing him with the opportunity to reenter the entertainment industry. As chief executive of Seagram, Bronfman had established Universal Music as the world's biggest music company. After Bronfman sold Seagram to Vivendi, he tried to buy back Vivendi but lost out to GE.

9. The sale was likely to reduce TW's debt from $28 billion to $20 billion.

Disney's movie successes in Eisner's early years (1985–1989) had been based on low-cost comedies that relied on less-well-known actors, writers, and directors. In the mid-1990s, Disney switched to high-budget action films, many of which like *Con Air* in 1997, flopped.

ABC's disappointing results. ABC had been the number-one-ranked network in viewers in 1995, the year it was acquired. After the merger, prime-time results were disappointing. ABC trailed NBC and CBS in the ratings. It actually lost money in 1998 when audiences continued to splinter and program costs kept rising (NFL rights, for instance).

Fox, not Touchstone, Disney's own television studio, produced the biggest hits on ABC (e.g., "The Practice," "Dharma and Greg," etc.).[10]

In 1999, Disney merged Touchstone with ABC in the hope it could revive Touchstone. Disney's aim was to produce and distribute more of its own content; however, the merger created tension between ABC executives who chose the shows and Touchstone executives who made them, which in turn led to further loss of talent.

ABC programmers claimed that bringing Touchstone into the fold sealed them off from other studios and only contributed further to ABC's decline. The programmers wanted to continue relationships they had formed with such firms as Dreamworks prior to the merger, but Katzenberg's move to Dreamworks made this plan unworkable.

In 1999, ABC experienced a temporary revival with the show "Who Wants to Be a Millionaire?" but the network soon fell again to third in the ratings. As the fall 2003 TV season started, ABC was committed to a menu of family comedies to turn itself around, but it was still looking for a monster hit. Other than "The Bachelor," " Monday Night Football," and "Who Wants to Be a Millionaire," the network had not had a show that ranked in the top five in viewership since the year before the merger. ABC executives lost faith in their in-house production studio. When studio executives came to network executives with ideas for shows that later became mainstays on other networks ("Scrubs," a hit comedy on NBC, and "CSI," a hit franchise with two spinoffs on CBS), the network executives turned the studio executives

10. Fox produced and owned most of its own shows and supplied other networks with many of their hits. These hits included "Dharma and Greg" and "The Practice," which it provided ABC, "Chicago Hope," which it supplied to CBS, and "Buffy the Vampire Slayer," which it gave to WB. Fox was the top TV studio, having achieved this position in the early 1990s by snaring talented comedy writers with lucrative salaries and thus tying up this resource. While a show actually ran, it might barely make a profit because of high production costs. The profits mainly came from syndication, especially syndication to cable, which provided most of the profits to TV studios.

down. The network executives showed poor judgment when they decided not to pursue "Survivor," which became CBS's top-ranked show, and "The Apprentice," a huge hit on NBC. The executives at ABC were hampered in what they could do on their own. They had to put up with Eisner's micromanaging and second guessing from Bob Iger, Disney's chief operating officer and second in command.

ABC's disappointing results were a serious headache for Eisner. Long-time board member and Disney family member, Roy Disney, as well as other prominent board members, called for him to resign. In 2004, Anne Sweeny took over the reigns at ABC. She had a history of turning around weak cable channels and revitalizing them, starting with Nickelodeon, owned by Viacom, for whom she once worked. She helped build the FX cable channel at Viacom, with its racy R-rated shows like "Nip/Tuck." Disney hired her in 1996 to reinvigorate the Disney Channel, which was losing out to Nickelodeon in the ratings. Rather than go head-to-head with Nickelodeon, Sweeney discovered a new audience for the Disney Channel—the so-called tweener, or young adolescent, not quite a child and not quite a full-blown teenager. Under Sweeney, the Disney Channel became the third highest rated cable channel in the American market. Sweeney's first year at ABC was proving to be a success, largely because of the popular Sunday night hit "Desperate Housewives," about a mythical suburb cul-de-sac called Wisteria Lane populated by women eager to kill their husbands and have sex with the gardener.

Whither the network? Even with Sweeney's success, ABC and the other national networks had been declining for a long time. One indicator was that the combined audience share for nightly network news had fallen from a peak of 75 percent in 1980 to 47 percent in 1998. This decline was attributable to the fact that more news sources existed than previously. Cable news was on all the time. Cable catered to different political viewpoints and was attracting a larger audience than that of the networks; there was CNN (liberal), Fox News (conservative), and MSNBC (in the middle).

As the choices multiplied, Americans watched less national network television. Cable channels like TBS, ESPN, and the Disney Channel were the most profitable parts of such companies as TW and Disney because they provided two sources of revenue—subscriptions and advertising.

Disney had lost popularity with younger audiences. Its "wholesome" image was viewed as a weakness among kids who grew up quickly. Network executives were concerned that young viewers (18–32 year olds) were defecting at a record pace. In a movement more than a decade old, prime-time TV watching by young viewers had been declining by 1 percent to 2 percent per year. To the extent that this group continued to watch TV, it increasingly did so on its own terms; for instance, it recorded the shows and skipped the commercials. This trend made advertisers—upon which the networks were almost entirely dependent for their revenue—very nervous.[11]

ESPN. Disney's most profitable holding continued to be ESPN. Founded as the Entertainment and Sports Programming Network in 1979, ESPN was always on the lookout for new programming.

ESPN's original offerings—auto racing, college basketball, and college football—never took off. Critics made jokes about arm wrestling and other less-than-central sports needed to fill the network's 24-hour schedule.

The NFL's decision to put more of its games on ESPN gave ESPN the momentum it needed. Acquiring the rights to Sunday night NFL football, which ESPN initially shared with Turner Broadcasting, was especially important. Because cable ratings for football games were so high, the fees ESPN could charge cable operators were among the highest in the business. Cable operators were willing to pay these fees because they could not persuade customers to sign up for cable without ESPN in the package.

ESPN knew that people would continue to watch major-league football, baseball, and basketball games, but the network had to fill in the rest of its program time with something other than sports. It could not rely on second-tier sporting events because people did not want to watch them. The network had to hedge its bets with as much original programming as possible. It therefore extended and developed its own programs with new offerings such as "SportsCenter," a daily sports-highlights program that tried to be irreverent, fast paced, and down-to-earth. It was also successful with "Pardon the Interruption" and "Around the Horn," sports-talk programs hosted by sportswriters and columnists.

---

11. To retain the billions of dollars advertisers spent each year (in 2002, advertisers spent more than $17 billion), the networks were looking for new ways to attract young viewers. Among the options they had started to create were video on demand (services that let viewers watch shows whenever they wanted), DVDs, and video games. But they faced the problem of sorting out who owned the rights to shows if they were incorporated into a DVD, video game, or video-on-demand format.

Two original ESPN movies also did very well: *A Season on the Brink*, about college basketball coach Bobby Knight, and *The Junction Boys*, about Alabama football coach Bear Bryant. ESPN confined lower-profile sports and reruns to its smaller cable channels, ESPN2 and ESPN3. It had a successful radio network, a Website, a magazine, and restaurants. ESPN was also developing high-definition television and Spanish versions of its offerings. It needed these revenue sources to prevent being held hostage to the sports leagues.

Upending the wholesome image. A major issue Disney faced going forward was the extent to which its wholesome image might collide with its plans for ESPN. Was this image a liability that was interfering with Disney's ability to fully capitalize on ESPN's strengths? Family entertainment did not always sell. When Disney paid $5.2 billion to Fox to buy ABC's Family Channel in 2001, the company claimed that the deal would permit it to take advantage of its strengths in family fare. However, the Family Channel's acquisition proved to be a bust. Industry analysts estimated that the company overpaid for Fox's children's channels and a 6,500-episode TV library by as much as $1 billion. The Family Channel's prime-time audience did not meet Disney's projections, and provided evidence that family fare might not be a vehicle for growing cable.

Just as HBO transformed itself by adding "The Sopranos" and "Sex and the City," ESPN decided to push edgier programs that would attract new viewers—including women—and hold current viewers' attention when they were not watching games. The cable channel developed a new drama series called "Playmakers" that included stories about a football player in a crack house, a team doctor who gave shots to injured players who clearly should not be going back on the field, and players who, when pulled over by police, quickly hid cocaine in their glove compartments.

Other plotlines consisted of a cocaine-addicted running back who stole morphine from a sick child he visited in the hospital and another football player who was arrested for assaulting his wife. Unlike sports events, these shows could be repeated frequently.

Indeed, "Playmakers" had a very successful 11-episode run on ESPN prime time, with 2.6 million viewers and an average audience of 2.1 million over the length of the series. These figures were a fivefold improvement over what ESPN had been airing in the same Tuesday 9 P.M. to 10 P.M. slot the prior year.

Alienating professional sports. With ESPN operating five channels and constantly in need of new programming, the success of "Playmakers" was very important. The NFL, however, was worried about the negative impact the show could have on the league, and thus threatened that ESPN, which was in the sixth year of an eight-year, $4.8 billion deal to carry NFL football, might not be the winning bidder next time around. The NFL had other alternatives, specifically the USA Network, which NBC acquired as part of its deal with Vivendi, and Fox, which already broadcast some NFL games.

Relations between the NFL and ESPN were further strained because of radio personality Rush Limbaugh, who was forced to resign from ESPN because of inappropriate remarks he made about the Philadelphia Eagle's African-American quarterback Donovan McNabb.

ESPN's dealings with the National Basketball Association (NBA) also were turning sour. NBA officials were very concerned that ESPN was considering a reality show featuring former basketball player Dennis Rodman and tentatively called "Rodman on the Rebound." The NBA also was upset about ESPN's production of its games on ABC. The league disliked ABC's commentary and on-screen graphics, and overall considered the product inferior to that offered by the former owner of NBA rights, NBC.

Disney maintained that it was not certain about the future of "Playmakers" and that it was rethinking its plans for Rodman's show. ESPN was paying $600 million a year for its NFL rights, $400 million for basketball, and $135 million for baseball. ESPN was one of the most profitable cable networks because of the close relationships it had with these sports leagues.

The ESPN/professional sports leagues relationship was mutually beneficial. Both parties gained. Advertisers loved having the young male audience. As a consequence, ESPN was able to charge cable and satellite operators a high price to carry the channel.

However, the price for TV rights for major sports was continuing to rise as more cable networks were bidding for the leagues' games, and ESPN was having trouble passing on the additional costs to cable and satellite distributors. Shows like "Playmakers" and "Rodman on the Rebound" therefore were important parts of the mix. Would Disney have to abandon its foray into more salacious content?

Creating family friendly content. The other option—more family-friendly content on Disney's other venues—did not seem doable.

Audience tastes had shifted away from traditional animated films like *Ariel* and *Aladdin* and had moved to computer-generated (CG) products such as Pixar Animation Studio's *Finding Nemo* and DreamWorks' *Shrek.*

The big question for Disney was whether it could master this new technology. Most of its artists were more comfortable with traditional hand-drawn cartoons. Disney made the successful 2000 film *Dinosaur* in CG, and it cofinanced and distributed Pixar's CG hits, but hand-drawn animation had been at the core of what it had done and traditionally stood for. Now Disney had to take the plunge into CG programs because its continued relationship with Pixar was in doubt. Its contract with the company had come to an end and Pixar was open to bids from other studios. Disney's thrust into CG products was partly a hedge against the fact that its relationship with Pixar would dissolve when the contract ran out in 2005.

Eisner said that Disney was interested in turning animation back into the profit center it used to be, but most of Disney's hand-drawn films did not do well, not only because they were not produced by means of CG technology, but also because the stories and characters were not strong. For instance, unlike the 1989 *Little Mermaid,* the 2002 release of *Treasure Planet* was a dismal failure. It cost $140 million to make, but sold just $38 million worth of tickets in the United States.

The main challenge Disney faced in moving to CG products was that it had to retrain a host of artists devoted to drawing. CG characters were built as computer models in three-dimensional virtual sets. Disney's traditional artists didn't feel comfortable with this new technology. Could it make this transition?

The AOL/Time Warner merger

After the announced merger on January 10, 2000, AOL/ TW's market valuation was $290 billion, a figure buoyed by the Internet bubble and the premium AOL paid over TW's market value. However, it was apparent at the time that the two companies' 1999 earnings of $2.7 billion, including large gains on asset sales, would be unlikely to support this type of valuation. The new company would have to very quickly realize the benefits of their merger.

The quest for synergies. The merger was sold with the argument that the two companies' complementary assets would deliver synergies and unlock value that each company alone could not release. The merger's proponents claimed that there would be tactical synergy of the kind that was supposed to exist in nearly all mergers—reduced operating expenses from shared assets and activities such as marketing, IT, and subscription renewal management. The proponents also argued for greater revenues from cross-promotion from the large subscription base and advertising revenue.

The combined company had nearly 130 million subscribers to its various services—magazines, cable, and Internet. As the company collected data on these subscribers, it could sell subscribers additional products. With the larger subscriber base, the company was in a position to raise both advertising prices and margins.

The merger also made it possible for the combined company to promote TW's creative productions, such as a movie, across multiple, TW-owned and controlled channels from theaters to networks to cable and the Internet. The company considered additional strategic opportunities, such as combining publishing, music, and film, and delivering it on the Internet in a way that met the customers' individual needs.

Interests colliding. TW did not move fast enough to realize these benefits,[12] because it was run as a fiefdom of competing interests. For TW to realize the gains, real cooperation across the company's many independent and often feuding business units would be necessary.

However, after the acquisition was completed, crowding at the top and a dual leadership structure created numerous problems. Jerry Levin from Time Warner was CEO and Steve Case from AOL was chair. Robert Pittman from AOL was responsible for the networks, cable, magazines, and online businesses; he controlled 65 percent of the firm's revenue. Dick Parsons from Time Warner was responsible for TV, movies, and music production, and controlled 35 percent of the firm's revenue. Ted Turner, still a board member, was in the background. Levin, Case, Pittman, and Turner soon left the scene or were forced out, and Parsons, a lawyer known for his negotiating skills and not his vision, took over.

This result was not what Case envisioned when he and Levin announced the merger in January 2000. The scenerio that the two men

---

12. Management first projected growth of 25 percent annually in EBITA. Then it forecast double-digit growth. Then it scaled back its projections to 5 percent to 9 percent annual growth.

believed would unfold was a company that could deliver movies, music, and magazines over high-speed Internet connections. The company had all the assets to capitalize on the convergence of these disparate media forms that would result in consumer empowerment and choices. TW could be a leader in the media, entertainment, and communications industry.

Unfulfilled promise. But the promise of convergence did not come to fruition. Cross-promotion collided with the need of each unit to generate revenue. Combining the two companies could not prevent TW units from forging lucrative deals with other entertainment companies (e.g., AOL's $21 million agreement with CBS MarketWatch).

The individual pieces of the merged company faced challenges. CNN's ratings were falling (at one time they were down over 40 percent among 25-to-54-year olds). Audiences and critics viewed CNN as having second-rate programming, production, and talent. FoxNews had emerged as a strong competitor, as had MSNBC.

To realize the benefits of the combined company, the culture had to be speedy and collaborative. However, the company had a history of being slow moving and it suffered from conflict in decision making. The addition of AOL only added to the internal bickering. TW paid cash bonuses based on the performance of individual business units, while AOL's compensation was based on the stock gains of the company as a whole. TW reported quarterly earnings and used accounting data, while AOL reported results weekly and used a variety of business measures crucial for its success.

In combining the two companies, there had to be decisiveness, innovativeness, and cohesiveness to get the pieces to work together. But the pieces were often stronger than the whole. Power and status lay in individual business units that had strong brands and traditions of excellence. TW's talent, which was diffused throughout the organization, was the organization's most valuable asset. TW's top-management team could ill afford to antagonize this talent because of some central vision held.

The CEO and top-management team had little bargaining power when they tried to induce the separate units to work together. The company was best run by a negotiator, which was one of the main reasons that Parsons survived the rocky leadership battles that ensued after the two companies combined.

Reviving AOL. AOL became the weak link, so TW's main issue was what to do with it. How should TW revive the ailing Internet Service Provider (ISP)? AOL's third-quarter 2003 results continued in a downward spiral. Revenue was off by 4.5 percent and profits were down by 7 percent. With the rise of cable Internet access, the ISP business was in the midst of long-term decline.

AOL was the top ISP service provider in the United States (see Appendix F), but it was losing subscriptions to cheaper alternatives, including some ISPs that were providing basic dialup service free. People were moving to high-speed Internet connections or cut-rate dialup plans offered by competitors like NetZero.

Subscription numbers. Analysts had raised questions about how AOL generated its subscription numbers. Few doubted that AOL had the largest market share in the industry, but they had questions about how the company obtained that share.

For instance, it was common knowledge that AOL bulked up sales through agreements with retailers like Target, Sears & Roebuck, and J.C. Penney. The company gave the retailers the right to sell limited-use accounts for $1 to $3. Then, the retailers offered the discounted accounts to their employees for $10, making a $7 to $9 profit. With such bulk deals, AOL puffed up its subscriber numbers; the deals added as much as 15 percent of the total growth in the AOL subscriber list in 2001 and 2002.

These charges came at a time when AOL was proclaiming that its large customer base was its key business strength, and while the company was reporting a decline in subscriptions nearly every quarter. From more than 29 million subscribers at the time of the merger, the number had fallen to about 25 million. AOL said it lost 846,000 subscribers in the second quarter of 2003, mostly because it had to cut off the service of nonpaying members who took advantage of the ubiquitous free-trial subscriptions AOL offered. AOL estimated that its current subscriber base consisted of only 70 percent fully billed customers; 14 percent of its subscribers were on limited-use plans; and 16 percent were on trial plans.

With the drop in number of subscriptions, AOL advertising and e-commerce revenues also were off. In addition, the company was also under investigation by the Securities and Exchange Commission (SEC) for its accounting practices and advertising deals during the dot.com bubble. The SEC subpoenaed both Parsons and former chair Case to testify.

Bundling. With its subscription base declining and few avenues left to increase it, AOL had to change strategy. It moved from building up a huge base of subscribers through free trials and bulk sales to cutting costs, reducing the workforce, and obtaining more revenue per subscriber. AOL's top management believed that the latter option was indeed a real possibility. From the following fees, it could obtain as much as $159 a month from each subscriber:

$24 basic subscription

$30 broadband service

$30 home network

$20 unlimited music

$15 interactive games

$40 unlimited voice and wireless calls

AOL would receive this amount in return for a monthly dose of interactive entertainment, information, and communications services. But AOL would have to transform itself. It would have to change from a provider of online access into a one-stop shop for movies, music, interactive video games, phone service, Internet shopping, and more.

As of 2004, AOL had not made this transformation. Bundles, like the kind AOL was trying to create, were hard to sell; they created billing problems and posed technological challenges.

Divesting? AOL's troubles were leading to increasing calls for TW to divest the ailing unit. According to those who favored a divestiture, the merger simply had not worked. As a sop to critics, TW did drop AOL from its name. It was no longer called AOL Time Warner; instead it became Time Warner again.

However, the critics were making a more profound point that could not be cast aside by a simple name change. The promised convergence of the TV and the PC, of the old and new media, of magazines, movies, television, and music that would be distributed, cross-promoted, and sold on a single Internet platform was not coming to fruition. Very little of this nature had happened since the merger.

Why didn't TW spin off AOL? One reason was that Steve Case, AOLs founder, remained a board member and believed that the movement toward a more connected society via the Internet could not be halted and that TW was the vehicle to exploit it. People's use of the Internet for many different purposes would just keep increasing, and a company like TW was situated "to connect the dots" for them. Advertisers too preferred dealing with a single entity to market and sell products and develop rich Internet relationships with customers.

According to people like Case, TW should hold on to AOL to see what kinds of media convergence might develop from intercompany initiatives. Synergies would have to be greater than cross-promoting movies, magazines, TV shows, and music, as TW was already its own biggest advertiser.

In Case's view, the merger's promise was in cross-divisional innovation. AOL could set its content apart from other online services by using dedicated TW material in broadband applications.

Broadband costs. Digital convergence would happen only when high-speed broadband connections were more ubiquitous, but AOL had not been very successful at making this goal a reality. A main reason was the cost. Narrowband service over the telephone wires was a high-margin business; broadband was not. The equipment for broadband was expensive to install. The initial $40 to $50-a-month charge for broadband was low to attract early adopters.

Most of AOL's dial-up customers had yet to upgrade to broadband. Indeed, TW's cable lines penetrated less than 20 percent of American homes, and AOL provided broadband to just .5 million users. Its market share in high-speed Internet was under 5 percent.

Another 2.5 million AOL users obtained broadband from a competitor. They continued to pay full price for AOL so that they could access it from outside their homes—for instance, from a hotel room—but AOL executives recognized that these arrangements were not likely to last. At some point in time, AOL was apt to lose customers who in essence were paying twice for their Internet service.

AOL did not own any phone lines or cable running directly into its customers' homes. To reach these homes, AOL had to work out complicated deals with competing cable operators and phone companies, including those within AOL itself, such as Time Warner Cable and Roadrunner. The money AOL charged a customer for broadband had to be shared with these companies. AOL offered to be the marketer for the companies. It would maintain the customer relationship, which it hoped would translate to broadband add-ons. Success in this endeavor required that AOL have good working relations with TW's independent divisions, including Time Warner Cable and Roadrunner, which were among the market leaders.

Another of AOL's options was to buy, merge, or work out joint ventures with other cable companies. This option, however, was not practical because of TW's high level of debt and the likely intervention of antitrust authorities.

In fact, TW had lost out in its bid for AT&T's cable operations to Comcast, which was backed by Microsoft.[13] TW could not match Comcast's price and it was concerned that antitrust authorities would intervene.

What to Do Next?

The questions facing TW and Disney, then, were serious. What the two companies should do next was unclear. Their answers would determine their future.

Questions for Discussion

1. Is the entertainment industry an attractive one? Do a five-forces analysis.
2. Why did the entertainment industry have so much merger and acquisition activity?
3. Did GE make a wise choice when it bought Universal Studios from Vivendi?
4. What were the rationales used for owning production and distribution? What is your opinion of these rationales?
5. Do you believe that TW and Disney should be broken up? How would you break them up? What are the different pieces that you would spin off as separate entities? Why?
6. Which parts of TW and Disney were stars, question marks, cash cows, and dogs, and why? Do you agree with the analysis in the case?
7. Is Eisner really the problem, or is he Disney's most important asset? What is your opinion of his leadership of the company?

---

13. Comcast later made a bid to buy Disney, but Disney was able to thwart this bid.

8. What were the sources of ABC's problems? How could they be fixed?

9. Why were the cable channels so profitable?

10. Was Disney's wholesome image really an issue? Why?

11. Why did ESPN have to develop its own programming? Is this another example of the production-distribution problem? Explain your answer.

12. Is it really true that family entertainment does not sell? Why? What is your opinion?

13. What kind of programming should ESPN develop? Explain your view.

14. What kind of synergies were used to sell the AOL/TW merger? Why were these synergies not realized?

15. Should TW divest or sell off AOL? Why?

16. How dependent was AOL on the further diffusion of broadband? What could AOL do to help solve this problem? Why hadn't it taken these steps?

Exercises

1. Spend some time watching both network and cable television. What is your opinion of the programming? Which niches are being served? Which are ignored? How enjoyable was the experience? What can be done to improve it?

2. AOL/Time Warner's ability to confront companies like Disney depends on how it manages its diverse holdings. Provide advice to management.

3. Is Disney in a position to make gains on AOL/Time Warner? What should it do?

Video

"Merger between Disney and ABC." ABC News "Nightline."   MPI Home Video, 1995.

Bibliography

Angwin, Julia. "Road Runner, America Online Wage Unsisterly Rivalry." *The Wall Street Journal*. October 21, 2002:B1.

_____. "America Online's Fate Grows More Uncertain." *The Wall Street Journal*. January 14, 2003:B1.

Bradley, Stephen, and Erin Sullivan. "AOL Time Warner, Inc." Harvard Business School Case 9-702-421, September 2002.

Fabrikant, Geraldine, and David Kirkpatrick. "AOL's Need: A New Vision." *New York Times*. February 2, 2003, Section 3:1.

Flint, Joe. "ESPN to Blast Critics of Program Costs." *The Wall Street Journal*. October 23, 2003:B2.

_____. "ESPN's Risky New Game Plan: Relying Less on Pro Sports." *The Wall Street Journal*. October 24, 2003: A1.

Gunther, Marc. "The Wary World of Disney." *Fortune*. October 15, 2001.

_____. "Has Eisner Lost the Disney Magic?" *Fortune*. January 17, 2000.

Gunther, Marc, and Stephanie Mehta. "The Mess at AOL Time Warner." *Fortune*. May 13, 2002.

Kafka, Peter, and Peter Newcomb. "Late Bloomer." *Forbes*. March 3, 2003.

Levine, Tyrell, and Michael Rukstad. "The Walt Disney Corporation: The Entertainment King." Harvard Business School Case 9-701-035, July 2001.

Loomis, Carol. "AOL Time Warner's New Math." *Fortune*. February 4, 2002.

Lowry, Tom, Ronald Grover, and Catherine Yang. "Dashed Digital Dreams." *Business Week*. July 15, 2002.

Mehta, Stephanie, and Marc Gunther. "Dick Parson's Make or Break Year." *Fortune*. February 3, 2003.

Merrill Lynch. "Filmed Entertainment." September 2003.

Orwall, Bruce. "Tensions Persist Between Eisner and Roy Disney." *The Wall Street Journal*. October 21, 2002:B1.

_____. "Disney Decides It Must Draw Artists into Computer Age." *The Wall Street Journal*. October 23, 2003:A1.

Peers, Martin. "Time Warner's Quarterly New Jumps." *The Wall Street Journal*. October 23, 2003:B2.

Peers, Martin, and Ken Brown. "AOL's Winners and Losers." *The Wall Street Journal*. January 14, 2003:B1.

Stockton, Hilary. "AOL Time Warner." Graduate School of Business. Palo Alto, CA: Stanford University. February 2000.

Appendix A. Additional information on financial performance of Time Warner and Disney

EXHIBIT 1   Disney's annual income statement (in millions of U.S. dollars except per-share items)

	12 months ending 09/30/02	12 months ending 09/30/01	12 months ending 09/30/00	12 months ending 09/30/99	12 months ending 09/30/98
Total revenue	25,329	25,172	25,325	23,455	22,976
Cost of revenue	22,924	21,573	21,567	20,030	18,466
Gross profit	2,405	3,599	3,758	3,425	4,510
Depreciation/ amortization	21	767	1,233	456	431
Interest expense, net operating	723	544	599	—	—
Interest expense, (income) net operating	228	117	289	127	622
Unusual expense (income)	0	1,454	92	172	64
Other operating expenses, total	(34)	(22)	(489)	267	0
Total operating expense	23,139	23,889	22,692	21,052	19,583
Operating income	2,190	1,283	2,633	2,403	3,393
Net income before taxes	2,190	1,283	2,633	2,403	3,229
Provision for income taxes	853	1,059	1,606	1,014	1,307
Net income after taxes	1,337	224	1,027	1,389	1,922

Source: Yahoo! Finance (http://finance.yahoo.com).

EXHIBIT 2   Time Warner's annual income statement* (in millions of
U.S. dollars except for per-share items)

	12 months ending 12/31/02	12 months ending 12/31/01	12 months ending 12/31/00	12 months ending 06/30/00	12 months ending 06/30/99
Total revenue	40,961	37,166	7,605	6,886	4,804
Cost of revenue	24,315	20,533	3,866	3,458	2,669
Gross profit	16,646	16,633	3,739	3,428	2,135
Selling/general/ admin. expenses, total	9,916	9,079	1,864	1,638	1,233
Depreciation/ amortization	732	7,186	99	74	65
Unusual expense (income)	45,873	250	10	15	95
Total operating expense	80,836	37,048	5,839	5,488	4,354
Operating income	(39,875)	118	1,766	1,398	450
Interest expense, net nonoperating	(1,900)	(1,546)	(55)	—	—
Interest/invest. income non-operating	117	193	330	—	—
Interest income (exp.), net non-operating	(1,783)	(1,353)	275	—	—
Other, net	(2,776)	(3,521)	(208)	616	638
Provision for income taxes	140	139	712	782	334
Net Income after taxes	(44,574)	(4,895)	1,121	1,232	754

Source: Yahoo! Finance (http://finance.yahoo.com).
*The first year of the merger was 2001. Prior to that the income statement above reflects just
AOL's performance. The goodwill loses are shown under "other."

Appendix B

EXHIBIT 3   Top 12 theme parks in the world (based on attendance)

Tokyo Disneyland	Animal Kingdom Disney Florida
Disney World Florida	Universal Studios Florida
Disneyland Anaheim	Blackpool UK
Epcot Disney World Florida	Lotte World South Korea
Disney-MGM Florida	Yokohoma Sea Paradise
Everland South Korea	Universal Studios California

Source: Tyrell Levine and Michael Rukstad, "The Walt Disney Corporation," Harvard Business School Case 9-701-035.

Appendix C. Top-rated TV shows

EXHIBIT 4   Top eleven primetime broadcast TV programs
(for week of 11/17/03–11/23/03)

Rank	Program	Network	Household rating	Total viewers (in millions)
1.	"CSI"	CBS	16.6	26,640
2.	"E.R."	NBC	15.5	23,413
3.	"Friends"	NBC	13.4	20,660
4.	"Friends"	NBC	12.8	19,928
5.	"The Bachelor"	ABC	12.4	18,623
6.	"CSI: Miami"	CBS	12.3	18,870
7.	"60 Minutes"	CBS	12.0	17,957
8.	"Everybody Loves Raymond"	CBS	11.9	19,437
9.	"Survivor: Pearl Islands"	CBS	11.5	19,898
10.	"CBS Sunday Movie"	CBS	11.4	17,392
11.	"Law And Order"	NBC	11.4	17,525

Source: Nielsen Media Research (http://www.nielsenmedia.com).

Appendix D. The top syndicated networks, systems, and cable systems

EXHIBIT 5   Cable networks and cable systems

	Top cable networks (February 28, 2003)		Top cable systems (June 2003)	
Rank	Network	Basic subscribers (in 000)	Cable system	Basic subscribers (in 000)
1.	TBS Superstation	87,700	Comcast Corporation	21,364
2.	ESPN	86,700	Time Warner Cable	10,938
3.	C-SPAN	86,600	Charter Communications	6,487
4.	Discovery Channel	86,500	Cox Communications	6,279
5.	USA Network	86,300	Adelphia Communications	5,116
6.	CNN (Cable News Network)	86,200	Cablevision Systems Corporation	2,964
7.	TNT (Turner Network Television)	86,200	Bright House Networks	2,063
8.	Lifetime Television (LIFE)	86,000	Mediacom Communications Corporation	1,560
9.	Nickelodeon	86,000	Insight Communications*	1,296
10.	A&E Network	85,900	CableOne (&)	715
11.	Spike TV	85,800	RCN Corporation	431
12.	The Weather Channel	85,300	Cebridge Connections (e)	350
13.	MTV (Music Television)	84,900	Bresnan Communications**	309
14.	QVC	84,900	Service Electric	291
15.	ABC Family Channel	84,800	WideOpenWest (e)	289
16.	The Learning Channel (TLC)	84,700	Tele-Media Corporation (&)	227
17.	ESPN2	84,500	Armstrong Group of Companies	214
18.	CNBC	84,100	Midcontinent Communications	201

Source: Kagan Research, LLC. Data from Cable Program Investor (Top Cable Networks, February 28, 2003) and Cable TV Investor: Deals & Finance (Top Cable Systems, June 2003). "Unless otherwise noted, counts include owned and managed subscribers." N/a=not available, e=estimate, &=counts include recent acquisitions/dispositions.

*Customer data includes effecs of the swap of the Griffin, GA, system for the managed New Albany, IN, and Shelbyville, KY, systems. e=estimate, &=counts include recent acquisition/disposition.

EXHIBIT 6   Top cable TV programs, total day (week of 11/17/03-11/23/03)

Rank	Program	Network	Household rating	Total viewers
1.	NFL regular season (Redskins/Dolphins)	ESPN	6.6	9,661,000
2.	"NFL Prime Time"	ESPN	3.3	4,932,000

Source: Nielsen Media Research (http://www.nielsenmedia.com).

EXHIBIT 7   Top cable TV programs (week of 11/10/03-11/16/03)

Rank	Program	Originator	Household rating	Total viewers
1.	"Wheel Of Fortune"	Kingworld Media Sales	9.4	14,620,000
2.	"ESPN NFL Regular Season"	ESPN Sports Network	8.7	12,919,000

Source: Nielsen Media Research (http://www.nielsenmedia.com).

Appendix E

EXHIBIT 8   The top-grossing films in 2003 (as of 11/28/03)

	1. Disney	2. Warner	3. Universal	4. Sony	7. Dreamworks
No. of top 30 hits	7	6	5	5	1
Gross $ in billions	11.3	.8	.7	.6	.08

EXHIBIT 9   Top grossing films, 2003

30 top grossing films	Release date	Total gross (in millions)	Studio
1. *Finding Nemo*	5.30.03	$339,666	Walt Disney/Pixar
2. *Pirates of the Caribbean*	7.11.03	304,176	Buena Vista
3. *The Matrix: Reloaded*	5.16.03	281,554	Warner Bros.
4. *Bruce Almighty*	5.23.03	242,744	Universal
5. *X2: X-Men United*	5.2.03	214,869	20th Century Fox
6. *Terminator 3: Rise of the Machines*	7.4.03	150,327	Warner Bros.
7. *Bad Boys II*	7.18.03	138,541	Sony
8. *Anger Management*	4.11.03	135,561	Sony
9. *Bringing Down the House*	3.7.03	132,675	Buena Vista
10. *The Hulk*	6.20.03	132,123	Universal
11. *2 Fast 2 Furious*	6.6.03	127,084	Universal
12. *The Matrix Revolutions*	11.7.03	125,383	Warner Bros.
13. *Seabiscuit*	7.25.03	120,026	Universal
14. *S.W.A.T.*	8.8.03	116,878	Sony
15. *Spy Kids 3D: Game Over*			
16. *Freaky Friday*	8.8.03	108,935	Buena Vista
17. *Scary Movie 3*	10.24.03	106,469	Dimension
18. *The Italian Job*	5.30.03	106,059	Paramount
19. *How to Lose a Guy in 10 Days*	2.7.03	105,764	Paramount
20. *American Wedding*	8.1.03	104,445	Universal
21. *Daddy Day Care*	5.9.03	104,081	Sony
22. *Daredevil*	2.14.03	102,498	20th Century Fox
23. *Charlie's Angels: Full Throttle*	6.27.03	100,785	Sony
24. *Elf*	11.7.03	94,733	New Line
25. *Legally Blonde 2: Red, White and Blonde*	7.4.03	90,135	MGM
26. *Freddy vs. Jason*	8.15.03	82,557	New Line
27. *The Texas Chainsaw Massacre*	10.17.03	79,197	New Line
28. *The School of Rock*	10.3.03	77,727	Paramount
29. *Old School*	2.21.03	74,971	DreamWorks
30. *Brother Bear*	10.24.03	70,322	Buena Vista

Source: Movieweb (http://movieweb.com).

Appendix F

EXHIBIT 9 The top ISP providers

Rank Top dial-up ISPs 2003 (estimates)	Millions of subscribers	Market share	Top ISPs dial-up +cable+DSL 2003 (estimate)	Millions of subscribers
1. America Online	25.3	27.5%	America Online	25.3
2. MSN	8.7	9.4	Microsoft Network	9.0
3. United Online (NetZero + Juno Online)	5.2	5.6	NetZero	8.6
4. EarthLink	5.0	5.5	Spinway	6.7
5. Comcast	4.4	4.8	United Online	5.0
6. SBC	2.8	3.0	EarthLink	5.0
7. Verizon	1.9	2.1	Excite@Home	3.7
8. Cox	1.7	1.8	Prodigy	3.5
9. Charter	1.3	1.5	1stUp.com	3.5
10. BellSouth	1.2	1.3	Freei.Net	3.2
11. Cablevision	.92	1.0	RoadRunner	3.0
12. Adelphia	.78	0.8	AltaVista (via 1stUp)	3.0
13. Qwest	.56	0.6	SBC Communications	2.2
14. Covad	.50	0.5	Compuserve (AOL)	2.0
15. RCN	.39	0.4	Verizon	1.8
16. ATX (includes former CoreComm and Voyager.net)	.30	0.3	AT&T Worldnet	1.5
17. Other U.S. ISPs		35.7%		

Source: NetworkWork Fusion (http://www.nwfusion.com).

CASE 7

Globalization
Pepsi versus Coke[1]

The competition between Pepsi and Coke was heated. This case details the different approaches that the two companies took with respect to this competition and the results they achieved. The key question facing the companies' managers was where they should next take the competition between them. Was Pepsi's greater emphasis on the domestic market a mistake? Was there only so much more growth in sales and income that it could squeeze from the home front? Was Coke unduly engrossed in foreign markets and therefore vulnerable in the United States? How could Coke protect its domestic base while continuing to dominate abroad? Both Coke and Pepsi had to fine-tune their strategies in light of the rapid political and social changes that the global economy was experiencing.

The Recent Performance of Pepsi and Coke

On the basis of such parameters as market capitalization, revenue growth, margins, and net income, Pepsi still had quite a distance to go to catch up to Coke (see Table 7.1). Coke's market cap was higher and it had better margins and more net income.

From 1998–2002, Coke's revenue and income had not been growing as fast as Pepsi's. Total revenue and net income at Coke barely increased, while Pepsi showed positive movement in both numbers (see Appendix A: Exhibits 1 and 2). Pepsi outperformed Coke in the stock market from 1998 to 2003 by a substantial margin.[2]

---

1. This case was written by Alfred Marcus, University of Minnesota, Carlson School of Management. Copyright © 2005 by Marsh Publications LLC. All rights reserved.

2. Coke's December 2003 stock price was a full 45 percent below its 1998 high. Operating income had increased an average of just 4 percent in the 1998–2003 period, and revenues had grown by an average of just 3 percent.

TABLE 7.1   A comparison of Coke and Pepsi in 2003

	Coke	Pepsi
Market cap ($)	122.26 B*	78.18 B
Employees	56,000	142,000
Rev. growth	-2.60%	-6.80%
Gross margin	63.10%	54.08%
Operating margins	26.25%	19.69%
Net income ($)	4.35 B	3.66 B

Source: Yahoo! Finance (http://finance.yahoo.com).
*B = billions.

Coke's problems

Coke had problems domestically and globally. The company's 2003 increase of 6.5 percent in operating profit was mainly the result of a summer heat wave in Europe that added to demand, and a strong Euro that boosted returns. Pepsi, in contrast, came through with a 10 percent increase in operating profits in the same period. This increase, unlike Coke's, was not based on one-time events.

Without doubt, Coke's foundation was strong. It was one of the most recognized brands in the world, and among its largest shareholders was Warren Buffett, one of the world's most astute investors. However, in the United States, cola sales were stagnant. While the market for bottled water advanced to 26 percent and sports drinks increased to 15 percent, carbonated soft drinks sales were barely growing (less than 1%), and in the faster-growing beverage segments, Pepsi was doing better than Coke. Pepsi's bottled water, Aquafina, outsold Coke's Dasani.

Pepsi seized hold of 81 percent of the expanding sports drink market when it acquired Gatorade. In 2000, Coke's board instructed management to stop bidding for Gatorade's parent, Quaker Oats Company. Coke's Powerade had been unable to catch up with Gatorade.

Pepsi's Lipton teas bested Coke's Nesteas by 16 points in market share. Pepsi also had the best-selling orange juice in Tropicana, which topped Coke's Minute Maid in nearly every market in which they competed.

In the youth sports market, Pepsi introduced summer-only products like Mountain Dew Live-Wire to attract young people to highly profitable convenience store outlets. Coke countered with the launch of Vanilla Coke in 2002, which was a success, but in trying to achieve more rapid growth, Coke's sights still were set on international markets. In the United States, the annual consumption per person of soft drinks was about 840 servings, but in developing countries like China and India, the rate was less than 25.

Winning new markets in the global arena, where political, economic, and social surprises were all too common, was not an easy job. In Europe, Coke's sales fell off after a 1999 tainted-soda scare in Belgium. The company faced similar concerns in India in 2003, where people made accusations that Coke and Pepsi's bottled water had high pesticide levels.

Coke had to confront other telltale incidents. In 2003, in the United States, it admitted to deception in a marketing test carried out in Burger King, and agreed to pay the restaurant chain about $21 million. It had to pay more than a half million dollars to a former employee who claimed wrongful termination after revealing the fraud. It also had to deal with a Securities & Exchange Commission(SEC) investigation of its accounting practices.

The Soft Drink Industry at the Start of the 21st Century

At the start of the 21st century, the United States was the world's largest soft-drink market with a 27 percent global share in 2001, but the North American soft-drink market was saturated. Average consumption per person per year (see Table 7.2) was 157.2 liters (nearly 14 ounces per person per day). Growth in North America was the slowest in the world from 1996 to 2001 (see Figure 7.1). The fastest-growing regions in 1996–2001 were the Middle East, Eastern Europe, and Asia/Australia.

The fastest-growing countries were Asian. Pakistan's growth rate was the highest in the world. Between 1996–2001, the volume of soft drinks consumed in Pakistan was up 146 percent. Pakistan was expected to continue to have the highest percentage soft-drink consumption growth rate between 2002–2007, India was expected to make sizable gains, and Indonesia, China, and Vietnam were expected to be in the top five.

By 2007, Asia/Australia would have the world's largest soft-drink market with a 25 percent share, outpacing the North American market,

TABLE 7.2   2002 worldwide consumption of soft drinks

Region	Retail volume, liters per head
North America	157.2
Latin America	59.2
Western Europe	49.4
Eastern Europe	22.0
Asia Pacific	4.3

Source: Euromonitor International—The World Market for Soft Drinks, 2003.

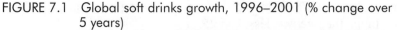

FIGURE 7.1   Global soft drinks growth, 1996–2001 (% change over
5 years)

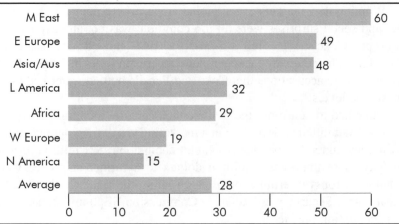

Source: Zenith International (http://www.zenithinternational.com).

which was expected to decline to 24 percent of the world's total. Strong growth was expected in a number of countries in Eastern Europe, the Middle East, and Africa.

Alternative beverage consumption

Soft-drink volume was projected to reach 467 billion liters in 2003, equivalent to 75 liters per person per year, or about 7 ounces per day (a liter is equal to 30.272 ounces). The 5 percent growth rate in consumption compared favorably with an expected rise of 1 percent for hot drinks and 2 percent for milk. In the carbonated soft-drinks and bottled-water segments, three countries (the United States, Mexico, and China) were the leaders.

In 2001, carbonated soft drinks were the biggest segment with 45 percent of global volume (see Figure 7.2), but bottled water was the fastest-growing sector, rising by 10 percent in 2001 and accounting for 53 percent of total growth in sales from 1996 to 2001.

Coke and Pepsi were not the only companies competing in this market (see Table 7.3). Entrepreneurs from Snapple to Nantucket Nectars to Arizona Iced Tea had shaken up the industry. Throughout the world, alternative beverage consumption was on the rise. The consumption of canned and bottled tea and energy drinks was growing, and the top carbonated soft-drink brands were in decline, their volume share stagnant or declining (see Appendix B: Exhibits 4, 5, and 6).

FIGURE 7.2   Global soft drinks consumption 2001

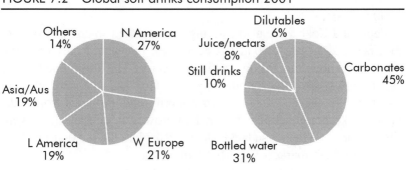

Others
14%

N America
27%

Asia/Aus
19%

L America
19%

W Europe
21%

Dilutables
6%

Juice/nectars
8%

Still drinks
10%

Carbonates
45%

Bottled water
31%

Total 412,000 million litres

Source: Zenith International (http://www.zenithinternational.com).

TABLE 7.3   Other major beverage companies (in billions)

Company	Products	Brands	2002 sales
Nestle Waters	Bottled mineral and spring waters	Perrier, Pellegrino, Aquarel	$5.5
Cadbury Schweppes	Soft drinks	A&W Root Beer, Squirt, RC	4.1
Groupe Danone World Water	Bottled water	Evian	3.9
Cott	Soft drinks, bottled water, juices, iced teas, sports drinks	Store brands	1.2
National Beverage	Colas, sparkling water, juices	Faygo, Shasta, Big Shot	.5
Northland Cranberries	Fruit juices	Seneca, TreeSweet, Awake	.1

Source: Compiled by the author from various sources.

Alcoholic (still) drinks were the third-largest segment. Rum, vodka, and tequila drinks in a variety of flavors—orange, pineapple, raspberry, mango, coconut, and banana—were exploding among young drinkers looking for easy-to-sip liquors. Fruit juice/nectars, and dilutables (powdered drinks) followed the still-drink category in popularity.

The next frontier was supposed to be "enhanced waters," drinks like Revive, which was a purple-tinted, fruit-flavored water laced with vitamin B and potassium. Energy Brands, a privately held concern, made the drink. It was trying to fill yet another gap in the industry. The company had just 1 percent of a market estimated to be worth nearly $8 billion annually, but its sales more than quadrupled from 2000 to 2001.

Pepsi and Coke were also entering the so-called smartwater market to offset declines in carbonated beverages, but would they have the marketing know-how to compete in this sector? The drinks had to have catchy titles like Eve, Endurance, Go-Go, Balance, Propel, and Essential. To succeed they needed celebrity endorsements from individuals like Sarah Jessica Parker. Hip crowds in coastal cities were first adopters. Whether sedate Coke or Pepsi had the moxie to make a go of it in these markets was uncertain.

The contest with Pepsi

Pepsi had the following six divisions:

* Frito-Lay North America (FLNA)
* Frito-Lay International (FLI)
* Pepsi-Cola North America (PCNA)
* Gatorade/Tropicana North America (GTNA)
* PepsiCo Beverages International (PBI)
* Quaker Foods North America (QFNA)

Snacks. Besides being a beverage company, Pepsi was the world's leading snack-food company with brands like Lays, Ruffles, Fritos, Doritos, Tostitos, Grandma cookies, Cracker Jacks, and Quaker granola bars. Its lead over its rivals in the snack-food industry was commanding (see Appendix C: Exhibit 8).

Pepsi's beverage divisions (PCNA, GTNA, and PBI), on the other hand, were locked in a close fight with Coke in the overall beverage market. When bottled water, juices, sports and energy drinks, tea, and coffee were added, Pepsi was neck-and-neck in the U.S. market with Coke.

However, snack foods, not beverages, were the mainstay of Pepsi. When Pepsi first merged with Frito Lay in 1965, the beverage divisions earned 2.5 times the net profits of the snack division and the Pepsi brand accounted for roughly 58 percent of net sales. By 2002, things were very different. Frito Lay constituted 57 percent of the company's net sales and profits. The beverage divisions contributed 37 percent of net sales and 34 percent of net profits, and the rest came from Quaker.

Bottlers. In the United States, Pepsi, like Coke, had sold almost all its bottlers. It had ownership interests of less than 50 percent in a few large bottlers (referred to as anchor bottlers). Like Coke, Pepsi did not consolidate the results of its bottlers into its financial statements.

Coke's finances were complicated because of its bottlers. These bottlers were the 38 percent-owned Coke affiliate, Coca-Cola Enterprises, and other parts of the global network that legendary CEO and former Chairman Robert Goizueta had sold in 1986. Technically, Coke did not control these companies, but because they were captive customers to Coke's syrup business, Coke actively managed them. Coke often pressured the bottlers to buy other bottlers and increase production capacity. Sometimes, Coke coaxed them into buying bottlers at high prices from itself. During the 1990s, Coke profited from buying and selling its bottlers. The company wanted to add capacity to keep up with increased demand and to keep the debt from its capital-intensive, low-margin bottlers from accumulating on its books. During this period, Coke enjoyed double-digit returns on assets, while the bottlers had to settle for less (see Table 7.4). In return, Coke paid the bottlers for marketing and support, which kept them afloat.

Coke, for instance, helped pay for the new vending machines and coolers that the bottlers needed. However, the SEC questioned the way Coke accounted for such transactions. If Coke had to combine its balance sheet with the bottlers, analysts estimated that the company might have to reduce its earnings by about 4 percent and slice its return on invested capital in half.

Customers. Pepsi's strategy focused first on supermarkets and second on convenience stores where it could put its sophisticated direct-store-delivery (DSD) system to best use (see Table 7.5). DSDO enabled the company to merchandise its products with maximum visibility and appeal.

Between its snacks and soft drinks, Pepsi was the second biggest supplier of U.S. supermarkets next to Kraft. On average, Pepsi's products

TABLE 7.4   Return on assets: Coke and its bottlers (percent)

	1997	1998	1999	2000	2001	2002
Coke	21.5	18.3	14.7	17.2	17.5	17.8
Bottlers	2.8	2.2	1.0	1.0	1.9	2.8
Combined	8.8	7.7	5.9	6.3	7.5	8.6

Source: BusinessWeek, 2002.

TABLE 7.5   U.S. soft drink share by customer classes in 2000 (percent)

Supermarkets	33.5
Fountain	22.3
Convenience stores	11.2
Vending	11.4
Other retail	10.0
Warehouse/mass merch.	8.7
Restaurants	2.9

Source: Adapted from Yoffie, "Cola Wars Continue," Harvard Business School Case 9-702-442, 2002.

were 3 percent of total supermarket sales and 20 percent of their cash flow. The operating margins were 9 percent, compared to 2 percent on other products supermarkets sold. The supermarket chains that Pepsi served, including Wal-Mart, pressured Pepsi to keep the margins low.

Coke also had to accept low margins to obtain the fountain business of large restaurant chains like McDonalds. For Coke and Pepsi, convenience stores and vending machines were high-margin businesses, and fountains and supermarkets low-margin ones. Pepsi dominated in the convenience stores and Coke dominated in vending machines.

International. Though Pepsi's international operations were extensive, the company was far less dependent on them than Coke. Frito-Lay products were marketed in 120 countries and the company's beverages were sold in more than 160 countries. Pepsi's largest operations were in Mexico and the United Kingdom, but just 31 percent of the company's total revenues came from non-North American markets. Pepsi's international beverage division produced just 8 percent of the parent company's total sales (see Appendix D: Exhibit 9).

In contrast, 68 percent of Coke's sales were in countries outside North America. Market share estimates prepared in 1999 suggested that Coke bested Pepsi in almost all global markets where the two companies competed (see Table 7.6). While in soft drinks in the United States, Coke had a 44 percent market share in comparison to Pepsi's 31 percent. Globally, Coke outsold Pepsi three to one.

Revenue in Pepsi's domestic beverage divisions was growing more rapidly than abroad. Domestic growth was driven mainly by Aquafina, product introductions (e.g., as Lipton Lemonade, Pepsi Blue, Pepsi Twist, Code Red, and Sierra Mist), and Gatorade.

Pepsi international was experiencing setbacks in Latin America. In Argentina, the setbacks were caused by the country's economic problems. In Venezuela, one of the few international markets in which Pepsi once had an advantage, the company's bottling partner, Cisneros

TABLE 7.6   Soft drinks: Selected international market shares, 1999

Country	Population (hundred thousands)	8-oz. consumption per capita	Annual growth (%) 1992–1999	Coke (%)	Pepsi (%)
United States	272.6	874	2	44	31
Mexico	100.3	590	2	70	19
Chile	15	392	5	81	4
United Kingdom	59	370	7	43	12
Germany	82	344	-3	56	8
Brazil	171.9	276	12	51	7
Italy	56.7	212	0	45	8
Philippines	79.3	205	9	70	18
France	58.9	158	3	60	8
South Korea	46.9	108	-2	54	13
Japan	126.2	92	-1	55	11
China	124.7	22	8	34	16

Source: Adapted from Yoffie, "Cola Wars Continue," Harvard Business School Case 9-702-442, 2002.

Group, had shifted allegiance to Coke. Pepsi immediately lost its 85 percent market share.

Though Pepsi was having trouble growing its global business, growth-in-operating profits were higher abroad than at home (see Table 7.7). In 2003, Pepsi's international sales were flat. Coke, on the other hand, had strong growth in such countries as China (29 percent), India (17 percent), and the Philippines (16 percent).

In response to its poor showing in Latin America, Pepsi was being more selective about where it invested abroad, focusing on China, India, and Indonesia, countries that had 2.4 billion people, nearly half the world's total population. These countries' gigantic populations,

TABLE 7.7   The growth of Pepsi's sales and operating profits in the United States and abroad: 2001–2002

	2002($)	Percent change 2002	2001
Pepsi-Cola North America			
Net sales	$3,365	6	20
Operating profit	987	12	7
Gatorade/Tropicana North America			
Net sales	3,835	4	5
Operating profit	590	1	6
PepsiCo Beverages International			
Net sales	2,036	1	2
Operating profit	261	23	32

Source: Pepsi Cola 10K Report, 2003.

increasing affluence, and underdeveloped soft-drink markets made them huge untapped opportunities for Coke and Pepsi. China's 1.2 billion consumers drank just five servings per consumer on average per year compared to 343 servings per consumer in the United States. However, both companies had numerous questions about how to approach these markets.

1. What relationship should Coke and Pepsi have with bottlers? Should they buy them, form joint ventures, or partner with them?
2. On what types of distribution channels should they rely—fountains, vending, supermarkets, and/or convenience stores?
3. What type of packaging should they mainly use—cans, glass, or plastic? What sizes should they sell?
4. How much should they charge?
5. What types of marketing campaigns should they employ?

Global Issues

In their attempts to expand globally, Coke and Pepsi faced serious issues in countries such as Japan and India. They also had to confront a general attack on American brands. In some parts of the world, local brands emerged that challenged the dominance of U.S. brands.

Japan. Coke's biggest issue was how to continue to do well in Japan. While Japan accounted for just 5 percent of Coke's global volume, it generated 20 percent of the company's operating profits.

Japanese consumers' infatuation with high-margin vending machines had propped up the market and helped Coke's profits, but an aging population was buying more and more of its beverages in low-margin supermarkets, a development that was not promising for Coke, whose profit growth in Japan in the first decade of the 21st century was expected to decline to about half of what it had been in the early 1990s.

Coke's response was to introduce new vending-machine technologies. It was also trying to get its bottlers to cut costs, but in the long term, the company could not be assured of smooth sailing in Japan. Coke still made mistakes. In the summer of 2003, it launched a low-calorie beverage in Japan which translated into "the big sag."

India. In India, Coke faced different issues. Controversy existed over tainted bottled water. In addition, Coke still could not be certain of the

ownership of its assets. It was facing growing pressure to sell 49 percent of its holdings in Hindustan Coca Cola to Indian investors.

Coke had abandoned India in 1977 after a socialist government
required that it cut its equity stake in its Indian holdings to 40 percent
and reveal its formula's secret. However, even after reentering the
market in 1993, Coke was subject to a government edict that applied
to all soft-drink companies to sell 49 percent of their equity to Indian
partners within two years of setting up business in that country.

Coke initially appealed the ruling and after the Indian government
relented, it bought 30 bottling plants and 10 franchises in the belief that
only scale operations would turn a profit. By 2003, it had acquired 56
percent of the Indian soft-drink market, but still was not making any
money. To create the distribution and manufacturing infrastructure it
needed cost more than Coke had anticipated.

Coke's total investment in India, more than $840 million, was one
of the largest by a foreign investor, but in 2002, Coke had to write off
$400 million in losses. The company had nothing but losses since
returning to the Indian market. Its plants and other operations
employed more than 5,000 people, and sales in 2002 reached 34 billion rupees ($702 million). With an anticipated 20 percent increase in
revenue, Coke believed it could achieve a modest operating profit. But
if Hindustan Coca Cola had to be sold right away, it would obtain a
poor price. Therefore, Coke again asked the government to "kindly
waive the divestment requirement." It hoped that by 2007, Hindustan
Coca Cola would be in better shape and it could get a decent price for
its shares. Indian investors pressured the government not to give in to
Coke. They wanted to buy the shares immediately while the price was
weak. Unless it could turn this situation around, Coke faced unattrac-
tive prospects in India.

The attack on American brands

Global brands like Coke were under attack throughout the world.
Consumers increasingly rebelled against Americanization. They
responded against a global market of uniform products.

U.S. companies had benefited from consumers who were eager to
sample American brands, taste American values, and enjoy a Western
lifestyle. By 2000, 62 of the most valuable 100 brands in the world
were American, but the pace of this Americanization was starting to
slow. In emerging markets from China to Eastern Europe, the appeal
of local brands grew while those from the United States faded.

Kola Real. As consumers reached saturation with U.S. brands, local brands found new life. An example was Kola Real, a family-run Peruvian company that started in 1987, did well in its home country, moved to Venezuela and Ecuador, and then targeted Mexico. In Mexico, the average person consumed 101 liters of cola a year, only slightly less than Americans at 113 liters, and far more than Brazilians, who drank just 32 liters a year.

Coke's control of Mexico had been solid with 70 percent of the market, which represented about 11 percent of the company's worldwide sales. The Mexican president, Vicente Fox, had been a Coke executive. Pepsi's market share was down to about 15 percent, but in the more affluent northern part of the Mexico, it had a strong presence with about 21 percent of the market.

Kola Real's entry into the market came in 2002. It had a state-of-the-art plant in an uninviting industrial park in a small town just east of Mexico City. It had success taking on Coke and Pepsi in one of the strongest soft-drink markets in the world.

What made Kola Real's entry easier was the switch to plastic bottles (see Table 7.8). Plastic bottles replaced glass bottles in the early 1990s, providing a less expensive alternative for firms entering the business.

TABLE 7.8   1998 world soft-drink volume shares by package
type (percent)

Cans	52.1
Plastic	46.8
Glass	1.1

Source: Beverage Marketing Corporation, 1998.

Supermarkets. Kola Real put its Big Cola product in large plastic bottles and sold it at a steep discount in supermarkets, an important outlet for new competitors as Coke and Pepsi dominated the small shops. Supermarket chains were using buying clout to squeeze suppliers. Thus, supermarket chains were not a favorite outlet of Coke and Pepsi. In Mexico, supermarkets amounted to less than 5 percent of soft drink sales, but they were the fastest-growing segment. Wal-Mart had arrived on the scene with supercenters that combined discount merchandising and groceries.

The pressure for low-cost alternatives to Coke and Pepsi was intense. Kola Real's entry strategy was to compete on price. The same bottle of Coke that cost about $1 in the United States cost about $1.40

in Mexico, a far poorer country. Kola Real had similar products that it sold for less money. Its family-sized, 2.6-litre bottle went for 9 to 10 pesos (80 to 90 cents).

Within a year of opening Kola Real's plant in Mexico, the company had a 3.5 percent market share. It quickly established a 17 percent market share in the country. Kola Real's operations were completely without frills and the company did little advertising. It relied instead on word of mouth and the pride that Latin Americans had in a product that came from their own region. Kola Real kept its distance from Coke and Pepsi's distribution systems. It established its own way to get product to market by leasing 600 trucks that moved product to 24 distribution centers that Kola Real owned and operated. It also had an 800-person sales staff that pushed its cola in large groceries and small shops in rural locations.

Coke and Pepsi respond. Coke and Pepsi counterattacked with aggressive marketing of their own, especially aimed at trend-setting Mexican teenagers. Coke's problem was that it was very aggressive: In response to complaints, Mexico's Federal Competition Commission found that the cola giant had paid retailers to exclude competitors' products.

Pepsi's problem was that it had no room to give on price. In Mexico, it had been trying to position itself as the low-cost alternative to Coke. Its 2.5 liter bottle sold for 12 pesos, just a bit more than Kola Real. It could not match Kola Real's prices without losing money.

Pepsi's Mexican volume was down by 5 percent in the third quarter of 2003 and its profits in the country for the full year were expected to be 40 percent lower than anticipated. Pepsi's disappointment was large, as it had spent more than $1 billion in 2002 to acquire a large Mexican bottler (Grupo Gemex SA).

In 2003, Coke's cola sales in Mexico were flat. Meanwhile, Kola Real's goal, to capture as much as 15 percent of the Mexican market in five years, did not seem out of reach. Coke and Pepsi had once competed against each other in Latin America with little local competition. Now, cheaper local rivals like Kola Real were seriously cutting into their profits and other companies were following Kola Real's lead. An Ecuadorian company, Fiemex SA, was launching a cut-price cola called El Gallito, or Little Rooster. Mexico's Guadalajara soccer club had its own Chiva Cola.

Mexico seemed to be going in the same direction as Brazil, the world's third-largest soft-drink market, where low-cost, local brands had expanded their market share from 3 percent in the early 1990s to about 30 percent in 2003.

So-called U.S. Cultural Imperialism

Throughout the world, customers were returning to local brands as their quality improved in response to global competition. Particularly in the Muslim world and Western Europe, activist groups called on consumers to boycott U.S. and British products and use local products in their place.

In Pakistan's North-West Frontier province, extremist vigilantes regularly destroyed signs advertising foreign consumer goods such as Coke and Pepsi that featured unveiled women. Across Europe, Muslim alternatives to Coke and Pepsi were sprouting up.

In 2003, the Iranian cola company, Zam-Zam, was an important emblem of opposition to the United States among Muslims. The Islamic Republic in Iran had banned Pepsi in 1979. It turned down Tawfiq Mathlouti, a Tunisian-born French businessman, to set up his own company, Mecca Cola, which sold a Coke look-alike product with the slogan, "Don't drink stupid, drink with commitment." Mecca Cola promised that 20 percent of its profits would go to charities, such as Palestinian causes and European Muslim organizations.

Other Islamic alternatives in the European market were Qibla Cola and Muslim Up. Qibla, named after the direction in which Muslims pray, started in the United Kingdom. It too was promising to use its profits to help Muslim charities. It estimated it could sell one million bottles in Britain and had plans to expand to Scandinavia, Turkey, Pakistan, and Egypt. Muslim Up, started by three Frenchman of Tunisian origin, was already operating in Britain, Germany, Belgium, and Italy as well as France.

Thinking and Acting Locally

Coke and Pepsi had to decide how to respond to these developments. In 2000 Coke announced that the company would have to listen more to its local business partners' advice and adapt products and advertising to local tastes. Coke would have to delegate more product development and marketing responsibility to local managers and develop and promote local executives rather than expatriates.

Coke also started to increase its acquisition of local brands. In Japan, two-thirds of its sales were from local brands. Worldwide, Coke owned more than 100 local brands. In Argentina, it launched a new soft drink called Nativa as part of a strategy to make products with indigenous ingredients. Nativa was flavored with the country's traditional yerba mate herbal tea. The Nativa advertising campaign, focused on the earthy qualities of the drink and the tea's status as a national icon. Ads were filmed from the semitropical north where yerba mate was grown to the southern tip of Tierra del Fuego.

Around the world, Coke was experimenting with drinks from Qoo fruit juice in Asia to an energy drink called Burn in Great Britain. Its best-selling beverage in Japan was Georgia coffee.

Tailoring advertisements. Coke was also continuing to try to tailor its ads to local markets. For example, its Chinese New Year television ad featured a dragon in a holiday parade, covered completely in red Coke cans. The ad concluded, "For many centuries, the color red has been the color for good luck and prosperity. Who are we to argue with ancient wisdom?"

In India, Coke hosted gatherings of up to 15,000 retailers to show off the coolers and refrigerators that the company loaned out. Coke's salespeople went house-to-house in New Delhi, handing out more than 100,000 free bottles of Coke and Fanta.

With resentment against the United States running high, Coke was repositioning itself as a supranational brand—global in nature, uniform throughout the world, and not so much American.

Distance from its country of origin. To improve its global image, Coke introduced a new worldwide graphic. The graphic was intended to convey the message that Coke was not just a drink, but a product with a special relationship to customers. The new look retained the company's core values, yet was meant to demonstrate to the teeming young people of the world Coke's authenticity, energy, and refreshment.

Coke maintained the stature and implied quality associated with the United States, but merged its products with local cultures by adapting the packaging, serving sizes, and flavors. It also enhanced local ties by doing community-service projects such as offering educational grants to the Palestinian Authority and making donations to Spanish environmental causes.

Pepsi acted similarly. In India, it sold the same products as in the United States but with a distinctly Indian orientation. It was a main sponsor of cricket. It relied on local celebrities in its ads. Senior management consisted of Indian talent, and the company had many community projects such as those in the Punjab of growing tomatoes and exporting the chili paste. Pepsi's slogan was *Yeh Dil Maange More!* (This Heart Wants More!). It was so popular that an Indian army officer screamed it after a victory against Pakistan in the 1998 Kargil War.

In India, Pepsi looked for the most prominent businessmen in each town and gave them exclusive distribution rights, tapping their connections to drive growth. From 1995–2000, its volume increased at a 26 percent annual rate, and it took 19 points of market share from Coke, bringing Pepsi's share to 47 percent, which was very close to Coke's 52 percent.

Coke's Leadership

The two companies had different leaders who coped with these issues. Since 1980, Coke has had four CEOs, each with somewhat different strategies. The strategies ranged from reorganizing the bottlers and eliminating nonsoft-drink businesses to instituting a culture of learning, shaking up the bureaucracy, and pushing aggressively into remote markets in developing countries.

Goizueta. Roberto Goizueta, who served as Coke's chair and CEO from 1980 to 1997, was a chemical engineer from Cuba. When he became head of the company in 1980, it had numerous unrelated ventures from shrimp farming to wine making. The bottler system was in disarray, with important markets in the hands of weak operators. The company's stock price was falling and it was barely profitable. In his first year at the helm, Goizueta made many changes that turned the situation around. Goizueta lifted sales from the time he became chief executive until his death in 1997 from $4 to $18 billion and increased market capitalization 3,500 percent.

Goizueta first worked on the bottling system, which was not keeping up with technology and changes in markets. He forced the bottlers to become leaner and more competitive. In a campaign to "refranchise" the system, Goizueta weeded out the weak operators. Coke would buy them, refurbish them, and resell them to stronger members of the system. The aim was to ensure that Coke's distribution system was superior to Pepsi's.

Goizueta also eliminated the nonsoft-drink businesses (wineries, water purification plants, plastics, and foods) that had weak financial results (less than 10 percent return on capital) and he held managers accountable to three-year goals. He tried to create more coordination and central planning among the global soft-drink divisions. Rather than using separate strategies in different countries—packaging innovations in Belgium, line extensions in Germany, and bottling investment in Spain—he sought a unified global strategy.

He ran the company by the numbers, the most important of which were rate of return, cash flow, and capital requirements. On that basis, Goizueta determined that Coke's concentrate business was it strongest element. Bottling was less attractive, because it demanded huge investments of capital. Ultimately, Goizueta sold the bottlers

Goizueta judged performance based on operating profit after deduction for the cost of capital. He was an innovator in the use of this indicator (EVA) as a corporate yardstick. He was focused on giving shareholders an above-average return, satisfying consumer tastes and needs, and being welcome in every country in which Coke did business. In the competition with Pepsi, Goizueta wanted leadership in all segments. He made mistakes, such as buying a Hollywood studio and introducing New Coke, but was also very successful in such ventures as entering Eastern Europe and recreating Coke's marketing strategies.

Ivester. Doug Ivester was Goizueta's successor. He lasted just two years on the job. At the age of 52, he suddenly resigned as chairman and CEO of Coke in 2000 under pressure from Warren Buffett, Coke's most powerful director, whose company, Berkshire Hathaway, owned about 8.1 percent of Coke's shares. Under Ivester, Coke's earnings declined, and its market value barely grew. Ivester took over the company in 1997 after Goizueta died of cancer. Foreign entanglements immediately got him into trouble: Asian currencies collapsed, and the weak dollar that had propped up Coke's earnings became stronger.

Ivester did not handle the foreign crises well. Board members considered him rigid and lacking in political skill. His emphasis was on discipline and control. His weak spot was creativity. Ivester had systems for everything. Everything was done according to schedule. Ivester was obsessed with data and analysis. His main initiative was to make Coke into a "Learning Organization." However, in the image and perception areas, which were critical to a marketing company like Coke, he was weak. He maintained that he was managing for the long run and therefore he should not overreact to immediate issues. According to the board, though, he had command of the details, but he did not have a good grasp of the big picture.

Globally, the problem was not only foreign exchange. Ivester's acquisition strategy, given increasing anti-American sentiment in

Europe, was inflexible. He could not get the European Union (EU) to accept Coke's attempt to purchased Orangina and Cadbury Schweppes. EU regulators instead went after the company for alleged anticompetitive practices. When the tainted cola crisis arose in Belguim in 1999, Ivester minimized it. He believed it was a minor problem, certainly not a health hazard. Thus, he was slow in addressing the issue.

Daft. Doug Daft, a 56-year-old Australian who had run Coke's businesses in Asia, was asked to replace Ivester in 1999. Daft tried to energize the soda-maker's bureaucratic culture, but the results were mixed. Daft laid off 20 percent of Coke's 29,000 employees and reassigned or fired 30 of the company's 32 top managers, but he could not get Coke's board to go along with a deal to acquire Gatorade, which Pepsi bought instead.

Moreover, he walked away from a joint snack-and-juice venture he had created with Procter & Gamble because of criticism that the terms favored P&G. Under Daft, mending relations with Coke's bottlers was coming at a cost to Coke's profitability.

Daft still did not have a good answer for Pepsi's aggressive move into noncarbonated beverages, though under his leadership Coke was making some progress. Dasani and Minute Maid were doing better, and the company was introducing brand extensions like Lemon Coke.

Daft was hired because as head of Coke's profitable Asian operations, he had been very good at exploiting new beverage trends. With Daft as CEO, the Asian divisions continued to do well, but the Latin American operations were in trouble.

Coke still relied mainly on its Coke and Diet Coke mainstays, but it had 1,500 different drinks, counting different sizes, around the world versus 1,000 before Daft took over. It also had many prototype beverages and innovations. However, many of these new product ideas still had not emerged from Coke's development teams.

The company failed to develop good products for the teen market to match Pepsi's Mountain Dew and good products for "new agers" to match SoBe, the nutrient-enhanced brand that Pepsi purchased. South Beach Beverage, the owners of SoBe, decided to sell to Pepsi, not Coke, because of what they perceived as Coke's lack of creativity.

Isdell. Daft's leadership came to an abrupt end when he was replaced by E. Nevill Isdell in 2004. Isdell was a 60-year-old, longtime Coca-Cola executive and former president of the company's European operations. He had led Coke's advances into India, Russia, and Eastern Europe in the 1980s and 1990s, as the company built its distribution network around the world. He pushed aggressively into those markets and established capacity ahead of demand based on the belief of Coke's earlier generation leaders that a soft drink had to be within "arm's reach" of customers.

Under Isdell, Coke was placing its bet on remote markets in China and India to help regain global momentum. It was expanding its production and distribution far from Asia's big cities, and marketing cheap sodas to a population that in the past had been considered too poor and difficult to reach.

Pepsi's Leadership

Since 1996, Pepsi had two CEOs. The company had stable leadership focused on winning the war with Coke. It brought out new products or acquired firms that had these products. Coke failed to match these moves.

Enrico. Roger A. Enrico was Pepsi's CEO from 1996–2000. The son of an iron-ore worker, Enrico grew up in Chisholm, Minnesota, and went to work for Pepsi after a brief stint at General Mills. He joined Pepsi's Frito-Lay division, where he eventually rose to the top. A bitter foe of Coke, Enrico believed that Coke's leadership had tried many times to put Pepsi out of business. Enrico made his name when he was head of Pepsi's U.S. soda business in the 1980s. At his urging, in 1983, the company paid $5 million so that Michael Jackson would do a Pepsi commercial. Pepsi made many major changes under Enrico:

1. In 1997, it spun off Taco Bell, Pizza Hut, and Kentucky Fried Chicken chains and created Tricon Global Restaurants, a company with a market cap of $4.7 billion.
2. In 1999, it sold its bottling in a $2.3 billion public offering, with Pepsi keeping 40 percent of the shares.
3. In 1998, Pepsi bought Tropicana for $3.3 billion.
4. In 2000, Pepsi got the better of Coke with a $337 million offer for SoBe and then a $14 billion offer for Quaker Oats.

In his time as CEO, Enrico completely transformed the company. He got Pepsi to focus on packaged foods and drinks. In snack foods, he played a hand in the near-total dominance that Pepsi achieved. In soft drinks, he helped Pepsi make a comeback by branching out into alternative beverages and introducing new products. He also brought back the effective "Pepsi Challenge" advertising campaign of the 1970s that asked consumers to compare Coke to Pepsi.

Enrico's strategic decisions were meant to focus the company on areas where it could dominate. The result of his decisions was that Pepsico had one-third less sales, but profits grew by more than $100 million. Operating margins increased from 10 percent to 15 percent, while return on invested capital shot up from 15 to 20 percent.

Pepsi still trailed Coke in the U.S. soft-drink market, but in 1999 Mountain Dew edged out Diet Coke for third place. Pepsi continued to lose global market share in soft drinks to Coca-Cola, but mostly because it overextended itself into too many countries in an attempt to outdo Coke.

Reinemund and Nooyi. In 2000, Enrico named his successor, Steven S. Reinemund, a former Marine who had successfully run Frito-Lay for eight years. Reinemund in turn tapped Indra Nooyi to be president and chief financial officer. Reinemund and Nooyi operated as a team. Reinemund was more the straight-laced efficiency expert and Nooyi more the marketing genius. Reinemund was analytical and Nooyi was creative but tough and was also known for her negotiating skills. She closed the 1998 deal to purchase Tropicana and played a critical role in the 2000 acquisition of Quaker, which brought Gatorade into the fold.

Reinemund had said that Pepsi's key to success was its "ruthless focus." Globally, the company was aiming "to go deep rather than wide." It wanted to build strong-scale profitable businesses in key markets. Then, there was the matter of the SoBe brand, which stretched Pepsi's reach into a new niche, but skeptics saw the trend toward such drinks as exaggerated.

What to Do Next?

Pepsi had mounted a successful challenge to Coke domestically, but questions remained about whether it could sustain this challenge on a global basis. Coke would have to defend its global lead, while at the same time ensuring that it did not have any further slippage domestically. How to balance global and domestic moves was foremost in the minds of the leaders of both firms. How they would achieve this balance would largely determine the future performance of their companies.

Questions for Discussion

1. Compare Coke and Pepsi's performance from 1998–2002. Who was doing better? Why?
2. Which company had stronger brands—Coke or Pepsi?
3. Why do you think Coke was having so many problems? Did the company's leadership have anything to do with the problems it was confronting? Size up the leaders of Coke and Pepsi. Which company was in better hands? Why?
4. Do you agree that soft-drink consumption in North America had reached its peak? Why or why not?
5. Why was alternative beverage consumption on the rise? What types of drinks were growing the fastest? What regions had the most rapid increases in sales?
6. Compare the growth in the consumption of alternative beverages with the consumption of conventional brands. What does the comparison tell you? Whose conventional brands were seeing the biggest declines? Which company should be most concerned?
7. Were Pepsi's Frito Lay divisions net pluses or net minuses for the company?
8. Why had Coke and Pepsi sold their bottlers? What advantage did they gain from this tactic?
9. How do Coke and Pepsi's customers differ? Who obtained better margins from its customers?
10. Which company dominated in international markets—Coke or Pepsi?
11. Why were international markets attractive to Pepsi? What global markets interested it the most? Why?
12. Compare Coke's problems in Japan and India. In what ways did these problems differ? How were they alike? Were there common actions Coke could take in both instances? Explain.
13. Explain the success of Kola Real. What lessons should Coke and Pepsi learn from this success?
14. How should Pepsi approach global markets? How should Coke

approach these markets? In what ways should the approach of the two companies be similar? In what ways should their approaches be different?

15. What could Coke and Pepsi have done to counter opposition to their products in Islamic countries?

16. Compare and contrast the orientations of Coke and Pepsi leaders toward global issues and markets.

Exercises

1. Go to a supermarket and/or convenience store. Walk around. See what beverage options there are. How are the products presented? How are they promoted? How are they priced? How much space has been allotted to Coke products? How much space has been allotted to Pepsi products? Which products are more prominently displayed? Which products are better displayed?

2. Why does Pepsi lag behind Coke in global market share? What should Pepsi do, *if anything,* to catch up with Coke in global market share?

3. Why does Coke lead Pepsi in global market share? What should Coke do, *if anything*, to maintain its lead over Pepsi in global market share?

Video

"The Colonel Comes to Japan." Enterprise Series. MTI Teleprograms. Distributed by Simon & Schuster Communications.

Bibliography

Armour, Lawrence. "Eau, Neau!" *Fortune*. March 17, 2003.

Bajpai, Rajendra. "Hard Times for Soft Drinks." *Fortune*. February 4, 2002.

Bruss, Jill. "A Gangbuster Year Leaves Pepsico Holding All the Right Cards." *Beverage Industry*. January 2002.

Byrne, John. "Pepsico's New Formula." *Business Week*. April 10, 2000:172.

Chang, Leslie, Chad Terhune, and Betsy McKay. "A Global Journal Report; Rural Thing—Coke's Big Gamble in Asia: Digging Deeper in China, India; As Growth Slows Elsewhere, Beverage Giant Targets Nations' Vast Hinterlands; New CEO Has Seen the Pitfalls." *The Wall Street Journal*. August 8, 2004:A1.

Chen, Christine. "Darius Bikoff vs. Coke and Pepsi." *Fortune Small Business*. February 2003.

Creswell, Julie, and Julie Schlosser. "Lost Its Fuzz." *Fortune*. November 10, 2003.

Foust, Dean and Geri Smith. "Repairing the Coke Machine." *Business Week*. March 19, 2001:86.

_____. "Has Coke Been Playing Accounting Games?" *Business Week*. May 13, 2002:86.

_____. "Coke: The Cost of Babying Bottlers." *Business Week*. December 9, 2002: 93.

Kermouch, Gerry. "Call It the Pepsi Blue Generation." *Business Week*. February 3, 2003.

Luhnow, David, and Chad Terhune. "A Low-Budget Cola Shakes Up Markets South of the Border." *The Wall Street Journal*. October 27, 2003:A1.

McKay, Betsy, and Suzanne Vranica. "Coke Readies New Campaign, Drawing on Its Own Tradition." *The Wall Street Journal*. October 4, 2002.

"Out with Vice, in with Virtue." *Economist*. May 13, 2003.

Slater, Joanna. "Coke, Pepsi Fight Product-Contamination Charges in India." *The Wall Street Journal*. August 15, 2003:B1.

Stevenson, Seth. "I'd Like to Buy the World's Shelf-Stable Children's Lactic Drink: Coca Cola Confronts a Global Marketplace That Has Lost Its Thirst for Bubbly Brown Sugar Water." *New York Times Sunday Magazine*. March 10, 2002.

Tehrune, Chad. "How Coke Officials Beefed Up Results of Marketing Test." *The Wall Street Journal*. August 20, 2003:A1.

Yoffie, David B., and Yusi Wang. "Cola Wars Continue: Coke and Pepsi in the 21st Century." Harvard Business School Case 9-702-442, January 11, 2002.

Appendix A. Coke and Pepsi's annual income statements: 1998–2002

EXHIBIT 1   Coca Cola annual income statement (in millions of U.S. dollars except for per-share items)

	12 months ending 12/31/02	12 months ending 12/31/01	12 months ending 12/31/00	12 months ending 12/31/99	12 months ending 12/31/98
Total revenue	19,564	17,545	17,354	19,284	18,813
Cost of revenue	7,105	6,044	6,204	6,009	5,562
Gross profit	12,459	11,501	11,150	13,275	13,251
Total operating expense	14,106	12,193	13,663	15,302	13,846
Operating income	5,458	5,352	3,691	3,982	4,967
Net income before taxes	5,499	5,670	3,399	3,819	5,198
Net income after taxes	3,976	3,979	2,177	2,431	3,533

EXHIBIT 2   PepsiCo annual income statement (in millions of U.S. dollars except for per-share items)

	12 months ending 12/31/02	12 months ending 12/31/01	12 months ending 12/31/00	12 months ending 12/31/99	12 months ending 12/31/98
Total revenue	25,112	23,512	22,337	25,093	22,348
Cost of revenue	11,497	10,750	10,226	10,326	9,330
Gross profit	13,615	12,762	12,111	14,767	13,018
Total operating expense	20,382	19,491	18,519	21,610	19,764
Operating income	4,730	4,021	3,818	3,483	2,584
Net income before taxes	4,868	4,029	3,761	4,275	2,263
Net income after taxes	3,313	2,662	2,543	2,505	1,993

Source: Yahoo! Finance (http://finance.yahoo.com).

Appendix B. The consumption of alternative beverages including teas and energy drinks and conventional carbonated soft drinks in 2002

EXHIBIT 3   Alternative beverages

Region	Retail volume, liters per head 2002	Percent growth 1997–2002
Functional beverages		
Western Europe	1.7	148.4
Eastern Europe	0.1	219.9
Asia Pacific	1.2	43.3
North America	11.5	14.7
Latin America	0.8	49.3
Fruit drinks (no juice content)		
Western Europe	0.1	97.4
Eastern Europe	1.3	60.1
North America	2.2	17.4
Latin America	0.1	13.8
Asia Pacific	0.0	-1.5

Source: Euromonitor International—The World Market for Soft Drinks, 2003.

EXHIBIT 4   Canned and bottled tea

Brand	Sales (in millions)	Percent change vs. last year	Market share
Lipton Brisk	113.2	(9.5)	18.6
Snapple	94.7	17.3	15.6
Arizona	93.6	18.5	15.4
Nestea Cool	75.7	(17.7)	12.5
Diet Snapple	72.4	18.6	11.9
Nestea	28.8	46.8	4.7
Lipton Iced Tea	23.2	11.0	3.8
SoBe	19.2	45.4	3.2
Lipton	17.2	17.7	2.8
Private label	14.1	17.4	2.3
Category total	607.9	4.2	100.0

Source: Euromonitor International—The World Market for Soft Drinks, 2003.

EXHIBIT 5   Energy drinks

Brand	Sales (in millions)	Percent change vs. last year	Percent of market share
Red Bull	68.6	40.4	54.8
SoBe Adrenaline Rush	12.6	11.7	10.0
Amp	11.6	74.2	9.2
KMX	6.6	(19.5)	5.2
Rockstar	6.2	290.9	5.0
Hansens	3.5	(25.6)	2.8
Monster Energy	2.3	16,499.0	1.8
Blue Ox	2.1	(18.8)	1.7
Snapple Elements	1.2	(8.8)	1.0
180	1.1	(31.2)	0.9
Category total	125.3	31.3	100.0

Source: Information Resources Inc., Total food, drug and mass merchandise, excluding Wal-Mart, for the 52 weeks ending June 15, 2003.

EXHIBIT 6   Carbonated soft drinks

Brand	Company	Volume (%) change
Coca-Cola Classic	The Coca-Cola Co.	(2.5)
Pepsi	Pepsi-Cola Co.	(3.6)
Diet Coke	The Coca-Cola Co.	0.7
Mountain Dew Regular	Pepsi-Cola Co.	(2.7)
Diet Pepsi	Pepsi-Cola Co.	2.8
Sprite Regular	The Coca-Cola Co.	(3.7)
Dr Pepper Regular	Dr Pepper/Seven Up Inc.	(1.3)
Caffeine Free Diet Coke	The Coca-Cola Co.	(1.9)
7 UP Regular	Dr Pepper/Seven Up Inc.	(5.3)
Diet Dr Pepper	Dr Pepper/Seven Up Inc.	4.2
Diet Mountain Dew	Pepsi-Cola Co.	3.9
Caffeine Free Diet Pepsi	Pepsi-Cola Co.	(1.2)
Mountain Dew Code Red	Pepsi-Cola Co.	64.4
Sunkist Orange	Dr Pepper/Seven Up Inc.	10.2
Vanilla Coke	The Coca-Cola Co.	NA

Brand	Volume share	Volume share change
Coca-Cola Classic	15.2	(0.5)
Pepsi	13.8	(0.6)
Diet Coke	7.3	0.0
Mountain Dew Regular	6.5	(0.2)
Diet Pepsi	5.3	0.1
Sprite Regular	4.9	(0.2)
Dr Pepper Regular	4.8	(0.1)
Caffeine Free Diet Coke	2.5	(0.1)
7 UP Regular	2.2	(0.1)
Diet Dr Pepper	1.5	0.1
Diet Mountain Dew	1.5	0.0
Caffeine Free Diet Pepsi	1.5	0.0
Mountain Dew Code Red	1.2	0.5
Sunkist Orange	1.2	0.1
Vanilla Coke	1.2	1.2

Source: Information Resources Inc. and A. C. Nielsen, total all channels for the 52 weeks ending December 31, 2002.

EXHIBIT 7   Major soft-drink companies' volume positions

	Volume % change	Volume share	Volume share change
Carbonated soft drinks	0.7	100	0.0
Coca-Cola Co.	2.8	37.0	0.7
Pepsi-Cola Co.	1.5	34.8	0.3
Dr Pepper/Seven Up Inc.	(1.4)	17.2	(0.4)
Private label	(7.7)	7.3	(0.7)

Source: Information Resources Inc. and A. C. Nielsen, total all channels for the 52 weeks ending December 31, 2002.

Appendix C. Pepsi's market share in snacks and beverages: 2002

EXHIBIT 8 Pepsi's market share sales and profit contribution

U.S. snack chip industry, % volume in supermarkets (includes potato chips, tortilla chips, extruded snacks and pretzels; excludes Wal-Mart).

U.S. beverage market share % volume in measured channels (includes carbonated soft drinks, bottled water, ambient juices and juice drinks, chilled juices and juice drinks, sports drinks, energy drinks, ready-to-drink tea, ready-to-drink coffee).

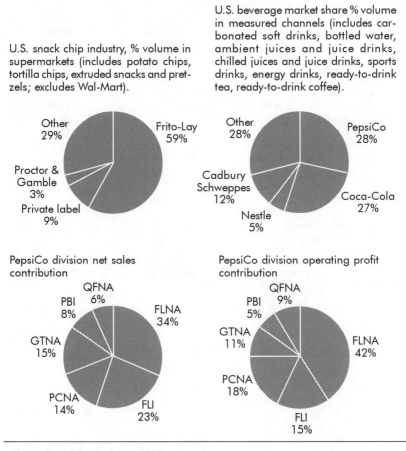

PepsiCo division net sales contribution

PepsiCo division operating profit contribution

Source: Pepsi Cola 10K Report, 2003.

Appendix D. Pepsi and Coke domestic and global sales in 2002

EXHIBIT 9   PepsiCo's 2002 Sales

	% of total
North America	
Frito-Lay North America	34
Gatorade/Tropicana North America	15
Pepsi-Cola North America	13
Quaker Foods North America	6
Other regions	31
Frito-Lay International	23
PepsiCo Beverages International	8
Divested businesses	1
Total	100

Source: Pepsi Annual Report, 2003.

EXHIBIT 10   Coke's 2002 sales

	% of total
North America	32
Europe/Eurasia/Middle East	27
Asia	26
Latin American	11
Africa	4
Total	100

Source: Coke Annual Report, 2003.

CASE 8

Corporate Leadership
Ecolab versus JohnsonDiversey[1]

JohnsonDiversey was formed in 2002 when an S. C. Johnson subsidiary, Commercial Markets Holdco, Inc. acquired a Unilever subsidiary in the institutional and industrial (I&I) cleaning and sanitation business. The new company was a direct threat to Ecolab. Both Ecolab and JohnsonDiversey were adding resources and capabilities, repositioning themselves, expanding globally, and innovating. Their performance would depend on how they well carried out these activities. The burden was on their top-executive teams to execute them well.

The Institutional and Industrial Cleaning Industry

JohnsonDiversey and Ecolab are in the I&I cleaning industry. JohnsonDiversey estimated the global market potential for I&I cleaning and sanitizing chemicals at $18.5 billion. Ecolab, with its additional product and service businesses such as pest elimination, equipment repair, pool and spa, vehicle care, and water care, estimated its total global market potential at $36 billion. Growth was driven by the need for multifunctional and biodegradable products that were cost-effective and for products that complied with government regulations. Shifts were toward higher value-added cleaning chemicals that boosted company margins. The use of these higher value chemicals had increased 6.5 percent from 2000 to 2004.

Seasoned leadership

Both companies had seasoned leadership in their top-executive teams. Ecolab's longtime CEO was Al Schuman. Schuman maintained

---

1. This case was written by Chris Morgan and Bryan Maser with the editorial assistance of Alfred Marcus. All information is from public sources. No information is taken directly from either JohnsonDiversey or Ecolab. Copyright © 2005 by Marsh Publications LLC. All rights reserved.

that though Ecolab had many ideas and people, it was a single entity with a common culture. In 1996, he created a vision to make the company more global and unified. The vision consisted of spirit, pride, determination, commitment, passion, and integrity.[2] In 2004, a 15-year Ecolab veteran, Doug Baker, who had served as president and chief operating officer (COO) since 2002, became Ecolab's new CEO.

JohnsonDiversey was a privately held company. S. Curtis Johnson III, the chairman, was a descendant of Samuel Curtis Johnson and the brother of Helen Johnson-Leipold, another company director. Prior to joining JohnsonDiversey, he had worked for S. C. Johnson & Son in its international divisions and had also been a venture capitalist.

Gregory E. Lawton was president and chief executive officer of JohnsonDiversey. He had also been a vice president and general manager at Procter & Gamble. The third top-management team member was Michael J. Bailey, the chief financial officer (CFO), who had worked for many companies including Ford Motor.

The recent performance of Ecolab and JohnsonDiversey. JohnsonDiversy was a relatively new company with a fresh management team eager to overtake Ecolab, but it had a long way to go. Its debt in 2003 was $2.6 billion as a result of its acquisition of DiverseyLever. In contrast, Ecolab's debt in 2003 was $675 million. DiverseyLever had a debt rating of *B,* while Ecolab had a debt rating of *A.*

JohnsonDiversey was spending more on R&D than Ecolab—$75 million in comparison to Ecolab's $53 million, but its revenues and operating margins lagged behind those of Ecolab. For the fiscal year 2003, JohnsonDiversy reported net sales of $2.9 billion and net income of $24 million, while Ecolab reported net sales of $3.8 billion and net income of $277 million (see Table 8.1).

Industrial segmentation. The I&I industry was segmented into four main categories: janitorial and housekeeping, food processing and industrial, foodservice, and laundry (see Table 8.2). The largest two segments were janitorial and housekeeping and food processing and industrial.[3] The three leading suppliers to these markets in 2000 were

2. Spirit was to motivate heart and soul, pride was to fulfill customer needs, determination was to compete, commitment was to be true to the cause, passion was to enthusiastically pursue company goals and objectives, and integrity was to be professional, reliable, trustworthy, and honest.

3. The latter is composed of dairy plants and farms as well as food and beverage processors.

TABLE 8.1   The performance of Ecolab and JohnsonDiversey in 2003

	Ecolab ($)	JohnsonDiversey ($)
Balance sheet items (thousands)		
Cash and cash equivalents	85,626	24,543
Inventories	309,959	263,397
Property, plant & equipment	736,797	595,483
Total assets	3,228,918	3,665,327
Short-term debt	70,203	124,228
Long-term debt	604,441	1,338,622
Income statement items (thousands)		
Net sales	3,761,819	2,947,772
Operating income	482,658	158,790
Net income	277,348	24,141

Source: Company reports.

TABLE 8.2   U.S. industry segmentation

Segment	$ million	% of total
Janitorial and housekeeping	2,800	37
Food processing and industrial	2,800	37
Foodservice	1,441	19
Laundry	550	7
Total	7,591	100

Source: B. Boynick and V. Kollonitsch, Food Service Cleaning Products USA 2000.

Ecolab, DiverseyLever, and Auto-Chlor (then a unit of Lever Industrial).

Janitorial and housekeeping market. JohnsonDiversey combined the assets of the number two and number three companies in the industry—DiverseyLever and Auto-Chlor with Johnson Worldwide Professional. Almost one-third of JohnsonDiversey's revenue was generated from its janitorial and housekeeping arm. Its strength was in floor-care products and solutions, which were the core technology of its primary brand, Johnson Wax.

JohnsonDiversey's strength was primarily in floor care due to its large investments in polymers and the Johnson Wax business. Known as an innovator in this area, JohnsonDiversey was a tough company with which to compete in the janitorial and housekeeping market. JohnsonDiversey continued to focus a significant amount of its effort on the development of new floor finishes and equipment. It had about 16 percent of the janitorial and housekeeping market compared to Ecolab's approximately 8 percent.

Foodservices market. Ecolab, on the other hand, was in a leading position in the foodservices market with 41 percent market share, while the JohnsonDiversey companies held the number two and three positions, with 9 percent and 8 percent market shares, respectively.

Ecolab's business strength had traditionally been in the institutional foodservice market. It dominated the cleaner and sanitizer business with more than double the market share of its nearest competitors. Ecolab maintained a leading share in the corporate chain account business in which its teams of sales and service professionals were able to reach customer locations throughout the globe.

Ecolab's robust level of service and proprietary dispensing equipment created high switching costs for clients. Restaurant managers, who were under daunting time and safety constraints, were reluctant to switch to competitors' systems. Switching would mean disruption from changes in equipment, cleaning products, service, and training. Ecolab therefore had an impressive customer retention rate of about 90 percent. Ecolab was also the recognized innovator in dishwashing. Its lead in this area was similar to JohnsonDiversey's in floor cleaning.

The foodservice business had seven customers types (see Table 8.3), and the segment's growth was projected to be about $1,656 million by 2005.

Ecolab had another advantage: It was national in scope. JohnsonDiversey's Auto-Chlor division was just starting to expand from its base in the South and West to markets in the Midwest and Northeast. It had consolidated routes to compete with Ecolab, but it still was not in a position to mount a frontal attack on Ecolab.

Ecolab maintained a strong lead in the provision of kitchen services throughout the United States. As shown in Figure 8.1, its strongest markets were colleges, lodging, industrial/offices, nursing homes, full-service restaurants, fast-food restaurants, and recreational facilities.

TABLE 8.3   Foodservice customers: Projected growth by 2005

End use	2000 $ million	2005 $ million
Full-service restaurants	618	721
Lodging establishments	117	133
Fast-food establishments	193	220
Nursing homes	119	133
Schools	95	106
Hospitals	87	94
Other	212	249
Total	1,441	1,656

Source: B. Boynick and V. Kollonitsch, *Food Service Cleaning Products USA 2000.*

Regional competitors. Both Ecolab and JohnsonDiversey faced strong regional competitors. Barriers to entry into the industry were low, which resulted in many small suppliers competing for the business. In the janitorial/housekeeping market, local competitors had established footholds in several metropolitan areas. Examples were Sunburst Chemical (Minneapolis, MN), Mount Hood (Portland, OR), and Midlab (Sweetwater, TN). Among the regional competitors in the foodservice market were Burns Chemical (Pittsburgh, PA), UNX (Greenville, NC), and ProClean (Houston, TX).

The regional players' business model was simple. The companies typically targeted a specific area, created low cost, but generally average performing products, went after independent accounts with a trained sales force, and then expanded the product line while maintaining an adequate or good level of service.

Regional markets had low barriers to entry, limited scale economies, moderate product differentiation, low capital requirements, and minimal switching costs. Thus, they were almost always up for grabs. These factors intensified the competition, enabling local and regional

FIGURE 8.1   U.S. market shares for Ecolab and the top three suppliers by end use: 2000

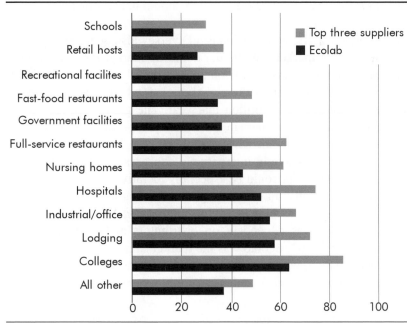

Source: B. Boynick and V. Kollonitsch, *Food Service Cleaning Products USA 2000.*

suppliers to compete for accounts. Usually, it was the independent full-service restaurants (only 25% of units were chain restaurants) that were open to the overtures of the regional players.

Ecolab asserted itself as a market leader in the national account chain business, where access to distribution channels and economies of scale were more important than in regional markets.

Solutions, not products. Both Ecolab and JohnsonDiversey tried to educate their customers to be concerned about the overall solutions rather than individual product costs. The two companies presented themselves as solution providers rather than purveyors of particular products.[4] This approach was very different than that of the regional players, who mostly provided low-cost detergents.

Ecolab and JohnsonDiversey made the claim to their customers that they were selling more than just detergents. They were dispensing equipment and service specialists, who were able to reduce a customer's overall costs through reductions in water consumption, energy use, labor, and detergent. The solutions they offered brought together safety, convenience, environmental protection, and ease of disposal. These solutions combined performance, service, and support in one package. From the customer and end-user perspective, the factor that should influence the purchase decision should not be price alone.

Global markets. Ecolab and JohnsonDiversey also aggressively competed in global markets. While the domestic market for I&I cleaning chemicals products was significant, an estimated $8.1 billion in 2004, it represented a fraction of the global market, which was estimated to be approximately $18.5 billion that year. The global market was of great importance to suppliers in this industry, especially because many of the industry's customers were multinational businesses. Landing global contracts to supply international concerns like McDonald's or the Hilton hotel chain could be especially lucrative.

However, establishing efficient global distribution channels was a major challenge for Ecolab and JohnsonDiversey. About 80 percent of all distribution was dependent on distributors and contractors (see Figure 8.2). In 2003, Ecolab was the market share leader in the North American market, while JohnsonDiversey was the market share leader in Europe, Latin America, and Asia (see Figure 8.3).

---

4. Ecolab had more than 11,600 employees (> half the total workforce) in the field in sales and service.

"Circle the globe, circle the customer." Ecolab's global strategy was based on the "Circle the Globe, Circle the Customer" idea. The company wanted to develop new products and services to fill a spectrum of customer needs, and then to expand to cover all a customer's locations around the world. As Ecolab's customers grew globally, the company wanted to grow with them. The circle the customer concept would only work if Ecolab was able to forge strong and successful partnerships with customers that spanned the globe.

JohnsonDiversey's large debt. In competing globally, JohnsonDiversey was hindered by its large debt. For this company, cost reductions had to be the main concern. It had to pay down the debt by capturing cash wherever it could.

Nonetheless, JohnsonDiversey also was an avid global competitor. The company was trying to be known as a preferred customer with distinctive partnership models and competitive offerings. It was attempting to strengthen its business portfolio with global programs that exploited growth possibilities in every region. A key tactic was its partnership with S. C. Johnson. JohnsonDiversy was using that com-

FIGURE 8.2   Distribution channels in industrial and institutional cleaning chemicals industry

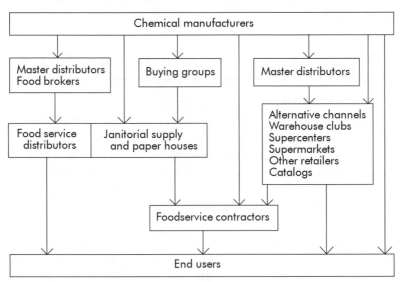

FIGURE 8.3   A comparison of 2003 domestic and global market
shares: Ecolab and JohnsonDiversey (percent)

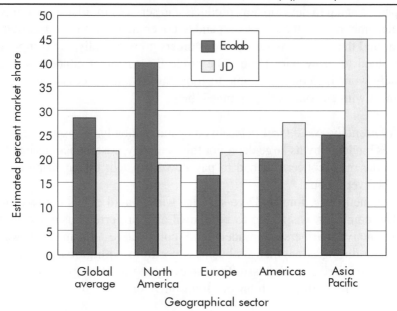

Source: B. Boynick and V. Kollonitsch, Food Service Cleaning Products USA, 2000.

pany's brand names (for example, Johnson Wax) to penetrate new global markets.

Mergers, Acquisitions, and Divestitures in Ecolab and JohnsonDiversey's History

Both Ecolab and JohnsonDiversey started as family-owned business-es. Ecolab (then Economics Laboratory) was created by Merritt J. Osborn in 1923 and JohnsonDiversey derived from S. C. Johnson and Sons businesses, which were founded by the clan's originator, Samuel Curtis Johnson I. Both companies grew by means of mergers and acquisitions. The companies they acquired and how they integrated and managed them were critical to their success.

Ecolab's history. Founded in 1923 and incorporated under Delaware laws in 1924, Ecolab began as a one-person company offering a single product. From these humble beginnings, it grew to become a leading global developer and marketer of premium cleaning and sanitizing products, pest elimination, maintenance and repair products, and services for the hospitality, foodservice, institutional and industrial markets. By 2003, Ecolab had over 20,000 employees servicing customers in more than 150 countries.

Over the years, Ecolab had been involved in a steady stream of mergers, acquisitions, and divestitures. Some of the more notable transactions are shown in Table 8.4.

Klenzade and Magnus. In 1961, when Ecolab acquired Klenzade Products, Inc. the company expanded into the area of dairy plant cleaning and sanitizing. The acquisition brought with it 90 technical, sales, and research personnel, and a new 80,000-square-foot facility in Beloit, Wisconsin.   Klenzade had pioneered in the area of Clean-In-Place (CIP) electronic systems. Its business extended into dairy farms, dairies, meat and poultry plants, bottlers, breweries, and canners.

In 1964, the acquisition of Magnus Chemical Company launched Ecolab into marine, aviation, and industrial cleaning.   Magnus brought in three manufacturing plants, and 22 international, independ-

TABLE 8.4   Ecolab's merger, acquisition, and divestiture history

1960	Ecolab created an international division.
1961	Ecolab acquired Klenzade.
1964–1966	Ecolab acquired various Magnus businesses, a detergent manufacturer.
1980	Ecolab acquired Apollo Industries and formed an industrial group.
1984	Ecolab acquired Lystads to form its pest elimination business.
1987	Ecolab acquired Airkem to form its professional products business.
1987	Ecolab acquired ChemLawn.
1991	Ecolab initiated a joint venture with Henkel.
1992	Ecolab sold its ChemLawn business.
1994	Ecolab acquired Jackson MSC, a dishmachine manufacturer.
1994	Ecolab acquired Kay Chemical, the primary suppliers of cleaning and sanitizing products to the quick-service industry.
1997	Ecolab acquired Grace-Lee, a major supplier of vehicle-care products.
1998	Ecolab acquired GCS.
1999	Ecolab acquired Blue Coral Systems, a major supplier of vehicle-care products.
2000	Ecolab sold its Jackson dishmachine manufacturing business.
2001	Ecolab bought the remaining 50 percent share of its joint venture with Henkel.
2001–04	Ecolab purchased four global pest elimination companies.

Source: Ecolab 2003 Annual Report and information compiled by case writers Chris Morgan and Bryan Maser from company sources.

ently-owned licensees that strengthened Ecolab's global presence. Later, in 1986, Ecolab sold Magnus to align its corporate focus more closely with the institutional marketplace.

Apollo. Ecolab's 1980 acquisition of Apollo Technologies quickly took a downward turn and had a very negative effect on the company. Apollo, combined with Klenzade, was going to be the foundation for Ecolab's industrial group. Apollo had divisions including Pulp and Paper, Electric Utilities, Mining and Metallurgy, Metal Processing, and Water Science. However, the high price Ecolab paid for Apollo ($71.2 million), plus poor economic conditions, created earning problems for the new division. In 1983, four days after Pierson M. "Sandy" Grieve became chairman and chief executive officer of Ecolab, he shut down Apollo, and recorded an operating loss of $42 million.

The sale of the consumer division and the acquisition and sale of ChemLawn. Ecolab sold its consumer division to Benckiser for $250 million in 1987. In the same year, it acquired ChemLawn, the nation's largest lawn-care services company for $378 million.

ChemLawn was the largest acquisition in the company's history at the time of its purchase. It gave Ecolab a nationally known brand name and more than 1.5 million residential customers. It also provided Ecolab with a ready-made residential services business that complemented its institutional operations. However, in 1989, Ecolab sold ChemLawn for $107 million. After several years of aggressive business development efforts that were not successful, Ecolab concluded that the operation did not fit its circle the customer strategy.

Kay Chemical. In 1994, Ecolab acquired Kay Chemical to enhance the circle the customer strategy. Kay was the leading cleaning product supplier to the quick-service market; the company provided a full line of products to quick-service restaurants, food retail stores, and convenience stores across the United States and in 100 international markets.

Vehicle-care products. From 1997 to 1999, Ecolab created its own vehicle-care (auto cleaning) division. Both the Grace Lee acquisition of 1997 and the Blue Coral acquisition in 1999 enabled Ecolab to offer fleet cleaning products and solutions to its current customer base.

The sale of Jackson. After purchasing Jackson Manuracturing in 1994, Ecolab sold its Jackson dish-machine manufacturing business in

November 2000 for about $36 million in cash.   This divestiture yielded a great return on the initial Jackson investment.

The acquisition of the Henkel joint venture. The most notable move Ecolab made was its 1991 fifty-fifty joint venture with Henkel, which enabled Ecolab and Henkel to share revenue by expanding Ecolab's product lines in Europe. Funding and resources were split between the companies. Ecolab's European presence grew from $150 million to $750 million by means of this joint venture.   In 2001, Ecolab acquired the remaining 50 percent interest in the joint venture from the Henkel Group for 485 million euros.

Strengthening pest elimination. Since 2001, Ecolab had invested in the growth of its Pest Elimination division by acquiring four global companies. This division provided customers with detection, identification, and guaranteed elimination of pests as part of the company's circle the customer strategy. In 2001, Ecolab bought Microbiotecnica, a Brazilian pest-elimination company with annual sales of $3 million. In 2002, it purchased Terminix Limited, a company in the United Kingdom with annual sales of $65 million.   In 2004, it bought Nigiko of France and Elimco of South Africa, companies with annual sales of $55 million and $4 million, respectively.

Evaluating its acquisitions. Ecolab evaluated its mergers, acquisitions, and divestitures from financial, competitive, and strategic perspectives.

- *Financial:* From a financial perspective, like many large corporations, Ecolab established hurdle rates for return on investment. The acquisition was examined with respect to how well the new business product or service would perform, as well as the opportunity it afforded to cross-sell current products or services.
- *Competitive:* From a competitive standpoint, Ecolab evaluated acquisitions based on their ability to reduce competitive threats. The acquisitions were assessed based on the degree to which they increased overall barriers to entry into customer accounts.
- *Strategic:* Strategically, Ecolab looked at acquisitions as an opportunity to expand the "circle the customer, circle the globe" strategy. Many small and unique businesses, it thought, would benefit from its global distribution and service network.

Ecolab also did remarkably well in integrating its culture into each acquisition.

A strong sales force. Ecolab's main strength was a strong, energetic, and motivated sales force. It had over 11,000 sales and service personnel (see Table 8.5). The company painstakingly trained its sales force, including the international salespeople, and made them a part of its culture.

The average compensation of a salesperson at Ecolab was between $40,000 and $50,000 per year with as much as 50 percent coming in commissions and incentive bonuses. Salespeople won additional fees for referrals and cross-selling.

The success of the "circle the customer, circle the globe" strategy depended on the ability of the sales force to sell more goods and services to existing customers and to bring new customers into the firm.

In 2003, Ecolab had annual sales of $3.8 billion and marketing personnel throughout the world who sold to customers in hotels and restaurants; healthcare and educational facilities; quick-service (fast-food and convenience stores) units; grocery stores; commercial and institutional laundries; the lighting industry; dairy plants and farms; food and beverage processing; pharmaceutical and cosmetic facilities; and the vehicle wash industry.

Ecolab's divisions. Ecolab's core and largest business was considered its Institutional division. It supported the cleaning and sanitation needs

TABLE 8.5   Ecolab's sales force: By division

Sales/service associates by division	2003 head count
Institutional	3,190
Kay	275
Pest Elimination	1,645
Professional Products	180
GCS Services	535
Textile Care	80
Food & Beverage	405
Water Care Services	95
Vehicle Care	100
Europe/Africa/Middle East	3,285
Asia Pacific	1,015
Canada	340
Latin America	540
Total	11,685

Source: Ecolab 2003 Annual Report.

of the foodservice and hospitality markets. The Professional Products division served the floor care and janitorial markets.

The GCS Service division was a pillar of the circle-the-customer strategy. It provided repair, maintenance, and parts distribution for the foodservice and healthcare markets. To capture laundry revenue not generated on the premises of hotels and healthcare facilities, Ecolab's Textile Care division focused on products for large commercial laundries. The focus of Ecolab's Food and Beverage division was markets including dairy, food and beverage processing, and dairy agricultural and pharmaceutical markets. The Water Care Services division provided unique products and advanced dispensing systems for customers' water treatment needs. Ecolab's Vehicle-Care division served a wide range of vehicles from passenger cars and trucks to commercial tractor-trailers with conveyor, in-bay, and self-service car washes.

JohnsonDiversey's (JDI's) history

JohnsonDiversey, Inc. (JDI) was formed in 2002 when JohnsonDiversey Holdings (then named S. C. Johnson Commercial Markets, Inc.) acquired the assets and equity interests of the DiverseyLever business. At the time, DiverseyLever was the institutional and industrial cleaning and sanitation business of Conopco, Inc., a subsidiary of Unilever (see Figure 8.4).

Unilever received a net cash payment of about $1 billion in various currencies, a one-third party interest in Holdings, and outstanding notes of about $241 million for DiverseyLever. To finance this purchase, JDI sold about $506 million of its 9.625 percent debt due in 2012. With JDI's subsidiaries and Holdings as guarantors, JDI took out three new term loans totaling $900 million and two revolving credit lines for about $300 million.

JDI postioned itself as a serious contender in the institutional and industrial market.

Acquisitions and divestitures. JohnsonDiversey made a number of acquisitions and divestitures after it was formed (see Table 8.6). In October 2003, it acquired assets of Southwest Auto-Chlor System, an Austin, Texas-based business that sold dishwashing, laundry, housekeeping, and kitchen products to the foodservice sector. In November 2003, it acquired the remaining shares of Daisan Kogyo Co., Ltd, which was "Japan's leading provider of commercial cleaning products and services to the food and beverage industry."

In June 2004, JohnsonDiversey sold its Whitmire Micro-Gen busi-

FIGURE 8.4   The creation of JohnsonDiversey

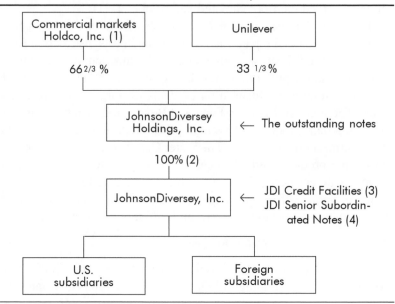

Source: JohnsonDiversey 2003 Annual Report.

ness, which manufactured and sold insecticides and equipment to the professional pest-management industry in the U.S. market. In selling this division, the company said that making pest-elimination products was no longer part of its corporate focus.

JohnsonDiversey's divisions

In 2003, JohnsonDiversey was made up of two main divisions: JohsonDiversey Professional and JohnDiversey Polymer.

TABLE 8.6   JohnsonDiversey acquisitions and divestitures

2003	JohnsonDiversey acquired certain net assets of Southwest Auto-Chlor System L.P., an Austin, Texas based business that markets and sells low-energy dishwashing systems, kitchen chemicals, laundry and housekeeping products and services to foodservice, lodging, healthcare, and institutional customers.
2003	JohnsonDiversey acquired 50.1 percent of the outstanding shares of Daisan Kogyo Co., Ltd. ("Daisan"), Japan's leading provider of commercial cleaning products and services to the food and beverage industry.
2004	JohnsonDiversey sold Whitmore Micro-Gen, which manufactured and sold insecticides and equipment to the pest-management industry in the U.S. market.

JohnsonDiversey Professional. The Professional division, which was by far the largest, marketed and manufactured cleaning, hygiene, and appearance products, and related services.[5] This division supplied foodservice, food processing, floor care, restroom and other house-keeping, laundry, and industrial products to a diverse group of end users, including food and lodging establishments, food-processing facilities, building service contractors, educational institutions, retail outlets, healthcare facilities, industrial plants, and governmental and other facilities. In addition, the Professional division provided a wide range of value-added services, including safety and application training, safety and hygiene consulting, and hygiene auditing.

JohnsonDiversey sold its professional products and related services globally to a broad range of customers in diverse industries, including companies such as Coca-Cola, Heineken, Hilton hotels, McDonald's, Royal Ahold, and Wal-Mart.

JohnsonDiversey Polymer. The Polymer division supplied environmentally compliant, water-based acrylic polymer resins to the industrial printing and packaging, coatings, and plastics markets.[6] Polymer resins worked within inks, paints, and floor coatings to disperse or carry colorants. They provided adhesion to the material being coated, protected the surface of the material, and resulted in a glossy finish. JohnsonDiversey sold these resins globally to customers such as Flint Ink Corporation, INX International Ink Co., and Sun Chemical Corporation.

JohnsonDiversey's commitments. JohnsonDiversey started via its acquisition of DiverseyLever. The size of the initial acquisition forced a substantial amount of long-term debt on the company, which limited its operating options.[7] The success of the acquisition ultimately would determine whether JohnsonDiversey could pay back these loans. Success for JohnsonDiversey depended more on branding, advertising,

---

5. JohnsonDiversey Professional had net sales of about $2.6 billion and a net loss of about $6.1 million for the 12 months ending in October 2003.

6. JohnsonDiversey Polymer had net sales of about $282.0 million and net income of about $14.6 million for the 12 months ending in October 2003.

7. The debt limited it from borrowing money or issuing preferred stock; paying dividends on, redeeming or repurchasing capital stock; making various investments; merging or consolidating with another company; and entering into various transactions with affiliates.

and merchandising than it did for Ecolab, whose success depended more on service.

JohnsonDiversey's sales and service force was only a fraction the size of Ecolab's.[8] Its approach therefore had to rely more on technology than did Ecolab's. Thus, it spent more than Ecolab on R&D, even though it was much more heavily in debt.

JohnsonDiversey had to accelerate product and solution innovation with new business models. It had to rely on efficient networking. The company had to implement and support a cost-effective infrastructure. Doing so meant the use of strategic IT systems, greater reliance on customer partnering, and a huge emphasis on staff productivity. One of JohnsonDiversey's main values was environmental leadership, which it also had to support. Doing all this was a great challenge.

Leadership

Leadership would largely determine which company would prevail. Both companies had relatively new people at the top. The future of each company would be determined by where these people took the companies. Both companies relied on mergers, acquisitions, and divestitures. Both were global in scope. The global economy had a huge impact on their performance. How would the leaders of these companies respond to these challenges?

Ecolab's corporate leaders had a culture of commitment to the customer and performing above expectations. The new CEO, Doug Baker, had worked in Institutional Marketing, Kay Chemical, and in Europe. His international experience was an example of Ecolab's increasing focus on global markets. Steve Newlin became the president of Ecolab's Industrial Sector in 2003. Previously he had been president and chief operating officer of the Nalco Co., where he spent 23 years in a variety of management positions. He had responsibility for Ecolab's North American Pest Elimination, Food & Beverage, Healthcare, Water Care Services, Vehicle Care, and Textile Care divisions. Tom Handley joined Ecolab as executive vice president, Specialty Sector. He bore the responsibility for Kay, Professional Products North America, and the GCS Services division. Handley had worked at Procter & Gamble

---

8. Ecolab had approximately three to five times as many institutional sales and service representatives in North America as JohnsonDiversey, which allowed Ecolab to offer more in-depth client training, more frequent customer visits, and faster response times to emergencies. Ecolab was supposed to dominate in the level of service.

for 22 years, where he held positions in marketing, general management, and strategic planning.

Ecolab's leaders were all professional managers. In contrast, S. Curtis Johnson III, the chairman of JohnsonDiversey, was a family member who directed a privately-held company. Johnson had been chairman of Commercial Markets Holdco. He had worked his entire life in family-held companies. He joined S. C. Johnson & Son in 1983 and became a general partner of Wind Point Partners, a $126 million venture capital partnership, which he cofounded and in which S. C. Johnson & Son was a major limited partner. Johnson also served as vice president for Global Business Development for S. C. Johnson & Son from 1994 to 1996, was vice president and managing director of Mexican Johnson, and a director of Worldwide Business. His experience in international business was extensive.

While Johnson was a family member, his top lieutenants were professional managers, not that much different from the top people at Ecolab. Prior to joining JDI, President and Chief Executive Officer Gregory E. Lawton had been president of NuTone, a supplier of residential ventilation products and electronics, and Michael J. Bailey, the chief financial officer (CFO) had been CFO of Standard Motor Products, a large manufacturer and distributor of automotive replacement parts. Both had worked with S. Curtis Johnson III for a number of years in Commercial Markets Holdco.

What to Do Next?

The main question confronting the corporate leaders at Ecolab and JohnsonDiversey was what to do next. As they battled to become the number-one supplier to the I&I industry, what would be the major factor in determining the winner? One question they had to consider was aquisitions. Would the acquisition of new businesses provide opportunities? What types of acquisitions did the companies need to make? What types of divestitures should they engage in? JohnsonDiversey's debt load precluded it from making necessary moves, but its connection to the S. C. Johnson consumer line was a decisive strength.

The global reach of the two companies was critically important as was the progress of the global economy. The industry in which they participated was closely tied to world economic conditions. Innovation would play a role. The leaders of both firms had to consider what role it would play.

Questions for Discussion

1. Does the fact that JohnsonDiversey was a privately held company have an effect on the two companies? What is that effect, if any?

2. Does JohnsonDiversey's high level of debt impede the moves it can make? Does the debt substantially limit its freedom of action?

3. Given its high level of debt, why was JohnsonDiversey spending more on R&D than Ecolab?

4. How valuable was it to have a high market share in an industry as diverse as I&I?

5. Which part of the industry was more attractive—janitorial and housekeeping or foodservices? Why?

6. Why were switching costs so high in foodservices?

7. What threat did regional competitors pose to JohnsonDiversey and Ecolab?

8. What gave Ecolab a strong competitive position in national accounts?

9. What were some of the major obstacles both companies faced in achieving increased market share in the global market? How valuable was the global market? How much would you invest in the global market (on a comparative basis) if you were JohnsonDiversey? How much if you were Ecolab?

10. How was Ecolab dealing with the global challenges? What did its slogan about circle the globe and the customer really mean? Why would it be successful globally using this strategy?

11. What strengths and weaknesses did JohnsonDiversey have in global competition?

12. What role had mergers and acquisitions (M&As) played in Ecolab's development? What role had divestitures played?

13. Why was the joint venture with Henkel so important?

14. Why do you think Ecolab was concentrating on the pest-elimination service business? Is this really an attractive business? Why had JohnsonDiversey exited the pest-manufacturing business instead of adding a service business to compete with Ecolab? What differences between the pest-elimination service and the pest-manufacturing business makes one more appealing than the other for two such similar firms?

15. What do you think of Ecolab's method of evaluating M&As?

16. Compare the relative strengths and weaknesses of the top execu-

tives of the two companies. Which company was better suited for winning in the I&I business? On which company would you bet your money? Why?

Exercises

1. Ecolab's success depends on how its executive team manages its existing holdings and decides to grow or contract via mergers, acquisitions, and divestitures. In light of the threat posed by the newly constituted JohnsonDiversey, what should the executive team do?

2. JohnsonDiversey may be in the unique position of having the ability to challenge Ecolab, but its executive team has loaded it down with so much debt that it might not have the time or latitude to make a sustained advance. How should JohnsonDiversey manage its existing holdings and grow or contract its business via mergers, acquisitions, and divestitures?

Bibliography

Boynick, B., and V. Kollonitsch. *Food Service Cleaning Products USA, 2000.* Kline & Company, Inc., 2000.

Ecolab. "Celebrating 75 Years." *Ecolab Inc.* January 1999.

_____. "2003 Annual Report." February 4, 2003.

_____. "Ecolab Inc. at Deutsche Bank Securities Inc. Global Services Conference." (http://www.ecolab.com). September 13, 2004.

Freedonia Group. "Industrial & Institutional Cleaning Chemicals—Market Size, Market Share, Demand Forecast, Sales, Company Profiles, Market Research, Industry Trends." (http://www.freedoniagroup.com). April 2000.

JohnsonDiversey. "2003 Annual Report." March 25, 2003.

_____. "Honson Holdings Inc. Senior Debt Notes Due 2013." Exchange offer. January 12, 2004.

Juvekar, P., and W. Gambardella. "ECL: We See a Great Defensive Growth Story." Citigroup Smith Barney. October 2003.

Simpson, B., and P. Elgrably. "Ecolab Inc. Leading Service Franchise in Cleaning and Sanitizing." William Blair & Company, LLC. April 2003.

CASE 9

Innovating
Monsanto versus DuPont[1]

This case examines why the need to apply biotechnology to agriculture originally arose and how Monsanto and DuPont became involved. Given the opposition that exists to this technology, the case asks what these companies should do next.

Monsanto and DuPont had seen a weakening in their revenues and profits (see Table 9.1). They were spending less on R&D and were not doing as well as competitors that were less committed to biotech (see Table 9.2).

With the Internet filled with sites such as MonsantoSucks and with references to MonSatan, Greenpeace urged both companies to give up biotech and embrace organic farming. How should these companies react? How should they cope with the situation they faced?

The Demand for Food

Demand for grains and other food was expected to increase by 40 percent by the year 2020. Since 1953, when James Watson and Francis Crick discovered the structure of the DNA that carries the information cells need to build proteins, scientists had generated detailed maps of the genes of hundreds of organisms and the data-analyzing capabilities to understand and use them.

Genetic modification is a special set of technologies that alter the makeup of living organisms including animals, plants, and bacteria.[2] In the late 1990s, Monsanto and DuPont made a serious commitment to

---

1. This case was written by Alfred Marcus, University of Minnesota, Carlson School of Management. Copyright © 2005 by Marsh Publications LLC. All rights reserved.

2. Scientists cut bits of DNA from one cell and splice them into another to make genetically modified products. When insulin started to be made this way in 1983, this method became an accepted practice in medicine. Biotechnology, a more general term, refers to using living organisms or their components to make products. Current products or products in the pipeline include vaccines, foods, food ingredients, feeds, fibers, and medicines.

using this technology to bring genetically modified (GM) foods to the market.

TABLE 9.1   A comparison of Monsanto and DuPont's income statements: 1999–2002 (in millions of U.S. dollars except for per-share items)

Monsanto	12 months ending 12/31/02	12 months ending 12/31/01	12 months ending 12/31/00	12 months ending 12/31/99
Total revenue	4,673	5,462	5,493	5,248
Cost of revenue	2,493	2,817	2,770	2,556
Gross profit	2,180	2,645	2,723	2,692
Research & development	527	560	588	695
Total operating expense	4,354	4,803	4,926	4,638
Operating income	319	659	567	610

DuPont	12 months ending 12/31/02	12 months ending 12/31/01	12 months ending 12/31/00	12 months ending 12/31/99
Total revenue	24,522	25,370	29,202	27,892
Cost of revenue	16,159	16,727	18,207	16,991
Gross profit	7,847	7,999	10,061	9,927
Research & development	1,264	1,588	1,776	1,617
Total operating expense	22,398	18,526	25,755	26,202
Operating income	2,124	6,844	3,447	1,690

Source: Yahoo! Finance (http://finance.yahoo.com).

TABLE 9.2   DuPont, Monsanto, and competitors: January 2003

	Dupont	Monsanto	BASF AG	Dow
Market cap ($ billion)	45.4	7.5	31.4	37.9
Employees	79,000	13,200	88,728	49,959
Revenue growth (%)	-3.30	-27.80	16.90	-0.70
Revenue ($ billion)	24.5	3.4	34.1	27.6
Operating margins (%)	1.62	13.13	8.02	2.27
Net income ($ billion)	.71	.05	1.2	1.0

Source: Yahoo! Finance (http://finance.yahoo.com).

GM crops were grown commercially or in field trials in over 40 countries on more than 100 million acres.[3] The principal ones were

---

3. In 2000, the countries that grew 99 percent of the GM crops were the United States (68 percent), Argentina (23 percent), Canada (7 percent), and China (1 percent).

TABLE 9.3   GM products: Benefits and controversies

Benefits	Controversies
Crops	Safety
Enhanced taste and quality	Unintended transfer of genes
Reduced maturation time	through cross-pollination
Increased nutrients, yields, and	
stress tolerance	Ethics
Greater resistance to disease, pests,	Mixing of genes from species to
and herbicides	species
New products and growing	
techniques	Labeling
	Should it be mandatory?
Animals	
Increased resistance, productivity,	Access & intellectual property
hardiness, and feed efficiency	Need to protect intellectual
Better yields of meat, eggs, and milk	property rights of developers while
Improved animal health and	at the same time providing access
diagnostic methods	to farmers in developing countries
	who are most in need
Environment	
Reduced use of herbicides,	
insecticides, and fungicides	
Conservation of soil, water, and	
energy	
Society	
Increased food security for growing	
populations	

herbicide- and insecticide-resistant soybeans, corn, cotton, and canola.[4]

Technologies for GM foods offered dramatic promise for meeting some of the twenty-first century's 21st centuries' greatest challenges, but like all new technologies, they posed various risks. Controversies surrounding GM foods and crops focused on human and environmental safety, ethics, labeling, access, and intellectual property rights (see Table 9.3).

The green revolution. In 1970, Norman Borlaug won the Nobel Prize for work in high-yield agriculture that allowed farmers to obtain more

---

4. Others grown commercially or being field tested were a sweet potato resistant to a virus that can decimate the African harvest, rice with enough increased iron and vitamins to alleviate malnutrition in Asia, and a variety of plants that were able to survive weather extremes. On the horizon were bananas that produced human vaccines against infectious diseases such as hepatitis B, fish that developed more quickly, fruit and nut trees that matured years earlier, and plants that might be able to produce feedstock for plastics.

food from the same amount of land or less. Among his accomplishments were "shuttle breeding," which sped immunity between strains of crops, and the perfection of dwarf spring wheat—stout short-stalked kernels that expended less energy growing inedible sections and more growing valuable grain.

The "green revolution" that Borlaug inaugurated increased yields throughout the world. Largely because of it, Pakistan became self-sufficient in food production in 1968 and India in 1974.[5] India, indeed, became the world's second largest producer of wheat and rice.

In 1950, the world required 1.7 billion acres to grow 692 million tons of grain to feed 2.2 billion people. In 1992, total acreage was virtually the same (1.73 billion acres) but the world was growing almost three times as much food (1.9 billion tons of grain) to feed more than twice the number of people (5.6 billion).

As global grain yields shot up from .45 tons per acre to 1.1 tons per acre, average daily per-capita calorie intake grew from 2,063 calories to 2,495 by the year 2000. Malnutrition, still a problem, was reduced. The greater crop yields per acre meant that less deforestation was occurring to open up new land for farming.

Decline in crop yield growth. However, since the 1980s, crop yield growth had started to decline. The world's population was increasing by 73 million persons per year. By the year 2020, analysts projected that there would be 7.5 billion people living on the planet and that world demand for rice, wheat, and maize would increase by 40 percent.

The high-yield crops, which Borlaug and his colleagues created, did not prosper without fertilizers. In some regions of the world, farmers found it difficult to get access to the fertilizer and other chemicals needed to grow crops. Water for irrigation was becoming scarce and there had been substantial depletion of the water table. Soil salinity and erosion had resulted in a loss of arable land, a 15 percent decline since the late 1970s.

Increasingly, scientists thought that genetic engineering would be needed to improve crop yields. If scientists could use biotechnology to code plants against insects so that farmers would not have to spray, this would be a real boon. Scientists might be able to devise plants that could survive in salty soil and dry conditions.

---

5. Pakistan went from 3.4 million tons of wheat grown annually to 18 million, and India from 11 million tons to 60 million. Dwarf rice yields in China were 1.6 tons per acre, close to the world's best of 2.0.

With genetically modified organisms (GMOs), it might be possible to pack more protein and minerals into grains as well as making them more pest resistant. The potential existed to add input traits to crops that would make farmers more productive by reducing the need for pesticides and fertilizers. In addition, farmers could potentially add quality traits such as better taste or more nutrition that made for higher-quality food.

Monsanto Turns to Biotechnology

Monsanto was not new to controversy.[6] Some of the products with which it has been associated over the years were saccharin, aspirin, fertilizers, carpets, PCBs, dioxin, and the defoliant Agent Orange.

In 1995, Monsanto had 20,000 employees., Robert Shapiro, who became CEO that year, wanted to transform the company into a biotechnology powerhouse. In a 1996 interview in the *Harvard Business Review*,[7] he articulated a vision for a world that was entering into a period of "unprecedented discontinuity" for which business had to plan with "cold and rational logic." The discontinuity existed because of population growth. By about 2030, the world's population would approach 10 billion people, and there would be almost twice as many mouths to feed.

With about a quarter of the world's population living in "abject poverty" in 1996, and as many as 800,000 people malnourished, Shapiro believed that feeding additional people on the planet would be an immense challenge. The only way out of the dilemma was to obtain additional productivity from each acre of soil that was harvested.

Monsanto's role would be to create more value without using more "stuff." The idea was to use intellectual capital to replace physical cap-

6. Founded in St. Louis in 1901, Monsanto describes itself as "a leading provider of agricultural products and integrated solutions for farmers." It portrays itself as follows on its Website: "We make Roundup®, the world's best-selling herbicide, and other herbicides. We produce leading seed brands, including DEKALB® and Asgrow®, and we provide farmers and other seed companies with biotechnology traits for insect protection and herbicide tolerance. With our unique combination of products and our unparalleled innovation in plant biotechnology, we create integrated solutions that bring products and technologies together to improve productivity and to reduce the costs of farming. We manage our business in two segments: Agricultural Productivity, and Seeds and Genomics. Our Agricultural Productivity segment includes Roundup® and other herbicides, our lawn-and garden herbicide business, and our animal agriculture business. The Seeds and Genomics segment consists of global businesses in seeds and related biotechnology traits, and technology platforms based on plant genomics, which increases the speed and power of genetic research" (http://www.monsanto.com).

7. Robert Shapiro, "Growth through Sustainability," *Harvard Business Review,* January-February 1997, p. 82

ital. Genetic modification would enable human beings to increase soil yields with fewer inputs.

Farmers had always saved the seeds of plants that lasted, looked better, tasted sweeter, and grew more vigorously. If the cross-pollinating of plants to create more robust hybrids was common, it did not make sense to accelerate this process by shooting snippets of DNA into plant walls with a tungsten-coated gene gun.

Innovation from the bottom up. Under the previous CEO, Richard Mahoney, Monsanto had assembled a high-quality group of molecular biologists, who had started to develop the ability to transplant DNA from organisms such as bacteria into plants to make plants hardier, better tasting, higher yielding, and more resistant to pests and disease.

Monsanto had a series of off-site meetings in the early 1990s that brought together critical thinkers in the company, about 80 employees who formulated a new approach for appraising environmental issues. Eventually about 140 employees took part. They organized themselves into seven "sustainability" teams, three concerned with enhancing productivity, three concerned with new-product development, and one concerned with communication. The "eco-efficiency" team was devoted to measuring and optimizing raw material use. The "full-cost accounting" team's mission was to take into account full environmental costs during the product life cycle. The "index" team was committed to establishing metrics to balance economic, social, and environmental factors.

There was also a general "new product development" team, a team devoted to meeting global water needs, and a team dedicated to solving the problem of world hunger. The final team communicated the vision to Monsanto's employees and offered them a role to play. These employees created a contagious bottom-up movement in the company. The following are some of the examples of what Monsanto accomplished:

- The *NewLeaf potato,* which Monsanto scientists had bioengineered to protect itself against a destructive beetle, was capable of eliminating the manufacture and application of millions of tons of potent pesticides made from oil-based raw materials. The pesticides typically were sprayed from the air with less than 5 percent actually coming into contact with target insects. The rest were toxic wastes that sat for long periods of time in an inert and hard-to-break-down form in the soil.

- *Bt corn* was being modified with the bacterium *bacillus thurungien-sus* (Bt). Naturally found in the earth, Bt made a poison that harmed the digestive tracts of various pests but did not hurt other living things. Organic farmers had used it for decades. Rachel Carson, the environmentalist who created the modern movement with her best-selling book, *Silent Spring,* had been a proponent of its use. The problem was that when Bt was applied manually, it decomposed in sunlight and washed away in rain. A far better idea was to insert Bt genes in a plant, thus protecting the Bt and making its use more effective. Bt cotton, which Monsanto scientists had bioengineered, repelled a destructive budworm that otherwise had to be destroyed by spraying. It eliminated the 10-to-12 times each growing season that farmers had to spray cotton, reduced risk, and left no poisons in fragile ecosystems.
- Monsanto scientists had also devised corn, soybean, and canola seeds that made crops that did not perish when they were exposed to Roundup herbicide. Farmers, therefore, did not have to plow to eliminate weeds left from the prior year's harvest before planting, thus ensuring that there would be less topsoil erosion. After the new plants sprouted, the farmers again could spray without having to worry about a herbicide killing their crops.

Acquisitions, joint ventures, and partnerships. To further enhance its biotech capabilities, Monsanto spent $8 billion on a series of acquisitions, joint ventures, and partnerships. In 1996, it bought Calgene for $50 million because the company had developed a gene for a slow-ripening tomato. In the same year, it bought DeKalb Genetics for $160 million, because of the corn seeds DeKalb was creating. In 1997, it bought Holden Foundation Seeds for $945 million because of the company's seed-marketing and sales capabilities. In 1998, it bought Cargill's international seed operations for $1.4 billion for this reason.

These acquisitions gave Monsanto the ability to both manufacture and market genetically enhanced seeds. Thus, Monsanto, which was the first on the market with the new seeds, moved to the top spot among companies in agricultural biotechnology. In 1997, 14 of the 24 genetically engineered seeds approved by U.S. regulatory agencies in the prior two years belonged to Monsanto or its partners.

In addition, Monsanto formed a joint venture with Cargill called Renessen for the purpose of creating and marketing new products using biotechnology. This joint venture focused on enhancing the quality of animal feeds made from corn, soybeans, and canola. Renessen's goal was to increase the amino acid levels in the feed and thereby diminish the need for artificial enhancement.

Monsanto's life sciences division was growing three times faster than the rest of the company, so in 1997, Shapiro decided to spin off the company's slower-growing commodity and specialty chemicals operation to shareholders as a separate concern. The new firm was called Solutia and had $3 billion in revenues.

Monsanto used the proceeds from the divestiture to buy additional companies such as Ecogen, Inc. with its large library of Bt genes, Synteri, which had access to gene expression analysis technology, Millenium Pharmaceuticals developers of genetic markers for corn and soybeans, and Mendel Biotechnology, which also had technical capabilities in agricultural genomics.

After the spin-off, Monsanto had three remaining divisions, which had annual revenues of about $7 billion (see Table 9.4). These divisions were agriculture, with about half of the company's revenues; pharmaceuticals, from the company's G. D. Searle subsidiary, with about a third of the company's revenues; and food products, dominated by the artificial sweetener NutraSweet, which made up about 20 percent of the company's revenues.

Paying for the changes. To pay for the changes, Monsanto was relying on the herbicide Roundup as its cash cow. Roundup had revenues of over $2 billion in 1998 and it was providing about 40 percent of the company's total operating income.

For the future, Celebrex, an arthritis drug that Searle made, was showing considerable promise, but ultimately, Monsanto's aim was to dominate in GMOs.

The path Shapiro set was for Monsanto to remake itself as a "life sci-

TABLE 9.4   Monsanto's three main divisions after the spin-off of Solutia

Monsanto	1997 net sales (bill $)	1997 operating income (bill $)	1996 net sales (bill $)	1996 operating income (bill $)	1995 net sales (bill $)	1995 operating income (bill $)
Agriculture	3.1	.11	2.5	.52	2.1	.48
Pharmaceuticals	2.4	.32	2.0	.08	1.7	.13
Nutrition	1.5	.21	1.5	.19	1.4	.19
Company total	7.5	.5	6.3	.6	5.4	.7

Source: Monsanto 1998 Annual Report.

ences" enterprise, dedicated to improving the environment and human health by creating new food, drug, and combined food-drug (neutracitical) products. Monsanto's changes were well received. From 1994–1997, the firm's stock nearly tripled in value. Shapiro believed that the company would continue to do very well if it could rapidly introduce environmentally advanced products that people wanted into the marketplace.

The food-drug combinations were especially promising. One day, it might be possible to put a vaccine for hepatitis B and for diarrhea into the cells of a banana. The advantages in countries short on refrigerators, sterile needles, and hygiene were immense. Another possibility was incorporating vitamin A into rice and thus reducing or eliminating the problems of millions of children worldwide who lose their eyesight or die from infections caused by vitamin A deficiencies.

DuPont Turns to Biotechnology

In 1997, DuPont was the world's largest chemical producer with sales of $46.7 billion, profits of $2.4 billion, and 98,000 employees.[8] Not to be outdone by Monsanto, it made a similar turn to biotechnology under newly appointed CEO Chad Holliday. On becoming CEO in 1998, Holliday announced that the company would cut back capital for its chemical businesses and make life sciences "the centerpiece." Life sciences had the highest margins of any of DuPont's businesses (see Table 9.5).

Holliday was aware of the successful turnaround carried out by Shapiro and decided that DuPont also had to bet its future on biotech. He was trying to execute a complex corporate transformation, changing the 197-year-old company from a highly regarded, but humdrum chemical concern, into a leading edge bioengineering corporation.

In 1999, a cyclical downturn in commodity chemicals combined with a decline in sales in Asia to mar the company's earnings. The

---

8. On its Website DuPont describes itself as follows: "DuPont is a science company. We put science to work solving problems in ways that make life better and safer. When we were founded in 1802, DuPont was primarily an explosives company. One hundred years ago, our focus turned to chemicals, materials and energy. Today, we deliver science-based solutions that make real differences in people's lives around the world in areas such as food and nutrition, health care, apparel, safety and security, construction, electronics and transportation . . . Our ability to adapt to change and our foundation of unending scientific inquiry has enabled DuPont to become one of the world's most innovative companies. But, in the face of constant change, innovation and discovery, our core values have remained constant: commitment to safety, health and the environment; integrity and high ethical standards; and treating people with fairness and respect." (http://www.dupont.com)

TABLE 9.5   Sales and margins of DuPont's businesses: 1996–1999

	1999 net sales (bill $)	1999 operating margins	1998 net sales (bill $)	1998 operating margins	1997 net sales (bill $)	1997 operating margins	1996 net sales (bill $)	1996 operating margins
Petroleum (Conoco)	19.7	4	19.3	4.0	20.9	5.1	20.1	4.3
Diversified (e.g., Polyester)	3	16	2.9	16.5	2.8	nil	3.1	16.5
Chemicals (e.g., Suva refrigerants)	4.5	14.5	4.5	13.5	4.3	14.2	4.1	13.6
Polymers (e.g., Teflon)	7.1	12.1	7	13.5	6.8	13.5	6.7	13.6
Fibers (e.g., Nylon, Lycra, and Kevlar)	8.1	12	8.0	11.5	7.7	13.5	7.2	11.1
Life sciences (prior to Pioneer purchase)	4.5	14.5	4.4	13.5	4.3	14.1	4.1	18.6
Company total	45.4	9.5	44.5	9.1	45.1	9.2	43.8	9.2

Source: DuPont Annual Report, 2000.

stock fell from a 12-month high of more than $80 per share to under $60, an event that only reinforced Holliday's conviction that he had to remake the company.

DuPont's entry into biotech was late compared to Monsanto, and its approach was somewhat different. Rather than selling off its mature businesses (nylon and polyester) right away, as Monsanto did when it sold its commodity and specialty chemicals, DuPont intended to use the surplus cash from these businesses to fund genetic research.

Besides emphasizing such applications as agricultural, pharmaceuticals, food, and health, as Monsanto did, Holliday had hopes that biotech could replace polymer chemicals as a feedstock for DuPont products.

Holliday believed that in the future the company would be relying less on petrochemicals for its raw materials and more on bioengineered crops. For such DuPont staples as polyester, auto paints, films, resins, and industrial chemicals, Holliday hoped that DuPont could use GMOs. If successful, the company would be less reliant on nonrenewable resources, whose prices fluctuated unpredictably, and more reliant on renewable resources that put less stress on the environment. In the meantime, DuPont had many biotech products to commercialize. The company could emulate and compete with Monsanto.

Restructuring. The transition to being a biotech leader would be a long one, but Holliday believed DuPont had to take this path. To show his commitment to biotech, Holliday made a number of important decisions. In 1981, DuPont had acquired Conoco, the world's 9th largest petroleum company. DuPont bought Conoco at the tail end of an oil shortage to secure a steady supply of raw materials. In 1998, it sold Conoco in the largest Initial Public Offering (IPO) for a U.S. company to that date.

In Conoco's place, DuPont spent $7.7 billion to buy the remaining 80 percent that it did not yet own of Pioneer Hi-Bred, the biggest seed maker in the world. This acquisition enabled Pioneer's research scientists to interact more freely with those of DuPont on gene technology.

To capitalize on the synergies available in pharmaceuticals and biotech, DuPont also spent $2.8 billion to buy Merck's share of a joint pharmaceutical venture. These acquisitions fortified DuPont in what was expected to be ongoing competition with Monsanto. They opened an array of possibilities—scientific discoveries in the workings of the gene, business opportunities for new markets, and the need for additional realignments and partnerships.

A history of innovation. Holliday maintained that moves of this type were not atypical for DuPont. After all, the company had switched from making gunpowder to chemicals at the end of the 19th century and had risen to prominence based on innovations developed in its labs such as nylon, Dacron, rayon, Teflon, Mylar, and Lycra.

Edgar Woolard, DuPont's CEO from 1989 to 1995, had paved the way for what Holliday was doing. Woolard had been an outspoken corporate environmentalist, who rose through the ranks to become vice president for environmental affairs. As CEO, Woolard had delivered many speeches about DuPont´s commitment to protecting the environment; and he had presided over the first "greening" of DuPont's portfolio, its voluntary exit from chlorflorocarbons (CFC) production in light of the controversy over ozone depletion, and its introduction of the SUVA brand of refrigerants and coolants, which were less harmful to the environment.

Under Holliday, the life sciences division became one of the fastest-growing and most profitable parts of the company. DuPont had promising research projects in the works that if successful would generate up to $25 billion in revenues and double the company's size by 2007. The projected after-tax margins of these projects were estimated to be 20 percent, about twice what the company was earning from its businesses in 1999.

A major player in crop protection. Like Monsanto, DuPont had become a major player in the crop-protection business. It manufactured herbicides, insecticides, and fungicides that farmers used to keep weeds, insects, and fungi at bay. This market was attractive because of the patenting needed, the proprietary knowledge on which it was based, and the high margins achievable once a product was under patent.

More than 60 percent of the market consisted of herbicides, another 25 percent insecticides, and about 10 percent fungicides. The remainder was miscellaneous. A company kept the strong position it acquired in a specific crop application for a long period of time. The research to achieve such a position usually was protracted and the risk was great; no more than 2 percent of chemicals tested were effective. The Environmental Protection Agency (EPA) supervised testing for safety and efficacy and the process, a very expensive one, could take more than five years to complete. After approval, a product's remaining patent life would be about 10 years.

DuPont had pursued the crop-protection market since the early 1980s, lured by the high potential margins and the research-intensive nature of the business. It purchased Shell's chemical protection business in 1986 and took its first steps in the life sciences shortly thereafter. In the late 1980s, it had fewer than 100 scientists engaged in biotech work at its central research department in Wilmington. The research was exploratory and was not being coordinated with crop protection. After executives came to the conclusion that biotech had commercial potential, they merged it with agricultural products. About half the scientists in biotech moved to the commercial side. Several patents were approved in the early 1990s, and DuPont established research agreements with other firms and academic staff at universities.

Like Monsanto, DuPont did field research on plants that were resistant to the weed killers it sold. In 1992, it marketed an herbicide that was resistant to tobacco seed through Northrup King. Other programs were underway to develop herbicide-resistant genes. Toward the end of the 1990s, most observers concluded that DuPont had the potential to compete with Monsanto.

Food research. Soybean research was very important at DuPont because the soybean was a ubiquitous product that was found in everything from baked products, to egg and meat alternatives, to animal feed. Scientists had produced a soybean that had 80 percent oleic acid content as opposed to the normal 24 percent. The oil from this soybean was more stable, cheaper to make, healthier, and tasted better. It added between $25 and $115 to the farmer's income for each acre grown.

At a Ralston Purina unit in St. Louis, Protein Technologies International (PTI), which DuPont acquired in 1997, was doing research to improve the taste and consistency of soybeans. PTI had cost DuPont $1.5 billion and next to Pioneer HiBred, was its most influential life sciences acquisition.

At its other labs, the company was working on both the input traits that would allow crops to withstand damage from pests and the output traits that would add to their taste, color, consistency, and nutritional content.

DuPont's executives were particularly enthusiastic about nutraceuticals. These potential health enhancers, increasingly called "functional foods," represented a market that could explode. Signs of change were already in grocery stores—calcium-fortified orange juice, herbal tea with antioxidants, and eggs with fish-derived fatty acids to help avert heart disease.

Many more foods of this nature were likely to be introduced. If, as research suggested, men with early prostate cancer could slow the disease's progress by eating soy-based foods, bioengineers might eventually be able to remove the genes that made the tumor-stopping chemicals and introduce them into wheat, corn, and other grains and in this way create a profusion of anticancer foods.

Predictability of the research. By 1997, 30 percent of DuPont's 10,000 research scientists were engaged in some form of life sciences work.[9] Breakthroughs seldom happened as planned, so the company was trying to put more predictability into the process. [10]

DuPont reviewed research projects to determine their commercial potential and when their results would be available. In 1997, DuPont

9. The remaining 70 percent were doing research in polymers, electronics and imaging, and other areas.

10. At Pioneer's headquarters in Des Moines, scientists were evaluating corn varieties that would improve yield and reduce disease. They were in the process of creating a new type of chicken feed that made the chickens taste better and reduced the smelly phosphorous content of the chicken manure. DuPont had been moving in these directions for a long time.

took an inventory: about 400 projects appeared to have the potential for commercial application. Many were complicated projects that drew on a variety of disciplines. The company chose 100 for further development.

From the most promising 100, DuPont made a list of the top 10. In the future, these projects would be among those on which the company would draw to create plants that could be grown for chemicals, which, for DuPont, was the ultimate prize.

Obstacles to Achieving the Vision

By 2001, more than 30,000 products were being sold that had been made from modified crops. These included soy sauce, bread, pasta, ice cream, candy, meats, and cornflakes. Worldwide, GM seeds had been planted on 74 percent of soybean acres, 76 percent of cotton acres, and 27 percent of corn acres. Monsanto protected corn-increased yields by an average number of bushels per acre.[11] It also had lower levels of fungal toxins, a possible human carcinogen.

DuPont and Monsanto had achieved many other successes, such as a genetically modified papaya that resisted the ring rot virus that had devastated the Hawaiiain crop. But no one at Monsanto or DuPont thought that going forward with additional innovation was going to be easy. A number of obstacles had emerged.

Cost. Both companies charged more for the protection their seeds offered. The justification for the higher price was that even a slight infestation by the corn borer could reduce yields.

Resistance in developing countries. In addition, farmers had to sign agreements that they would not resell the seeds, keep them without planting, or set them aside from one harvest to the next. Most U.S. farmers accepted these conditions without grumbling. They did not put up resistance as they were used to repurchasing their seeds every year. They had to buy new seeds because the hybrid seeds they used lost vitality if they came from last year's crop. However, farmers in developing countries counted on using last year's seeds for each year's new harvest. Implementing Monsanto's regime in developing countries therefore was going to be infinitely more difficult than in developed nations. Without a way to protect Monsanto's intellectual

---

11. The product was called YieldGard.

property, using GM seeds in developing nations was not going to happen.[12]

Warnings. Another obstacle was that from the start numerous scientists felt uncomfortable with GMO technology. The Union of Concerned Scientists (UCC) had issued working papers on strategies to counteract the potential "catastrophes" that could occur. One possibility raised was that pests, frustrated by new plant strains, eventually would adapt. Once they adapted, they would create a hazard that would be nearly impossible to control.

However, there was a clear solution to the specter of "super" pests. When growing GMO crops, Monsanto required that farmers create a "refuge" area—adjacent fields that were planted with nongenetically modified seeds of the same crop. Pests that grew resistant would mate with "regular" ones and the offspring would not be able to survive pesticide spraying.

Superweeds. In 1997, a Canadian farmer reported that some Roundup-ready seeds had "escaped" and mixed with a related species of weed on a field's edge. Suddenly, a "superweed" existed and appeared not to be controllable by conventional weed killers.

Monsanto retorted that the farmer had neglected the agreement he signed to establish a refuge area to prevent the transmission of genes from species to species. In the developed world, this threat was not large because similar weeds were rarely found next to most crops, but in the developing world, crops often had close relatives growing nearby.

Threats to human beings. Environmentalists said that they were uneasy about GMOs because of the tremendous rush to market them. In addition to what was known about GMOs, environmentalists were alarmed about possible unidentified threats. Testing done by environmental authorities could not pick up negative results affecting one in a million persons, but in a large enough population these effects could be serious. On these grounds, environmentalists raised issues

---

12. Even in the United States there was some opposition to the way Monsanto went about protecting its intellectual property. Farmers that used Roundup had to put up with unannounced audits to guarantee compliance. If caught violating the terms of their agreement, they could be fined by as much as $10,000. In 2003, a federal court in St. Louis awarded Monsanto $780,000 in a patent-infringement suit against a farmer who had saved seeds for planting next year. The devastated farmer faced bankruptcy because he had chosen to defy Monsanto.

about human consumption. They wanted the "precautionary principle" to be fully applied, that is, potential risks had to be given greater weight no matter how remote and how much greater the expected benefits.

The environmentalists picked up on a 1995 incident where Pioneer HiBred tried to splice together a Brazilian nut gene with a soybean. The purpose was to increase the level of the amino acids methionine and cystine and make the bean more nutritious for animal feed, but environmentalists pointed out that many people were allergic to the Brazil nuts and that these people might die if unbeknownst to them they consumed a soybean or soybean product with the spliced gene. Because of the pressure the incident generated, Pioneer HiBred had to abandon this project.

The monarch butterfly. In 1999, environmentalists publicized another incident. A Cornell University scientist's research showed that the eggs of the monarch butterfly would perish if exposed to the pollen of Bt-modified corn. In a laboratory study, the pollen destroyed three-day-old monarch larvae 44 percent of the time. Environmentalists claimed that these results provided definitive proof that GMOs were "deadly." Other scientists questioned these findings. They pointed out that it was just a lab study and they showed that in the field the Bt-infected pollen diminished rapidly a few meters outside the planting area and that pollination typically was complete before monarch butterflies fed. They also pointed to a simple antidote—the refuge area around a GMO field that manufacturers prescribed.

Terminator genes. Another controversy was brewing at almost the same time. In 1998, Delta & Pine Land Company, the biggest U.S. cottonseed producer, filed for a patent from the U.S. Department of Agriculture for a set of molecular switches that could turn genes off and on. Among the genes that the switches could manipulate were those for reproduction. The Canadian environmental organization Rural Advancement Foundation named the switches "terminator genes" after the mechanical murderer that Arnold Schwarzenegger portrayed in movies. The foundation claimed that the genes showed that biotech was an immoral technology synonymous with corporate greed. Biotech was a critical threat to poor people in the developing world for whom saving seeds was essential.

Monsanto, at the time, was in the midst of negotiations to acquire Delta & Pine. Monsanto stood to benefit from using the so-called terminator gene to protect its intellectual property. However, the terminator gene also had other uses such as solving the troublesome problem that GMO seeds might cross-pollinate with related species. Once a plant lost its ability to reproduce, there was little likelihood it would-transfer its genes elsewhere. The switches, in addition, could be used to turn on or off a variety of characteristics, such as the ability to fight drought, repel frost, protect the plant from the sun, or help the plant absorb the sun's rays. The switches ultimately would allow for "designer seeds," in which farmers would pay for precisely the traits they wanted.

The pressure on Monsanto to withdraw its offer to buy Delta & Pine was intense. Gordon Conway, an agricultural ecologist, who was head of the Rockefeller Foundation, and a supporter of GMOs, urged Monsanto to relent and give up on the gene. Though he believed that biotech would play a critical role in raising the level of prosperity in the developing world, Conway felt that Monsanto had best put this controversy behind it. Monsanto therefore withdrew its offer to buy Delta & Pine.

European opposition. Arguments made about the importance of GMOs for feeding the world's poor had little impact in Europe. The Europeans wanted their produce fresh, but genes that extended ripening times meant little because in developed countries refrigeration was common and inexpensive, and good roads to get produce to the market were everywhere. On the other hand, in developing countries, almost 40 percent of the fruit and vegetables rotted in fields and never got to market.

GMOs had the potential to address such issues as hunger and disease, but Europeans were neither hungry nor sick. Rather, they were fearful of new technologies that potentially tampered with the food supply after such incidents as an outbreak of mad-cow disease in Britain in 1996 and an attempted government cover-up of tainted eggs and chicken in Belguim in 2001.

GMOs were also a trade and diplomatic issue. They allowed the Europeans to seek protection of their domestic agriculture by other means. The European press portrayed companies like Monsanto as evil manipulators of nature who were creating grotesque frankenfoods that they were trying to shove down the throats of millions of unsuspecting people.

Labeling requirements. In 1997, the European Union (EU) issued a "novel food" directive that required labeling on all foods "containing," "consisting," or "derived from" GMOs. In addition to making labeling mandatory, the EU said that if there is still DNA or protein resulting from genetic modification present in a product, the product would be subject to labeling requirements.

The EU was insistent on recognizing the consumer's right to information and it used labeling as a tool for the consumer's right to make an informed choice.[13] Europe's opposition was important because it was the world's largest importer of soybeans. It accounted for 40 percent of soybean imports from all sources. Since the 1997 EU directive, there has been a virtual moratorium on the importation of new products that have GMOs into EU countries.

Other companies pull back. Because of the opposition in Europe, the Swiss pharmaceutical company, Novartis, and the British pharmaceutical, AstraZeneca, decided to combine their agricultural divisions and sell them. Under pressure, Novartis also stopped using genetically modified soy and corn in its Gerber baby food. CEO Daniel Vasella said: "We are not missionaries. We sell things. No company can prosper by telling customers what is good for them."[14]

In 1999, other large European companies—Unilever, Nestle, and Cadbury—announced they would no longer use GM products. Deutsche Bank told its clients not to invest in companies that were involved with GM products. In Italy, seed companies had to present a certificate to farm co-ops that said their products did not contain GMOs.

Everywhere in Europe, food processors, distributors, and supermarkets had to provide signed affidavits showing that their products were "biological," that is, not GMOs. Responding to this situation, food

---

13. David Byrne, the commissioner for health and consumer protection, in a 2002 speech to the European Parliament, suggested that the EU should require the mandatory labeling of food, food ingredients, and feed produced from a GMO even when the modified material is not directly detectable in the food, feed, or ingredient. The example Byrne gave was table oil that comes from GMO maize, soybeans, or rapeseed. Through the refinement process, all modified material is removed. Nonetheless, Byrne argued for labeling for the "purpose of informing consumers and users and allowing them to exercise choice."

14. See Michael Specter, "The Pharmageddon Riddle," *The New Yorker,* April 10, 2000.

retailers in Iceland and the U.K.'s Sainsbury decided to remove GM foods from their shelves.[15]

U.S. concerns. Generally, U.S consumers did not have the same attitudes as those found in the rest of world. But in 1999, the Food and Drug Administration (FDA) did hold a series of open meetings on the labeling issue based on survey results that showed that 70 percent of the U.S. public wanted some type of labeling. The problem with labeling, as these hearings demonstrated, was where it stopped. Products made from GM-derived grains had an extensive reach. Corn syrup and soy-based products were ubiquitous in the food chain; they were found nearly everywhere.

But the worldwide opposition to GMOs did not leave the United States. entirely unaffected. U.S. food manufacturers like Heinz and Frito Lay began to ask for non-GM products. Natural food chains refused to sell GM products, and McDonalds, while it purchased only non-GM potatoes, fried them in GM canola oil. In addition, Archer Daniels Midland (ADM) was starting to ask farmers to segregate modified crops and haul them to market in separate containers.

Has the Tide Shifted?

Was the opposition going too far? In 2002, six African nations devastated by drought refused U.S. food aid because the food had been genetically modified to resist pests. They did not accept the GM corn out of concern that Europe would reject their agricultural exports, which might become "contaminated" by the U.S. food. To many, the rejection of help was outrageous. Europe was heavily criticized for pushing its highly precautionary approach to GM crops onto poor countries.

The U.S. challenge to the EU. In 2003, the U.S. government formally challenged the EU's policies. U.S. Trade Representative Robert Zoellick argued that the EU moratorium was not only getting in the way of U.S. shipments of GM corn to the EU, but it was also preventing the spread of GM crop technologies to needy farmers in the developing world. The EU had created these restrictive policies despite a

15. Even China was showing signs of shifting from wanting to be the developing world's leader in biotech to fearing that it would lose key export markets in Europe and the rest of the world if it pushed ahead too quickly. Domestic consumers in China were beginning to indicate they would rather have food that had not been genetically modified.

2001 study done by its own research directorate that showed absolute-ly no added harm to humans or the environment from approved GM crops or foods.[16] Appendix A summarizes the outrage of Greenpeace's cofounder, Patrick Moore.

How should companies like Monsanto and DuPont deal with the public's fears? People were afraid of frozen foods when they were first introduced and tried to ban them. Advances like antibiotics and vac-cines were opposed because they entailed some risk. Aspirin continues to contribute to many diseases and deaths. The top managers at Monsanto and DuPont did not understand why they did so poorly in public relations battles. When asked, Shapiro said he was not a bully and if he was he was not a very successful one. But some Monsanto executives believed that Shapiro thought his job was to persuade, and that too often he had not been a good listener.

Whither Monsanto and Dow?

While the Dow Jones Industrial Average soared from 1998–2000, Monsanto's stock lost half its value. In 2000, the company combined with Pharmacia & Upjohn after talks to merge with AHP (now Wyeth Pharmaceuticals) broke down. It was rumored that Celebrex, Monsanto's arthritis drug, which might play a role in cancer preven-tion, was the sole reason Pharmacia made the deal; Monsanto's biotech's properties, it was thought, had very little value.

The "new" Monsanto. Pharmacia transferred all its agricultural assets and liabilities to a new company that went public in 2000. This com-

---

16. Charles Kessler and Ioannis Economidis, eds., *EC-sponsored Research on Genetically Modified Organisms: A Review of Results.* Brussels: Research Directorate-General, European Commission, 2001. Robert Paarlberg has written that European food safety regulators, "having under-regulated BSE, dioxin, and hoof and mouth disease," were "hoping to restore their credi-bility...by over-regulating GM foods." According to Paarlberg, the EU, "without any scientific evidence of risk," was going ahead with a tracing and labeling system that would "impose cost-ly new requirements on exporters." Mandatory labeling would extend to animal as well as human food, and even processed products where there was no longer any physically detectable GM con-tent. Paalberg asserted that "the biggest losers from a continued spread of European-style GM crop regulations will be poor farmers in the developing world, who will miss the opportunity to enjoy the future productivity gains that might otherwise come from this technology." "Let Them Eat Precaution: Why GM Crops Are Being Over-Regulated in the Developing World," Robert L. Paarlberg (rpaarlberg@wellesley.edu); see also Commission of the European Communities, Brussels, "Proposal for a Regulation of the European Parliament and of the Council Concerning Traceability and Labelling of Genetically Modified Organisms and Traceability of Food and Feed Products Produced from Genetically Modified Organisms and Amending Directive 2001/18/EC," Brussels, July 25, 2001.

pany was called the "new" Monsanto. The new Monsanto consisted solely of agricultural productivity, seed, biotech traits, and genomics businesses.

The CEO of the company, Hendrik Verfaille, said that he was committed to being forthcoming and engaging. The company would listen, respect, and consider legitimate concerns in its decision making.

Supporting biotech investments. A huge issue with which Verfaille had to deal was whether the new Monsanto's agricultural chemical business could continue to support its investments in biotechnology. The shift from traditional agricultural chemical approaches to biological approaches was still in its infancy. The first wave of GMO products had been designed to improve the efficiency and productivity of crop production. The breakthroughs that had occurred were mainly in this area.

Fewer breakthroughs had taken place in applications that delivered direct benefits to consumers. Such products were in Monsanto's pipeline. For instance, Monsanto had a product that added omega-3 fatty acids to foods, and enhanced the protein, vitamin, and mineral quality of animal feeds.

Roundup. Roundup was coming off patent in the U.S. market in 2000. How could Monsanto best manage Roundup's decline? Monsanto had to protect the brand by lowering its costs and developing improved formulations to fend off aggressive Chinese manufacturers. Monsanto had to continue to lower its costs so it could sell Roundup's primary ingredient, glyphosate, to other companies.

The initial use of Roundup to clean up a field before planting was a low-tech use of the product, where cost was the key concern and generic brands were highly competitive. However, after crops had begun to grow, spraying them without harming them was a more difficult task that required a precise product formulation. For the initial use of Roundup, Monsanto was developing a more concentrated version that allowed for extended spraying from a single tank. For later use of the product, Monsanto was developing formulas and mixtures that might be both patentable and fetch a high price.

Managing Roundup's decline was critical now that Roundup was off-patent. The product continued to have a 57 percent global market share and 81 percent U.S. share. But between 1997–2004 Roundup's price had fallen between 7 percent and 21 percent each year, and its gross margins were down from 71 percent in 1998 to 50 percent in 2004.

In 2002, 61 percent of Monsanto's earnings before interest, taxes, and dividends (or $822 million) came from Roundup. By 2007, this breakdown was expected to change with 29 percent coming from Roundup, 24 percent from agricultural productivity products, 17 percent from seeds excluding traits, and 30 percent from biotech traits.

DuPont's commodity businesses. DuPont faced different challenges than Monsanto. Should it continue to use its commodity chemical businesses as a cash cow to finance biotech given the opposition that had arisen to this technology, or would it do better as a pure biotech firm like Monsanto rather than being so diversified?

In 2003, DuPont made a dramatic announcement: It agreed to sell its textiles unit to Koch Industries Inc. for $4.4 billion. The sale of the nylon, polyester, and Lycra fiber businesses came during a sharp decline in the U.S. textile and apparel industries, mostly because of foreign competition. The sale reduced DuPont's dependence on high-cost raw materials made from petroleum byproducts. It signaled the company's intent to focus mainly on biotechnology for crop protection and food additives.

DuPont's CEO promised an unwavering commitment to these areas. In 2002, the textiles unit had $6.3 billion in revenue and 18,000 worldwide employees. But while this unit was the source of about a quarter of DuPont's annual revenue, it was the company's least profitable unit and had been subject to many job cuts and plant closings. The sale was expected to be neutral or positive with regard to earnings. DuPont would have less debt and a higher potential for growth and be more able to compete with other biotech leaders like Monsanto.

What to Do Next?

Now that DuPont had made this announcement, the question was what should its management and the management of Monsanto do next.

Both Monsanto and DuPont had made radical breaks with their pasts. Monsanto had gone much further. It now was nothing more than an agricultural biotechnology company, while DuPont was still relatively diverse. These newly reconstituted firms were the major large competitors left in agricultural biotechnology markets and their top managements would have to decide how they would compete. What were the critical moves that the two companies would have to take to ensure their success?

Questions for Discussion

1. What should the executives of Monsanto and DuPont learn from the controversy about GMOs? How should this learning affect what they do next?
2. To what extent should the strategies the two companies develop differ from each other? To what extent should Monsanto and DuPont band together and cooperate?
3. How can Monsanto and DuPont mitigate the opposition to GMOs? How can they avoid making matters worse?
4. Which biotech markets should the two companies emphasize? Which applications are most promising—agriculture, health, nutrition, industrial materials, and so forth?
5. Why did Monsanto and DuPont become involved in biotech in the first place? Why did the need for it arise?
6. What is the basis for the opposition to GMOs? How legitimate is this opposition? Draft a defense of GM food that you would present to the EU. Sketch out a defense you would bring to a meeting with environmentalists.
7. What special burdens does biotech innovation put on a company's managers? What issues do they have to address? What types of questions must they answer?
8. What role does corporate restructuring play in biotech innovation? Why does it have such a prominent role?
9. To support their involvement in biotech, Monsanto and DuPont have had to rely on other profitable corporate activities. How have the companies managed the balancing act of exploring biotech's potential and maintaining current revenue and income?
10. Why did DuPont sell its textile division? Was this decision a good one? Why or why not?
11. How can Monsanto cope with the loss of Roundup's patent? What should it do?

12. Was the entry of Monsanto and DuPont into the biotech business folly or brilliance? Relative to other chemical producers, will these companies be in a better or worse position 5-10 years from now? If you had to choose, would you invest in them or their competitors? Why or why not?

13. To what extent should Monsanto and DuPont work with the U.S. government to advance their interests in biotech? Are the benefits of an alliance with the U.S. government likely to exceed the costs?

14. What role do private foundations, nonprofits, and NGOs play in innovating biotechnologies? How can Monsanto and DuPont best manage their relations with these entities?

15. If developing nations like China are not supportive, chances are low that Monsanto and DuPont can be successful. How should the two companies handle their relations with developing nations?

16. Is the world just not ready for GM food? Should Monsanto and DuPont exit this business as soon as possible? What is your opinion?

Exercises

1. Visit anti-GMO Websites such as www.greenpeace.org, www.psrast.org, and www.purefood.org. Talk to an environmental advocate. What are the reasons for the opposition to GMOs? To what extent do you believe these reasons have validity?

2. Write a memo to DuPont management. What can DuPont learn from Monsanto's experience of being singled out as the nemesis of environmental organizations and anti-GM food activists? What should it do to ensure its long-term success with these groups?

3. What moves should Monsanto make next? How can it succeed in commercializing useful biotech products that can help humankind?

Videos

"Gary Hamel: Creating the Future." Palo Alto, CA: Stanford Business School. Executive Briefings, 1998.

"Clayton Christensen, Opportunity and Threat." Palo Alto, CA: Stanford Business School. Executive Briefings, 2000.

Bibliography

Barrett, Amy. "At Dupont, Time to Both Sow and Reap." *Business Week*. September 29, 1997:107.

Conway, Gordon. "The Voice of Reason in the Global Food Fight." *Fortune*. February 21, 2000:82.

Goldberg, Ray. "Monsanto: Leadership in a New Environment." Harvard Business School Case 9-903-449. June 2003.

Grant, Linda, and Alicia Hills Moore. "Monsanto's Bet: There's Gold in Going Green." *Fortune*. April 14, 1997:116.

Graves, Jacqueline M. "Designer Genes Go for Your Plate." *Fortune*. July 10, 1995:22.

Hamel, Gary. "Strategy as Revolution." *Harvard Business Review.* July-August 1996:69.

Reinhardt, Forest. "Agricultural Biotechnology and Its Regulation." Harvard Business School Case 9-701-004. April 2001.

Schwartz, Nelson D., and Mark Borden et al. "Monsantophobia." *Fortune*. March 29, 1999:36.

Simanis, Erik. "The Monsanto Company: Quest for Sustainability." World Resources Institute, Washington, D.C., 2001.

Shapiro, Robert "Growth Through Global Sustainability." *Harvard Business Review*. January-February 1997:79.

Specter, Michael. "The Pharmageddon Riddle." *New Yorker*. April 10, 2000:58.

Stipp, David. "Engineering the Future of Food." *Fortune*. September 28, 1998:128.

_____. "Is Monsanto's Biotech Worth Less Than a Hill of Beans?" *Fortune*. February 21, 2000:157.

Taylor III, Alex. "Why DuPont Is Trading Oil for Corn." *Fortune*. April 26, 1999:154.

Watkins, Michael. "Robert Shapiro and Monsanto." Harvard Business School Case 9-801-426, January 2003.

West, Jonathan. "E. I. du Pont de Nemours and Company (A) and (B)." Harvard Business School Case 9-699-037, October 1999.

Appendix A. An article by Greenpeace cofounder, Patrick Moore

EXHIBIT 1   *"A personal journey: Why the cofounder of Greenpeace supports nurturing the promise of
agricultural biotechnology"*

Patrick Moore's statement of how he moved to opposing Greenpeace's position on GMOs is an extraordinary example of how complex and nuanced the issue is and how much passion it arouses. He speaks very frankly about Greenpeace, the organization he once directed. This excerpt is an adaptation from his recent writings.

As we begin the 21st century, environmental thinkers are divided along a sharp fault line. There are doomsayers who predict the collapse of the global ecosystem . . . And there are the technological optimists who believe that we can feed 12 billion people and solve all our problems with science and technology . . . There is a middle road based on science and logic . . .

I became a born-again ecologist, and in the late 1960s, was soon transformed into a radical environmental activist . . . I spent fifteen years on the front lines of the eco-movement as we evolved from that church basement into the world's largest environmental activist organization . . . We put ourselves in front of the harpoons in little rubber boats and brought the Save the Whales movement into living rooms around the world. That really put Greenpeace on the map. By the mid-1980s Greenpeace had grown from that church basement into an organization with an income of over $100 million per year, offices in 21 countries, and over 100 campaigns around the world . . .

All social movements evolve from an earlier period of polarization and confrontation . . . For the environmental movement this transition began to occur in the mid-1980s. The term *sustainable development* was adopted to describe the challenge of taking the new environmental values . . . and incorporating them into the traditional social and economic values . . . Every day 6 billion people wake up with real needs for food, energy and materials. The challenge for sustainability is to provide for those needs in ways that reduce negative impact on the environment.

Not all my former colleagues saw things that way . . . They ushered in an era of zero tolerance and left-wing politics . . . They are anti-science and technology . . . Environmental extremists are anti-trade, not just free trade but anti-trade in general . . . They are anti-business . . . The liberal democratic, market-based model is rejected even though no viable alternative is proposed to provide for the material needs of 6 billion people . . . In their Brave New World there will be no more chemicals, no more airplanes, and certainly no more polyester suits . . . The environmental movement's campaign against biotechnology in general, and genetic engineering in particular has clearly exposed their intellectual and moral bankruptcy . . . It seems inevitable that in time, the media and the public will see the insanity of their position . . . the accusations of Frankenstein food and killer tomatoes are as much a fantasy as the Hollywood movies they are borrowed from.

In 2001, the European Commission released the results of 81 scientific studies on genetically modified organisms conducted by over 400 research teams at a cost of $65 million.[1] The studies, which covered all

---

1. http://europa.eu.int/comm/research/quality.of.lif/gmo/index.html.

areas of concern, have "not shown any new risks to human health or the environment, beyond the usual uncertainties of conventional plant breeding. Indeed, the use of more precise technology and the greater regulatory scrutiny probably make them even safer than conventional plants and foods . . ."

The environmental movement has been very clever at inventing campaigns that make us afraid of our food. They conjure up invisible poisons that will give us cancer, birth defects, mutations, and otherwise kill us in our sleep . . . scare tactics are now being employed in the campaign against biotechnology and genetically modified foods . . . there is no evidence of negative human health effects and environmental concerns . . . the campaign of fear now waged against genetic modification is based largely on fantasy and a complete lack of respect for science and logic . . . the real benefits of genetic modification far outweigh the hypothetical and sometimes contrived risks claimed by its detractors.

Certainly any science or technology can be used for destructive purposes . . . But the programs of genetic research and development now underway in labs and field stations around the world are entirely about benefiting society and the environment . . . We will never know everything and it is impossible to create a world with zero risk. The real question . . . is whether the risks of banning genetic modification are greater or less than the risks of pursuing it . . . The case of the Golden Rice provides a clear illustration of this point . . . a commercial variety of golden rice [is] now ready and available for planting. Hundreds of millions of people in Asia and Africa suffer from vitamin A deficiency. Among them, half a million children go blind each year and millions more suffer from lesser symptoms. Golden Rice has the potential to greatly reduce the suffering. But . . . it will be at least five years before Golden Rice will be able to work through the Byzantine regulatory system that has been set up as a result of the activists' campaign of misinformation and speculation . . . The only difference between the Golden Rice and conventional rice is that Golden Rice contains a gene from daffodils, the gene that makes daffodils yellow, the color of beta-carotene, and the precursor to vitamin A. What possible risk could there be from a daffodil gene in a rice paddy? Yet Greenpeace threatens to rip the rice out if farmers dare to plant it . . .

Golden Rice is not the only example of civilization being held hostage by activists who some believe should be held accountable for crimes against humanity . . . farmers from South Sulawesi (Indonesia) who had just completed a trial of Bt cotton on their farms . . . reported that yields had risen from the normal 600 kilos per hectare to an average of 2500 kilos per hectare, a four times increase . . . At the same time they had reduced pesticide applications from eight sprayings to one spraying . . . But none of this seems to matter to the activists . . . . On June 3, 2002, Greenpeace issued a media release announcing the publication of a report on the "adverse environmental impacts of Bt Cotton . . ." In typical Greenpeace hyperbole we were advised that "farmers growing this crop are now finding themselves engulfed in Bt-resistant superbugs, emerging secondary pests, diminishing natural enemies, destabilized insect ecology," and that farmers are "forced to continue the use of chemical pesticides . . ." Anyone who has studied the introduction of Bt cotton into China and other countries knows that it results in reduced chemical use, reduced impact on non-target organisms, including other insects, reduced exposure to chemicals by farm workers, increased productivity, and increased financial benefit to farm owners . . .

Of course the most tragic circumstance is that of southern Africa where Zambia has refused U.S. food aid because it contains GM corn . . . Greenpeace has the nerve to declare on their website that "Starving people still deserve the dignity of choice . . ." Surely there is some way to break through the misinformation and hysteria and to get a more balanced picture to the public . . .

I believe the main reason for the failure to win the debate decisively is precisely because the supporters of GM technology have not acted decisively themselves. The activists are playing hardball while the GM side is soft-pedaling the health and environmental benefits of GMOs. Biotech companies and their associations use soft images and calm language . . . How can that possibly be an effective counter to the Frankenfood fears and superweed scares? . . . Stronger medicine must be prescribed . . . Imagine an advertising campaign that showed graphic images of blind children in Africa, explained vitamin A deficiency, introduced Golden Rice, and explained how Greenpeace's actions are preventing the delivery of this cure. Imagine another ad showing impoverished Indian cotton farmers, explained Bt cotton, and gave the statistics for increased yield, reduced pesticide use, and betterment for farmers. Again it would be clearly stated that activists were the reason for the late and slowed adoption of the technology. How about an ad that graphically portrays the soil erosion and stream siltation caused by conventional farming versus the soil conservation obtained by using

GM soybeans and canola? And another one that shows workers apply-ing pesticides without protection in a developing country versus the greatly reduced applications possible with Bt corn and cotton? What if all these ads were hosted by a well-known and trusted personality, wouldn't this change public perspectives? (http://www.greenspirit.com)

CASE 10

Judo Strategies
Wal-Mart versus Spartan
Stores, Inc. (SSI)[1]

This case is about the clash between the retail titan Wal-Mart and a relatively small grocery distributor and retailer Spartan Stores, Inc. (SSI), which is mainly active in Western Michigan and Ohio. It deals with the threat that Wal-Mart poses to this small distributor and retailer and the use of various strategies that can be labeled judo by the protagonists in their struggle with each other.[2]

Wal-Mart

Wal-Mart's goal has been to grow at all costs. With about a quarter of its sales coming from its grocery business, it has become the largest food seller in the United States in only 10 years' time.

Before his death in 1992, Sam Walton, the company's charismatic founder, pointed Wal-Mart in this direction, seeing the fragmented retail food industry as an ideal target for the further growth of his company. While Wal-Mart had less than 6 percent of the total grocery market in 1995, by 2003, it had more than 10 percent.

David Glass, the CEO after Sam Walton's death, had grown the company from $44 billion in sales to over $200 billion 10 years later (see Table 10.1). Lee Scott, who succeeded Glass, intended to do as well. For Scott to equal Glass meant that Wal-Mart would become a trillion dollar company by 2011.

---

1. This case was written by Alfred Marcus, University of Minnesota, Carlson School of Management. Copyright © 2005 by Marsh Publications LLC. All rights reserved.

2. Judo strategies are based on these principles: move rapidly to uncontested space to avoid direct conflict; be flexible and give way when directly attacked by a much stronger opponent; and exploit leverage to use the weight and strength of an opponent against itself. See David Yoffie and Michael Cusumano, "Judo Strategy," *Harvard Business Review*, January-February, 1999.

TABLE 10.1   Wal-Mart's annual income statement: 2003
(in millions of U.S. dollars except for per-share items)

	12 months ending 01/31/03	12 months ending 01/31/02	12 months ending 01/31/01	12 months ending 01/31/00	12 months ending 01/31/99
Revenue	244,524	217,799	191,329	165,013	137,634
Total revenue	246,525	219,671	193,116	166,809	139,208
Cost of revenue	191,838	171,562	150,255	129,664	108,725
Gross profit	52,686	46,237	41,074	35,349	28,909
Selling/general/ admin. expenses, total	41,043	36,172	31,550	27,040	22,363
Total operating expense	233,806	208,920	183,000	157,726	131,885
Operating income	12,719	10,751	10,116	9,083	7,323
Net income before taxes	12,719	10,751	10,116	9,083	7,323

Source: Yahoo! Finance (http://finance.yahoo.com).

Where would this growth come from? Two-thirds was projected to come from domestic sales and a third from foreign markets. A high percentage of the domestic growth would be at the expense of domestic supermarkets.

The grocery industry

The grocery industry that Wal-Mart entered consisted of more than 31,000 supermarkets that brought in more than $400 billion in annual sales. Chains generated about 80 percent of the industry's revenues and independents about 20 percent.

The largest chains were Kroger ($44.7 billion 2003 sales), Safeway ($29.4 billion 2003 sales), and Albertson's ($28.5 billion 2003 sales). The 1990s were a period of consolidation in the industry with Kroger buying Fred Meyer, Safeway buying regional chains such as Randalls in Texas, and Albertson buying American stores.

Large European players such as Ahold (from Holland) and Delhaize (from Belgium) also entered the U.S. market. Ahold was the fifth largest chain in the United States ($25 billion in 2003 sales) and Delhaize the sixth ($14.7 billion in 2003 sales). Ahold had 294 Bi-Lo stores, 293 Super Stop and Shop stores, and 267 Giant food stores. Delhaize controlled 1,184 Food Lion stores. The European firms were known for their sophisticated marketing and supply chain management and their strong private label programs.

The average supermarket had about 28,000 square feet of selling space, annual sales of slightly more than $12 million, and sales per square feet of about $400. Gross profit margins were low—in the 20 percent to 35 percent range—and operating margins were lower—just 3 percent to 6 percent of sales.

The supercenter concept. After some experimentation, Wal-Mart created the supercenter concept in 1992 to sell groceries. The concept brought together a discount mass merchandise store with a grocery store. In contrast to the average supermarket, a supercenter had 100,000 to 200,000 square feet of space. It had the 36 general merchandise departments found in Wal-Mart's traditional discount store, but it also had all the items found in a traditional supermarket including a bakery, fresh produce, meat, and dairy products.

Most of the supercenter stores had separate grocery and general merchandise entrances, but common checkout stands. They were open 24-hours a day, and about 500 Wal-Mart "associates" worked in them. In contrast to the $12 million in annual sales a grocery might bring in, a supercenter might have annual revenues of more than $75 million.

Wal-Mart derived 40 percent of the revenues of its supercenters and 30 percent of those of its flagship discount stores from groceries. It had about 4,500 stores worldwide of which about 26 percent were foreign, 37 percent were its classic discount stores, 24 percent were supercenters, 11 percent were Sam's Clubs, and about 1 percent were the new concept with which it was experimenting, its neighborhood markets.[3]

The supercenters generated about 32 percent of the company's revenues, the discount stores about 31 percent, the international operations about 21 percent, Sam's Clubs about 15 percent, and the neighborhood markets less than 1 percent of 2002 revenues.

Since 1999, customer visits per year to supercenters were up 40 percent, while visits to supermarkets were down 12 percent. The average customer bought $12 more per-store for food at a supercenter than at a traditional grocer. Target, Kmart, and Meijer together had less half Wal-

---

3. The newest twist was Wal-Mart's low-volume neighborhood markets. Devoted exclusively to retail food, they had pharmacies, self-checkout, film processing, and an honor system that allowed a shopper to buy coffee and pastries as he or she shopped.

Mart's business in the superstore category. Wal-Mart was clearly the dominant player.

The attraction of the food industry

As of 2002, around a fifth of Wal-Mart's total sales came from food. This number expanded by over 20 percent in 2003. What attracted Wal-Mart to the food business? Obviously not the margins, which were among the lowest to be found in any industry.

The attraction was the traffic that food generated. People tended to shop for groceries once or twice a week as opposed to coming to Wal-Mart's stores for general merchandise about once a month. Once in the stores, people tended to buy general merchandise items on impulse. Thus, the additional traffic translated into higher sales growth overall. Though margins were low, Wal-Mart was in the position to further force down prices. It was able to do so because of customers' impulse purchases of higher margin goods found in the rest of its stores. The giant retailer was willing to accept gross margins in food of around 16 percent, while most supermarkets worked with gross margins of about 24 percent. The company drove down food prices by an average of 13 percent in the markets it served.

In most markets, analysts estimated Wal-Mart's food prices at 20 percent less than those of its competitors. A pricing study done by UBS Warburg in Dallas, Tampa, and Las Vegas found that Wal-Mart, in head-to-head competition with its main competitors (Albertson's, Kroger, Safeway, Winn Dixie, and Publix) offered discounts of between 21 percent and 29 percent for an identical basket of groceries.

Wal-Mart's plan. Wal-Mart's plan was to build 925 more supercenters and 300 more neighborhood markets by 2006. It was going to convert many of its discount stores to supercenters so that it could take better advantage of the concept it had pioneered.

If this plan were fully realized, Wal-Mart's supermarket sales would be more than double what they were in 2003, or more than $106 billion in 2006. This increase would amount to more than a quarter of all U.S. grocery sales.

Most analysts believed that the supermarket business was a zero-sum, or nearly a zero-sum, game. Thus, many current stores would have to be shut down if Wal-Mart achieved its aggressive expansion plans. Already, between 2001–2003, many U.S. supermarkets had shut their doors. If Wal-Mart added 54-million-square-feet of space (the equivalent of 1,800 new supermarkets by 2006), then 1 in 18 super-markets operating in 2003 would need to be closed to accommodate Wal-Mart's growth.

Spartan Stores, Inc. (SSI)

These facts were a wake-up call to Spartan Stores, Inc. (SSI). What should Spartan do to respond to the threat that Wal-Mart posed? The 43rd largest supermarket chain in the United States, SSI was a leading regional grocery distributor and retailer in western Michigan and Ohio. With total revenues of about $2 billion per year, it was a tenth the size of Wal-Mart.

SSI had started in 1917 as a distributing cooperative owned by a group of small and mostly independent retailers. In 2003, it continued to be the 9th largest grocery distributor in the United States behind such giants as Supervalu, Fleming, Nash Finch, and Roundy's. Its grocery distribution segment provided 400-plus stores with a selection of over 40,000 products.[4] If Wal-Mart expansion plans succeeded, it followed that 350–400 grocery stores in the United States would be shutting down each year. SSI's goal was to defend itself against this threat.

Acquiring stores. SSI's shift from being a distributor to owning and operating its own stores was fairly recent. Its new strategy, inaugurated in 1999, was based on the idea that vertical integration would allow it to achieve improved distribution, transportation, merchandising, and marketing leverage and gain greater purchasing power.

Since 1999, SSI had acquired 127 retail stores. Slightly less than $1 billion of SSI's total sales in 2003 came from its retail grocery chains, which it operated under names like Family Fare, Glen's, Food Town, and Great Day (see Table 10.2). It had also acquired a chain of deep-discount pharmacies that it operated under the Pharm name.

Vertical integration would permit SSI to provide better services to its company-owned stores and independent customers. The services SSI provided included market analysis and promotion, technology, human resources, information assistance, coupon redemption, and product reclamation. It also had its own Spartan, Home Harvest, and Pharm brands that it sold in its company-owned stores and distributed to its independent customers.

---

4. These products included dry groceries, produce, dairy products, meat, frozen food, seafood, floral products, general merchandise, pharmacy and health, and beauty care items.

TABLE 10.2   SSI's annual income statement: 2003
(in millions of U.S. dollars except for per-share items)

	52 weeks ending 03/29/03	52 weeks ending 03/30/02	52 weeks ending 03/31/01	52 weeks ending 03/25/00	52 weeks ending 03/27/99
Revenue	2,148.1	2,270.0	2,360.9	2,238.6	1,958.2
Total revenue	2,148.1	2,270.0	2,360.9	2,238.6	1,958.2
Cost of revenue	1,774.4	1,865.3	1,980.8	1,917.9	1,760.5
Gross profit	373.7	404.7	380.1	320.7	197.7
Selling/general/ admin. expenses, total	360.8	369.6	337.7	291.8	181.4
Unusual expense (income)	47.7	1.0	1.1	(2.9)	5.7
Total operating expense	2,182.8	2,236.0	2,319.6	2,206.7	1,947.5
Operating income	(34.8)	34.0	41.3	31.9	10.6
Net income before taxes	(52.1)	19.0	23.9	20.2	6.7

Source: Yahoo! Finance (hhtp://finance.yahoo.com).

The stock market initially reacted favorably to SSI's acquisitions. The year 2001 was a very good one for the company. Its market performance spiked and for much of the year, it outperformed Wall-Mart. However, since 2002, the company's stock had been in a freefall. Its market performance took a nosedive, while that of Wal-Mart rose at a steady pace.

Trouble. By 2003, SSI was in serious trouble. SSI's plan to be a retailer as well as a distributor was not working as well as anticipated. In 2003, the company lost $34 million.

As a result, it had to close 31 stores it had bought. SSI sold a segment of the company that distributed goods to convenience stores, and it was in the process of selling an additional 26 supermarkets, many of them around Toledo, Ohio. Its 55 remaining retail grocery stores and 21 deep-discount drugstores were located mostly in small metropolitan and rural areas in Michigan and Ohio. This region was obviously a target for Wal-Mart's next moves.

SSI's main competitors were Meijer (the 12th largest grocery in the country), the Great A&P Tea Company (the 10th largest), and Kroger (the 2nd largest). Meijer was SSI's main competitor in western

TABLE 10.3   SSI and its major competitors

	SSI	Meijer	Great A&P	Kroger	Wal-Mart
No. supermarkets > $2 mill sales	94 (includes stores SSI has sold)	156	488	2,482	1,336
Annual sales ($ billions)	.98	6.1	7.8	44.8	48.7
Sq. feet selling area	3,034	9,453	16,968	98,616	82,106
No. full-time employees	5,177	65,929	30,280	196,195	428,108
Store names (no. of stores)	Food Town (39) Glenn's Market (23) Family Fare (13)	Meijer Super-market (156)	Farmer Jack (109) A&P (84) SuperFresh Food (77)	Kroger (1,030) Ralphs (298) Kroger Superstore (156)	Super-centers (1,285) Neighbor-hood markets (51)
Chief trading area by census region (no. of stores)	East North Central (94)	East North Central (148)	Mid Atlantic (249) East North Central (140) South Atlantic (41)	Pacific (653) East North Central (499) Mountain (388)	West South Central (335) South Atlantic (324) East South Central (195)

Source: "Progressive Grocer's Annual Report of the Grocery Industry."

Michigan (see Table 10.3). In this region, SSI's market share held steady at about 55 percent, while Meijer's was around 30 percent.

A former member of SSI's cooperative had set up the Meijer Company in 1934. Meijer had more than 20 years' experience running superstores, some of which were as big as 200,000 square feet and had 100,000 SKUs, compared to around 65,000 square feet and 35,000 SKUs for a typical SSI store.

Though SSI was having trouble, it remained committed to being both a wholesale distributor and an owner and operator of retail outlets. Indeed, Craig Sturken, the newly appointed CEO in 2003, was an industry veteran with more than 40 years' experience in retail, where he had worked mainly in the Midwest for A&P and other large grocery chains.

Wal-Mart's Move into SSI's Territory

Wal-Mart had made most of its inroads in the retail grocery business in the west south central, south atlantic, and east south central portions of the United States, while SSI's stronghold was the east north central region, which Wal-Mart had failed to fully penetrate.

The challenge facing SSI's new CEO was a huge one as Wal-Mart continued to have its competitive guns aimed at regions like the one in which SSI was active (see Figure 10.1).

Good reasons for penetration. Wal-Mart had good reasons to try to penetrate the western Michigan and northern Ohio territory. The strategy of the retail giant was to be where it currently was not and in this part of the country its penetration rate was relatively low.

Wal-Mart considered a state that had at least one discount or supercenter store for every 125,000 persons to be fully penetrated. By this standard, 33 of 50 U.S. states had been fully penetrated, with Arkansas in the lead. The home of Wal-Mart's first store had one discount or supercenter store for every 35,000 persons.

But the states where most SSI's stores were located had been poorly penetrated by Wal-Mart thus far, making them a good target for Wal-Mart's advances. Michigan had one discount or supercenter store for

FIGURE 10.1   The region in which SSI was most active

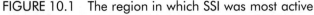

Source: Mapquest (http://www.mapquest.com).

every 175,000 persons, and Ohio had one discount or supercenter store for every 130,000 persons.

Wal-Mart considered metro areas with less than one store per 125,000 persons ripe for the penetration of its neighborhood stores, the 45,000 square-foot, no-frills supermarkets it was introducing. In metro areas in SSI territory, the number of existing Wal-Mart stores per person was low.

In Grand Rapids, where SSI was headquartered, there was one Wal-Mart store for every 210,000 persons; in Kalamazoo, one Wal-Mart store was present for every 225,000 persons; in St. Joseph, one Wal-Mart store existed for every 160,000 persons; and in Saginaw, there was one Wal-Mart store for every 135,000 persons.

Adjacent expansion. Though Wal-Mart's penetration was low in areas where SSI was active, the retail behemoth was expanding rapidly in adjacent areas. In this way, it was closing in on SSI, encircling its foe, and then going in for the "kill."

In nearby Indiana, Wal-Mart's penetration rate was high. It had one discount or supercenter store for every 72,000 people. In parts of Ohio, it also had high penetration rates. In Lima, Ohio, for instance, there was a Wal-Mart store for every 75,000 persons, and in Mansfield, Ohio, there was one store for every 85,000 persons.

SSI, meanwhile, was struggling, and it was questionable whether it could maintain itself in an environment in which Wal-Mart was becoming an ever-larger force.

Judo Strategies

Wal-Mart used so-called judo strategies to gain an advantage in market after market. These strategies consisted of movement, maintaining balance, and using leverage to defeat rivals. Small competitors like SSI had no alternative but to use similar strategies in kind. They had to operate under the radar. They had to be flexible, and occupy spaces where their opponents were not.

Under the radar. The markets Wal-Mart originally won were relatively uncontested because they were on the fringes of major population centers. Other retailers did not consider rural areas in regions of Arkansas attractive because the populations were neither dense enough for volume sales nor sophisticated enough for high markups.

Wal-Mart deliberately deployed a market saturation strategy in these areas, thereby gaining strength and experience to expand elsewhere.

The supercenter concept, along with the neighborhood store, was a fresh one-two punch, a market saturation strategy designed to gain not only mainstream customers, but to capture overflow shoppers looking only for groceries in neighborhood stores. Through such dense market concentration, Wal-Mart discouraged competitors from resisting its encrochments.

Big and flexible. Wal-Mart tended to blitzkrieg the opposition. It was flexible enough to occupy relatively unoccupied spaces where it could use its weight and strength to its advantage, yet big and strong enough to overwhelm opponents in sumolike matches if it had to fight under these conditions. Small players without a fighting spirit did not stand a chance.

Where your opponent isn't. Firms trying to resist Wal-Mart also had to use judolike strategies to defend themselves. They had to have as their main objective "to be where Wal-Mart wasn't."

The idea was to be flexible, give way when attacked by a superior force like Wal-Mart, move rapidly to uncontested ground to avoid head-to-head conflict, and use Wal-Mart's weight and strength against it. The problem was how to put these principles into practice. For SSI, doing so meant finding target customers that Wal-Mart was unable to serve well and addressing the needs of these segments in a very compelling way.

SSI also had to be more innovative than Wal-Mart. Its innovations had to be hard or disadvantageous for Wal-Mart to copy. Developing such innovations was not simple, however, for Wal-Mart had erected formidable barriers against being attacked.

Wal-Mart's Strengths

Wal-Mart's low-price image and its ultraefficient distribution system were hard to challenge. They provided something for everyone—a formula that existing companies in the industry found very hard to beat. Wal-Mart's strong and demanding culture, its closeness to customers, efficient distribution, and the way it simplified relations with suppliers, gave it the strength to overcome rivals.

A strong and demanding culture. Wal-Mart had a very demanding culture in which its nonunionized employees (called "associates") were expected to work very hard for low wages. In contrast, more than 20 percent of SSI's workforce was unionized.

The payoff for the hard-work ethic of Wal-Mart's employees was that they could become rich if the stock price went up because they were guaranteed a certain part of their compensation in company stock. On the other hand, employee morale was hurt when the stock price failed to advance as expected.

Other parts of the culture were also unique. Wal-Mart relied on what it called "servant leadership." It provided employees what they needed—merchandise, capital, information, and inspiration—to serve customers, and it developed in its managers and employees an almost perverse pride in acknowledging mistakes and correcting them.

Closeness to customers. Heavy competition had forced Wal-Mart to be constantly vigilant about keeping costs down. The company did so through a well-developed information infrastructure designed to customize merchandise at individual outlets.

Wal-Mart had pioneered a detailed point-of-sale (POS) replenishment system based on tracking more than 6,000 customer purchasing variables, including the time of day customers made their purchases. The goal was to customize each linear foot of shelf space in each department at each store so that the right quantity of goods was always available at the right time.

Wal-Mart's strategy was to try to provide each consumer with exactly what the person wanted at the precise time and exact price he or she wanted to pay. To achieve this result, the company mined the data it accumulated combining variables such as weather, holidays, and school schedules with a decade of past sales records. It relied on just-in-time sales information and point-of-sales figures to inform vendors which items to replenish and to provide optimal product supply for specific stores under a range of different circumstances.

Efficient distribution. Wal-Mart also introduced a more efficient distribution system than the one found in the grocery industry. In entering the grocery business, Wal-Mart pursued a strategy that did not follow accepted industry standards; this strategy capitalized on supply chain inefficiencies in the industry.

Channel pricing had encouraged early purchases ("forward buying") of significant quantities of goods at promotional prices. Manufacturers gave retailers a wide assortment of allowances and rebates, whose complexity made it hard to figure out a product's actual cost. Besides leading retailers to push overinventoried products consumers might not want, these inducements promoted speculation and provided incentives to earn arbitrage profits rather than to meet consumers' real needs.

Wal-Mart invested heavily in distribution, opening four dry-grocery distribution centers and two fresh-produce distribution centers in the United States. At the beginning of the 1990s, its distribution costs were estimated to be about 3 percent of total sales, while those of the average grocer were estimated to be about 6 percent.

Simplifying supplier relationships. With suppliers, Wal-Mart aimed to simplify relationships. The company allowed no slotting or display fees, damage allowances, handling charges, advertising costs, or late penalties. Wal-Mart also did not permit special sales and rebates.

Wal-Mart negotiated with suppliers to support a low-price strategy and therefore maintain its low-price reputation. It tried to boil down its supplier relationships to a one-number negotiation. It insisted that both sides swap information to streamline the flow of goods. Being the largest outlet for most of its suppliers gave Wal-Mart great clout in these negotiations.

Instead of rebates and promotions to move products, Wal-Mart offered everyday low prices. In return, suppliers got volume that kept their manufacturing facilities running smoothly, predictably, and efficiently.

The productivity of Wal-Mart's suppliers increased along with that of Wal-Mart's. The relationships between them were win-win with operating margins of the firms that supplied the grocery industry—household product makers, food processors, and soft-drink makers—growing between 1992–2001, even with Wal-Mart's entry into this arena.

The Grocers' Response

Observing Wal-Mart's success, the grocery industry tried to reengineer its supply chain by creating new alliances and incentives that would save costs. The industry started a nationwide campaign in "efficient consumer response" (ECR) to keep up with the practices Wal-Mart had established. The purpose was to bring about leaner inventories, lower inventory costs, and improved logistics via more cooperation and an enhanced flow of information from manufacturers to suppliers and retailers.

The grocers' goal was a responsive, consumer-driven system in which distributors and suppliers worked together as business allies to maximize consumer satisfaction and minimize cost. Analysts estimated that retailers and manufacturers could reduce total channel inventory levels by 40 percent to 50 percent.

New capabilities. To realize this goal, supermarkets had to acquire new capabilities. They needed capabilities in point-of-sale scanning, store ordering and inventory, category management, continuous replenishment, and electronic data exchange. They had to upgrade their information systems.

Supermarkets made a sustained effort to acquire these capabilities in the 1990s. SSI was an enthusiastic participant in this initiative. In 1993, it was a cooperative with 238 independent companies that varied in size, sophistication, and the strategies they pursued. A very high percentage of them were freestanding, one-store only operations.

Independent grocers. Independent grocers thought independently. For SSI to get a majority or a consensus to do anything was difficult. A tension was built into the cooperative structure between the company and the stores with which it was affiliated over the allocation of costs and profits.

The owners claimed that they trusted and respected the cooperative, but it was still difficult for them to act together and respond quickly. One of the first initiatives they took was to do a detailed analysis of their business processes. Starting with a clean slate, they identified 324 business processes and redesigned their companies around 104 of them.

SSI's executives were at the center of the undertaking and they were responsible for five processes: (1) customer support, (2) business support, (3) inbound operations and logistics, (4) outbound operations and logistics, and (5) business development.

In response to the ECR initiative, the affiliated companies also started to gather point-of-sale (POS) data for the analysis of buying habits and trends, and for inventory control. They had to take steps to try to ensure that the POS data was accurate, as clerks at checkout counters tended to make errors that invalidated the veracity of the data.

Coordination problems. Coordinating these efforts was difficult because the companies were members of a cooperative and did not belong to a chain that could centrally dictate policies it wanted its stores to follow. The cooperative structure made the problem of systems integration complicated, as each store was free to choose what it wanted to do and often stores chose to install disparate technologies that did not fit together well.

SSI tried to make changes. It had especially good relations with Procter and Gamble (P&G), whose brands accounted for nearly 10 percent of the sales of the companies in the cooperative. SSI endeavored to achieve a high degree of financial and information technology integration with P&G. It also helped to set up a frequent shopper program, but only some companies chose to participate.

SSI urged member companies to move to a modified high/low pricing strategy that combined everyday low prices with some specials, but it was only moderately successful in getting these companies to take that path. It experimented with other systems such as ABC accounting. With five of its suppliers, SSI developed a vendor-managed inventory system. SSI helped the companies administer new programs they were introducing for a fee, but many of them opted out of the system and decided not to participate.

Slow in coming. The changes were slow in coming. SSI provided up to 140 separate services and developed a "university," which served as a training center, but it was unable to transform the cooperative quickly. This experience taught SSI's executives an important lesson. They learned how difficult it was to coordinate the behavior of affiliated companies when the companies' ties were voluntary in nature. They believed that consolidating the companies under centralized leadership might yield many benefits.

This factor motivated them to acquire retail outlets where they could dictate policies rather than ask member companies to participate. In the intensely competitive environment of retail food, they felt that this route was more likely to ensure their survival.

SSI's Choices

Though the hopes of SSI's executive were high when they acquired retail outlets, success so far had eluded them and they were struggling with the problem of what to do next. They faced a number of fundamental choices. They could get bigger quicker, become lower cost, and/or differentiate.

Get bigger quicker. One option was to get much bigger very quickly. By scaling up to achieve economies of scale, SSI would be better able to meet the challenges emanating from large chains like Wal-Mart, Kroger Albertson, and Safeway.

SSI could aggressively snap up remaining small and independent markets to keep pace. The problem here was that not many small players were left that were worth snapping up.

SSI's executives were not particularly keen to follow this route after the experience they had had with recent acquisitions. Some of the stores they purchased had proven to be nonviable and the company was in the process of reversing its decisions and selling them. Moreover, for SSI, a small player with a weak financial position, this strategy might not be realistic. Would the company ever have the financial muscle to make bids on stores that were worth the purchase price?

On other hand, SSI could hope to be acquired by a large chain, but what were the prospects of this taking place given SSI's financial condition? It was not a particularly attractive takeover target.

Keep costs down. Though getting bigger certainly would help, regardless of what happened, SSI would have to fight a relentless battle to keep costs down. It had to streamline the way it ran its stores. The large chains could serve as models. They were struggling to keep pace with Wal-Mart and had sweeping plans to reorganize the way they managed their stores.

Kroger, for instance, was in the process of centralizing buying to lower margins in an attempt to close the gap between its costs and those of Wal-Mart. Albertson's had a similar program in place. These programs, however, were proving hard to implement, even for the large chains. Kroger, for instance, was having difficulty deploying the technology needed to centrally stock and manage its stores.

Wal-Mart's lead, moreover, was so great that even after companies eliminated substantial amounts of money from their operating costs, they were still behind. Wal-Mart, after all, did not need to profit that much from selling food. It could sell groceries almost at cost because it made up the difference in the sale of other items.

In competing against Wal-Mart, it was very hard to beat it on price, which did not mean that some companies were not making progress in this area. In trying to keep pace, companies could rely on shoppers' cards that gave sizable discounts. In return, the companies would be better able to track customers' buying habits. Companies also could ramp up their coupon programs. However, these programs were expensive and it was unclear to what extent it was feasible for SSI to adopt them. Wal-Mart was likely to remain the price leader, no matter what SSI did. The ability to challenge Wal-Mart on price was limited.

Differentiate. Another option that SSI had to consider was differentiation. A company, for instance, could distance itself from Wal-Mart on quality and variety. Kroger was offering something to people interested in the whole package, not just price. It was attempting to do many things well. If its costs were not the lowest, its service would be better, its private label stronger, the variety of perishables it offered more appealing, and its selection of natural foods better.

In keeping with this approach, Kroger was developing "signature stores" where shelf selection was heavily determined by surveys mailed to the surrounding community before a Kroger store opened. One of the new "signature stores" was going out of its way to please a large Asian-American community. It provided 860 varieties of produce, including bitter melon, Chinese long beans, and flowering chives. Kroger's hope was that this attention to detail would be difficult for Wal-Mart to match. However, Wal-Mart too had the capability to mine its mountains of data to tailor individual stores to local tastes.

Examples of the two choices

The basic choices a firm had to defend itself against Wal-Mart were low cost and/or high differentiation. Examples where firms used these strategies to fend off the Wal-Mart juggernaut were Buy for Less and Crest Food, which tried low costs, and H. E. B. Butt, which employed differentiation.

Low cost. Buy for Less and Crest Foods were independent grocers in Oklahoma City. Wal-Mart initially started small in the Oklahoma City area. It opened just three supercenters on the periphery of the city in 1992, 1994, and 1995. It began its full-fledged assault on Buy for Less and Crest Foods only in 1998–2002 with the addition of nine supercenters, seven neighborhood markets, and two Sam's Clubs. It quite quickly achieved control of 35 percent of the grocery market. Its supercenters had control of 23 percent of the market, the neighborhood stores 10 percent, and Sam's Club 2 percent.

Price compression. All prices were down for groceries after Wal-Mart entered the Oklahoma City market and price compression was the rule.

As would be expected, 28 competitors had to close their doors, including 10 chain stores belonging to Albertsons and Homeland and 18 independents. Despite Wal-Mart's successful onslaught, Buy for Less and Crest Foods were successful in resisting the behemoth. They did so on the basis of price. They fought back and prospered.

Price perceptions. Wal-Mart's competitors' success was based on the fact that people did not perceive Wal-Mart's supercenters or the neighborhood stores as the lowest-priced alternatives, nor did they see them as being identically priced. Indeed, people perceived the neighborhood stores as among the higher-priced options in the Oklahoma City area. Consumers believed that they could get better deals at Buy for Less and Crest, a perception that led to continued high levels of traffic and sales at these grocers.

Convenience. The advantage of the Wal-Mart neighborhood stores was that despite the fact that they were viewed as having higher than average prices, they were convenient, close to home, provided easy parking, and had 24-hour operations. The supercenters were very successful then not because they were seen as being low priced, but because they had other advantages including the convenience of one-stop shopping and a wide selection.

The supercenters also were viewed as having a major disadvantage—slow checkouts—that they did not share with Buy for Less or Crest. Other perceived disadvantages of the supercenters were that they were too crowded, too big, slow on service, poor on layout, and not as clean as other stores. Buy for Less and Crest Foods took advantage of these perceived disadvantages.

Differentiation. Headquartered in San Antonio, Texas, H. E. B. Butt (H-E-B) was the nation's 11th largest grocery chain. Privately held, it was founded in Kerrville, Texas, in 1905. H-E-B was in a part of the country, Texas, with a relatively high concentration of Wal-Mart supercenters. In Texas, there was one such store for every 80,000 persons. Yet H-E-B was holding its own. It was differentiating itself from Wal-Mart by being strong in ethnic merchandising, having flashy perimeter departments, and selling high-end specialty items.

In-store shopping experience. H-E-B provided an exceptional in-store shopping experience at acceptably low prices. For products like ice cream made from Poteet strawberries, a local favorite that H-E-B froze in vast quantities, the store was a destination site. The comapny also had exclusive manufacturing partnerships with vendors that tended to further differentiate its stores. The typical H-E-B store had more varieties of national brand and private-label products than a Wal-Mart supercenter; it carried 25 percent to 30 percent more SKUs than a supercenter.

Private labels. H-E-B also had strong private labels that had considerable drawing power and better margins than national brands. It had two private labels, the very high-quality and high-priced H-E-B brand, and the more moderate quality and price Hill Country Fare brand.

H-E-B's premium private label products especially appealed to the tastes of south Texans in ways that Wal-Mart could not match. Wal-Mart's private label brands typically were low cost and less appealing alternatives that were sold under the Greater Value brand name. Wal-Mart had a limited assortment of higher-quality items sold under the Sam's Choice brand.

Different formats. H-E-B's stores came in three formats. Standard supermarkets, which were 45,000–90,000 square feet in size, handled approximately 50,000 SKUs. These stores had 20 checkout lanes and employed 350 people. Customers enjoyed one-hour photo finishing, large beer and wine departments, coffee shops, bakeries, and pharmacies. These supermarkets averaged from $35 million to $55 million in sales per year. In them, H-E-B tailored what it offered to the local market through a combination of everyday low prices and exciting special events.

H-E-B also had 86 Pantry Food markets mostly in the Houston area. These stores had a low-cost, low-price format. They were 25,000 to 35,000 square feet in size and did about $14 million in business per year.

Recently, H-E-B pioneered with a new concept that it called Central Market. In this new format, there was 60,000 square feet devoted to premium products. The Central Markets had elaborate produce departments with more than 600 items. They had glass showcases for meat and fish. The meat and fish they sold were not wrapped in cellophane. They had many ready-to-heat-and-eat products.

The Central Markets were meant to target food enthusiasts. They appealed to them with large wine and beer sections, self-service pasta and olive bars, international cheeses, and full aisles of vinegars, oils, and salsas.

The three stores that fit this format were meant to be a destination shopping experience for people within a 60-mile radius, not the one-to-five mile radius of a typical store. The Central Markets did not have standard items like Coke or Frito Lay, but they were attracting large crowds of people. The most successful store was across the street from a Wal-Mart supercenter, which was generating traffic for it.

H-E-B's motto was "each and every person counts." With these three formats, it was trying to create a shopping experience that met individual needs to counter the mass appeal of Wal-Mart.

Finding a Niche

A company had to find a niche. Not everyone wanted to shop at Wal-Mart. An example was Whole Foods Market, the natural and organic foods market, that was experiencing explosive growth. Another example was Trader Joe's, described by Gary Hamel as "a cross between a gourmet deli and a discount retailer . . . a fashion food retailer . . . [where] customers . . . shop as much for entertainment as for sustenance." [5]

These examples demonstrated that there were niche markets that Wal-Mart could not satisfy. A company could build its business around customers who were not enchanted by Wal-Mart's product selection or shopping experience. Finding a good niche depended on a number of key factors such as the following:

- *Picking customer segments that Wal-Mart was not positioned to win over.* Some of the options included customers that were particularly health or time conscious, ethnic groups, such as Hispanics or Asians, gourmet cookers, urban shoppers, tech-savvy shoppers, senior citizens, families with small children, and event shoppers—people who are especially interested in parties or weddings.
- *Identifying nongrocery items and services that could win over customers.* Options included highly knowledgeable and helpful employees, a whole health format combining a pharmacy, a nutritional department, produce, and healthy living initiative in alliance with a local health club or workout facility.

---

5. The store, Hamel reported, stocks "dozens of offbeat foods—jasmine fried rice, salmon burgers, and raspberry salsa—as well as carefully selected, competitively priced staples."

- *Surrounding shopping with a distinctive experience.* Options included an upscale, service/brand reputation based on exclusive arrangements with premium-brand manufacturers, very high-quality perishables, labor-intensive perks such as a carry-out service, an especially aesthetic architectural design as well as having concerts, a cooking school, a food court, or a hair salon.
- *Providing integrated customized solutions rather than component products.* Options included cross-merchandising food equipment and utensils for meal occasions, a new-product education center, prepared foods, a vegetarian menu, fast-tempo shopping (drive-through computer ordering and no waiting self-checkout), and home delivery.

Indeed, Wal-Mart's very size could be used against it. The pressured shopper might prefer a smaller store, which was more convenient and easier in which to shop. Perhaps a better alternative would be to run profitable, smaller supermarkets in prime locations rather than large stores with much higher breakeven points.

As of September 30, 2004, Wal-Mart had 1,383 Wal-Mart stores, 1,625 supercenters, 543 Sam's Clubs, and 76 Neighborhood Markets in the United States. Internationally, it operated units in Argentina (11), Brazil (145), Canada (240), China (39), Germany (92), South Korea (16), Mexico (648), Puerto Rico (54), and the United Kingdom (372). Ultimately, the ability to compete with Wal-Mart depended on many factors. Better technology surely was one of them. A company needed to have the precise data about what goods were likely to sell out at particular times at particular stores. An especially promising innovation was "Shop 'n Scan," handheld devices with which the Albertsons' chain was experimenting at its stores. These devices permitted customers to bag their groceries as they shopped and thus reduced the time spent at checkout counters. The devices alerted customers to other items that they might also want, such as mustard and pickles for their cold cuts, and gave customers discounts and promotional material designed for them. Most importantly, the devices offered the stores that used them instantaneous information about customers' buying habits. The devices revealed exactly what was selling and who was buying it. Thus, stores were better able to tie together what customers wanted with what they provided. Technology like "Shop 'n Scan" was a way that stores could outmatch Wal-Mart at what it had historically done best—gain an intimate knowledge of customers' needs and have the ability to meet those needs in an efficient way that increased both customer satisfaction and loyalty.

What to Do Next?

The executives of SSI and Wal-Mart had to decide what to do next in their contest for the western Michigan and northern Ohio food market. What strategies could SSI executives best employ to ensure their company's survival and what strategies could Wal-Mart's executives best employ to ensure that they succeeded in their continued expansion?

Were there weaknesses in the Wal-Mart shopping experience that the executives of SSI could exploit? Could Wal-Mart correct these deficiencies and effectively counter the moves that SSI might make?

Questions for Discussion

1. What is a judo strategy? How has Wal-Mart employed this strategy in the past? How can SSI use judo strategy to counter Wal-Mart's anticipated entry into SSI's territory?
2. Why did Wal-Mart find the grocery business attractive? Was this an attractive industry? Do a five-forces analysis.
3. What is a supercenter? How did it fit into Wal-Mart's plans for the future?
4. What advantage did Wal-Mart have in the grocery business?
5. What were the likely consequences of Wal-Mart's entry for other players in the grocery business?
6. What role do price wars play in this industry?
7. What was the rationale for SSI acquiring retail outlets and becoming vertically integrated? Do you agree with this decision? Should SSI try to reverse it? What advice would you give to Craig Sturken, SSI's CEO?
8. How likely was it that Wal-Mart would penetrate into SSI's territory? How soon would this penetration come? What form would it take?
9. Why was Wal-Mart such a formidable opponent?
10. How did the grocery industry respond to Wal-Mart entering its turf?
11. Why was it difficult for SSI to build new capabilities in the grocery industry?

12. Were SSI executives right to conclude that they had to acquire retail outlets of their own after their efforts to introduce new capabilities only partially succeeded?

13. Which option made most sense for SSI—get bigger quickly, compete on price, or compete on differentiation? Why?

14. Explain what the Buy for Less/Crest Foods and H-E-B examples might mean for SSI?

15. What niche should SSI occupy? Could it transform itself into a Whole Foods Market or a Trader Joe's?

Exercises

1. Visit a Wal-Mart and a local grocer. Compare the products displayed, the pricing, the services offered, and the overall experience. Where is Wal-Mart weak? What are its vulnerabilities?

2. What should SSI do next? How should it protect itself against the possible encroachment of Wal-Mart into its territory?

3. What should Wal-Mart do to respond to the actions SSI might take? What should Wal-Mart do to ensure the success of its continued expansion in the retail grocery business?

Videos

"Sam Walton: Bargain Billionaire." A&E Home Video. Biography Series, 1998.

"Judo Strategy: David Yoffie." Stanford Executive Briefings, 2003.

Bibliography

Bell, David, and Jeffrey Feiner. "Wal-Mart Neighborhood Markets." Harvard Business School Case 9-503-034, March 2003.

Clark, Theodore, and David Croson. "H.E. Butt Grocery Company: A Leader in ECR Implementation" Harvard Business School Case 9-198-016. May 1997.

Maglitta, Joseph. "Spartan Stores, Inc." *Computerworld.* May 16, 1994.

Rangan, V.K., Marie Bell. "H.E.B. Own Brands." Harvard Business School Case 9-505-053. May 2003.

Schiano, William and James McKenney. "Spartan Stores Incorporated: Reengineering for Efficient Consumer Response." Harvard Business School Case 9-396-263, February 1996.

Senauer, Ben. "The Food Consumer in the 21st Century." The Retail Food Center. University of Minnesota, April 2001.

Turock, Art. "To Take On the World's Biggest Retailer." *Progressive Grocer.* 5, January 2003.

Useem, Jerry, Julie Schlosser, and Helen Kim. "One Nation Under Wal-Mart." *Fortune.* March 3, 2003.

"Wal-Mart Food: Big, and Getting Bigger." *Retail Forward.* September 2003.

Weir, Tom. "Picking the Right Target Customers and Points of Differentiation..." Progressive Grocer. May 1, 2003.

Yoffie, David, and Yusi Wang. "Wal-Mart in 2001." Harvard Business School Case 9-702-466, March 2002.

Yoffie, David, and Michael Cusumano. "Judo Strategy." *Harvard Business Review.* January-February 1999.

Addendum. Internet landscape overview

Forrester projects Americans will spend nearly $230 billion online by 2008, a figure that will account for 10 percent of the nation's total retail sales (Executive summary, "The Growth of Multichannel Retailing," National Governors Association, Carrie Johnson, senior analyst, Forrester Research).

EXHIBIT 1   Worldwide Internet population

Area	Internet users
Asia	257,898,314
Europe	230,886,424
U.S.A.	222,165,659
Latin America	55,930,974
Middle East	17,325,900
Ocenia	15,787,221
Africa	12,937,100

Source: Internet World Stats, Usage and Population Statistics (October 5, 2004) (http://www.internetworldstats.com/stats.htm).

EXHIBIT 2   Top Internet shopping portals

Company	Unique monthly visitors (millions)	Total daily visitors (thousands)
eBay	72.2	13,958
Yahoo Shopping	19.7	1,100
Shopping.com	17.2	1,079
BizRate	10.3	534
NextTag	9.4	494
AOL Shopping	7.6	437
MSN Shopping	5.6	271
PriceGrabber	3.3	160
Ebates.com	2.7	298
MySimon.com	1.2	51
Froogle	0.472	24

Source: comScore Networks Inc., data for February 2004 (http://www.comscore.com).

EXHIBIT 3   Share of retail Web sales by type of company

Type of company	Top 300 Web sales by group	Share %
Retail chain	$16,383,655,557	41
Virtual (Web only)	9,721,602,363	24
Consumer brand manufacturer	8,139,419,315	20
Catalog/call center	5,852,526,176	15

Source: The Internet Retailer Top 300 (http://www.internetretailer.com/default.asp).

255

EXHIBIT 4   Leading categories within the top 300 sites

Category title	No. of sites	Web sales in category	% of total
Mass merchants	27	$11,853,610,489	29
Computers/electronics	28	10,921,202,275	27
Office supplies	4	5,237,176,750	13
Specialty apparel	70	3,312,944,840	9
Drug/health/beauty	11	1,590,679,640	4
Flowers/gifts/jewelry	31	1,332,490,250	3
Housewares/home furnishings	31	1,121,192,293	3
Toys/hobbies	28	1,175,859,090	3
Sporting goods	33	1,117,842,005	3
Books/CDs/videos/DVDs	15	999,347,500	2
Food	14	848,985,894	2
Hardware/home improvement	8	585,871,975	1

Source: The Internet Retailer Top 300 (http://www.internetretailer.com/default.asp).

CREDITS

Case 1: Intel versus AMD

Table 1.1. Unit market share in microprocessors. CREDIT: Brent Schlender, "Intel Unleashes Its Inner Attila," Fortune, October 15, 2001. © 2001 TIME INC. REPRINTED BY PERMISSION.

Table 1.2. Microprocessors' growth in speed. CREDIT: Source: Ramon Casadus-Masnnel and Michael Rukstad, "Intel Corporation: 1997–2000," Harvard Business School Case 9-702-420. Boston: Harvard Business School, 2002. Copyright © 2002 by the President and Fellows of Harvard College. Reprinted by permission.

Table 1.3. Gross margins earned by Intel and its rivals. CREDIT: Reprinted from the December 12, 1997 issue of Business Week by special permission. © 1997 McGraw-Hill Companies, Inc.

Table 1.4. Typical system price with the processors of Intel and its rivals. CREDIT: Reprinted from the December 12, 1997 issue of Business Week by special permission. © 1997 McGraw-Hill Companies, Inc.

Exhibit 2. Intel's annual income statement 1998–2002 (in millions of U.S. dollars except for per-share items). CREDIT: Reproduced with permission of Yahoo! Inc. © 2005 by Yahoo! Inc. YAHOO! And the YAHOO! Logo are trademarks of Yahoo! Inc.

Exhibit 3. AMD's annual income statement 1998–2002 (in millions of U.S. dollars except for per-share items). CREDIT: Reproduced with permission of Yahoo! Inc. © 2005 by Yahoo! Inc. YAHOO! And the YAHOO! Logo are trademarks of Yahoo! Inc.

Case 2: Barnes & Noble versus Amazon.com

Table 2.1 A comparison of major booksellers with regard to a number of key indicators (September 2003). CREDIT: Reproduced with permission of Yahoo! Inc. © 2005 by Yahoo! Inc. YAHOO! And the YAHOO! Logo are trademarks of Yahoo! Inc.

Table 2.2. Shares of adult books sold. CREDIT: Source: Ghemawat, Pankaj, and Bret Baird. "Leadership Online: Barnes & Noble vs. Amazon.com. (A)." Harvard Business School Case 9-798-063. April 2000. Boston: Harvard Business School, 2000 . Copyright © 2000 by the President and Fellows of Harvard College. Reprinted by permission.

Table 2.3. Typical division of the profits for a fairly successful hardback novel. CREDIT: WALL STREET JOURNAL. EASTERN EDITION [STAFF PRODUCED COPY ONLY] by JEFFREY TRACHENBERG. Copyright 2003 by DOW JONES & CO INC. Reproduced with permission of DOW JONES & CO INC in the format Textbook via Copyright Clearance Center.

Table 2.4. Amazon.com's revenue and gross profit percentages. CREDIT: Source: Stig Leschly, Michael Roberts, and William Sahlman, "Amazon.com—2002," Harvard Business School Case 9-803-098, February 2003. Boston: Harvard Business School, 2003. Copyright © 2003 by the President and Fellows of Harvard College. Reprinted by permission.

Exhibit 1. Amazon.com annual income statement (in millions of U.S. dollars except for per-share items). CREDIT: Reproduced with permission of Yahoo! Inc. © 2005 by Yahoo! Inc. YAHOO! And the YAHOO! Logo are trademarks of Yahoo! Inc.

Exhibit 2. Barnes & Noble annual income statement (in millions of U.S. dollars except for per-share items). CREDIT: Reproduced with permission of Yahoo! Inc. © 2005 by Yahoo! Inc. YAHOO! And the YAHOO! Logo are trademarks of Yahoo! Inc.

Exhibit 3. Barnes & Noble.com annual income statement (in millions of U.S. dollars

except for per-share items). CREDIT: Reproduced with permission of Yahoo! Inc. © 2005 by Yahoo! Inc. YAHOO! And the YAHOO! Logo are trademarks of Yahoo! Inc.

Exhibit 4. Borders annual income statement (in millions of U.S. dollars except for per share items). CREDIT: Reproduced with permission of Yahoo! Inc. © 2005 by Yahoo! Inc. YAHOO! And the YAHOO! Logo are trademarks of Yahoo! Inc.

Case 3: Dell versus Gateway

Table 3.2. Gateway and Dell annual income statements 1999–2002. CREDIT: Reproduced with permission of Yahoo! Inc. © 2005 by Yahoo! Inc. YAHOO! And the YAHOO! Logo are trademarks of Yahoo! Inc.

Table 3.3. Direct competitor comparison (September 2003). CREDIT: Reproduced with permission of Yahoo! Inc. © 2005 by Yahoo! Inc. YAHOO! And the YAHOO! Logo are trademarks of Yahoo! Inc.

Table 3.4. Global PC market shares in June 2003. CREDIT: Source: V. K. Rangan and Marie Bell, "Dell: New Horizons," Harvard Business School Case 9-502-022, October 2002. Boston: Harvard Business School, 2002. Copyright © 2002 by the President and Fellows of Harvard College. Reprinted by permission.

Table 3.6. World handheld PDA market shares in June 2002. CREDIT: Source: V. K. Rangan and Marie Bell, "Dell: New Horizons," Harvard Business School Case 9-502-022, October 2002. Boston: Harvard Business School, 2002. Copyright © 2002 by the President and Fellows of Harvard College. Reprinted by permission.

Table 3.7. Market shares in servers in June 2003. CREDIT: Source: V. K. Rangan and Marie Bell, "Dell: New Horizons," Harvard Business School Case 9-502-022, October 2002. Boston: Harvard Business School, 2002. Copyright © 2002 by the President and Fellows of Harvard College. Reprinted by permission.

Table 3.8. Global market share of Dell and major competitors in international markets (2000). CREDIT: Source: V. K. Rangan and Marie Bell, "Dell: New Horizons," Harvard Business School Case 9-502-022, October 2002. Boston: Harvard Business School, 2002. Copyright © 2002 by the President and Fellows of Harvard College. Reprinted by permission.

Case 5: Charles Schwab versus Morgan Stanley

Table 5.1. The performance of Morgan Stanley and Charles Schwab in comparison to other companies in their industry (Oct. 14, 2003). CREDIT: Reproduced with permission of Yahoo! Inc. © 2005 by Yahoo! Inc. YAHOO! And the YAHOO! Logo are trademarks of Yahoo! Inc.

Figure 5.3. Different business models in financial services. CREDIT: Source: Alfred Marcus, Management Strategy, 2005, McGraw Hill, reproduced with permission from McGraw-Hill Companies, Inc.

Exhibits 1 and 2. Morgan Stanley annual income statement (in millions of U.S. dollars except for per-share items) & Charles Schwab annual income statement (in millions of U.S. dollars except for per-share items). CREDIT: Reproduced with permission of Yahoo! Inc. © 2005 by Yahoo! Inc. YAHOO! And the YAHOO! Logo are trademarks of Yahoo! Inc.

Case 6: Time Warner versus Disney

Table 6.1. A comparison of Time Warner and Disney in 2003. CREDIT: Reproduced with permission of Yahoo! Inc. © 2005 by Yahoo! Inc. YAHOO! And the YAHOO! Logo are trademarks of Yahoo! Inc.

Exhibits 1 and 2. Disney's annual income statement (in millions of U.S. dollars except per-share items) & Time Warner's annual income statement (in millions of U.S. dollars except for per-share items). CREDIT: Reproduced with permission of Yahoo! Inc. © 2005 by Yahoo! Inc. YAHOO! And the YAHOO! Logo are trademarks of Yahoo! Inc.

Exhibit 3. Top 12 theme parks in the world (based on attendance). CREDIT: Source: Tyrell Levine and Michael Rukstad, "The Walt Disney Corporation," Harvard Business School Case 9-701-035. Boston: Harvard Business School, 2001. Copyright © 2001 by the President and Fellows of Harvard College. Reprinted by permission.

Exhibit 5. Cable networks and cable systems. CREDIT: Source: Kagan Research, LLC. Data from Cable Program Investor (Top Cable Networks, Februry 28, 2003) and Cable TV Investor: Deals & Finance (Top Cable Systems, June 2003).

Case 7: Pepsi versus Coke

Table 7.1. A comparison of Coke and Pepsi in 2003. CREDIT: Reproduced with permission of Yahoo! Inc. © 2005 by Yahoo! Inc. YAHOO! And the YAHOO! Logo are trademarks of Yahoo! Inc.

Table 7.5. U.S. soft drink share by customer classes in 2000 (percent). CREDIT: Source: David B. Yoffie and Yusi Wang, "Cola Wars Continue, Harvard Business School Case 9-702-442, 2002. Boston: Harvard Business School, 2002 . Copyright © 2002 by the

President and Fellows of Harvard College. Reprinted by permission.

Table 7.6. Soft drinks: selected international market shares, 1999. CREDIT: Source: David B. Yoffie and Yusi Wang, "Cola Wars Continue," Harvard Business School Case 9-702-442, 2002. Boston: Harvard Business School, 2002 . Copyright © 2002 by the President and Fellows of Harvard College. Reprinted by permission.

Exhibits 1 and 2. Coca Cola annual income statement (in millions of U.S. dollars except for per-share items) & Pepsico annual income statement (in millions of U.S. dollars except for per-share items). CREDIT: Reproduced with permission of Yahoo! Inc. © 2005 by Yahoo! Inc. YAHOO! And the YAHOO! Logo are trademarks of Yahoo! Inc.

Case 9: Monsanto versus DuPont

Table 9.1. A comparison of Monsanto and DuPont's income statements: 1999-2002 (in millions of U.S. dollars except for per-share items). CREDIT: Reproduced with permission of Yahoo! Inc. © 2005 by Yahoo! Inc. YAHOO! And the YAHOO! Logo are trademarks of Yahoo! Inc.

Table 9.2. Du Pont, Monsanto, and competitors: January 2003. CREDIT: Reproduced with permission of Yahoo! Inc. © 2005 by Yahoo! Inc. YAHOO! And the YAHOO! Logo are trademarks of Yahoo! Inc.

Case 10: Wal-Mart versus Spartan Stores, Inc. (SSI)

Table 10.1 Wal-Mart's annual income statement: 2003. CREDIT: Reproduced with permission of Yahoo! Inc. © 2005 by Yahoo! Inc. YAHOO! And the YAHOO! Logo are trademarks of Yahoo! Inc.

Table 10.2. SSI's annual income statement: 2003. CREDIT: Reproduced with permission of Yahoo! Inc. © 2005 by Yahoo! Inc. YAHOO! And the YAHOO! Logo are trademarks of Yahoo! Inc.

Figure 10.1. The region in which SSI was most active. CREDIT: The MapQuest.com logo is a registered trademark of MapQuest.com, Inc. Map content © 2005 by MapQuest.com, Inc. The MapQuest trademarks and content are used with permission.

Additional credits:

Case 5: Charles Schwab versus Morgan Stanley

Table 5.6. From *The Profit Zone* by Adrian Slywotsky and David Morrison, copyright © 1997 by Mercer Management Consulting, Inc. Copyright © 2001 by Mercer

Management Consulting, Inc. Used by permission of Times Books, a Division of Random House, Inc.

Case 6: Time Warner versus Disney

Appendix C. Top Cable and Top Syndicated Programs, November 2003. Source: Nielsen Media Research.

INDEX